THEOLOGY AND CHANGE

Essays in Memory of
Alan Richardson

THEOLOGY
AND
CHANGE

Essays in Memory of
ALAN RICHARDSON

EDITED BY
RONALD H. PRESTON

SCM PRESS LTD
LONDON

334 01640 1
First published 1975
by SCM Press Ltd
56 Bloomsbury Street London

© SCM Press Ltd 1975

Typeset by Specialised Offset Services Ltd, Liverpool
and printed in Great Britain by
Fletcher & Son Ltd,
Norwich

CONTENTS

Foreword   vii

1 After Liberalism: Reflections on Four Decades   1
Michael Ramsey, *lately Archbishop of Canterbury*

2 The Future Shape of Popular Theology   11
John Bowden, *Managing Director and Editor of SCM Press*

3 Alan Richardson and his Critics in the Area of Hermeneutics   25
Anthony Hanson, *Professor of Theology in the University of Hull*

4 Recent Studies on the Resurrection of Jesus   53
Robert Leaney, *lately Professor of Christian Theology in the University of Nottingham*

5 The Absurdity of God's Non-Existence: St Anselm and the Study of Religion   68
James Richmond, *Reader in Religious Studies in the University of Lancaster*

6 Lessing's Ditch Revisited: The Problem of Faith and History   78
David Pailin, *Senior Lecturer in the Philosophy of Religion in the University of Manchester*

7 The Authority of the Christian Faith   104
Richard Hanson, *Professor of Historical and Contemporary Theology in the University of Manchester, and Assistant Bishop in the Diocese of Manchester*

8 Love and Justice   128
John Bennett, *formerly President of Union Theological Seminary, New York*

9 Reflections on Theologies of Social Change   143
Ronald Preston, *Professor of Social and Pastoral Theology in the University of Manchester and Canon of Manchester*

10 The Sociology of Religion, Comparative Religion and the
New Apologetic Task   167
Arnold Nash, *Emeritus Professor of the History and Sociology of
Religion and Adjunct Professor in the Department of Pathology,
University of North Carolina*

11 Higher Education in the Post-Robbins Era   188
Roy Niblett, *lately Head of the Department of Higher Education in
the Institute of Education, the University of London*

Curriculum Vitae   204

Bibliography of the Writings of Alan Richardson   205

FOREWORD

This symposium was planned as a tribute to Alan Richardson on his seventieth birthday, 17 October 1975. The foreword was originally completed and signed on Ash Wednesday, 12 February 1975. On Sunday 23 February Alan Richardson collapsed in York Minster after Evensong and died in an ambulance which was taking him to hospital, so that what was a *Festschrift* now becomes a memorial. His death and the manner of it were not entirely unexpected, though his friends had hoped that he and Phyllis Richardson would have had some time together to enjoy his retirement, which was about to be announced. Their sense of thankfulness for his life and friendship is strong, as is their sympathy with Phyllis Richardson. It is clearly too soon to attempt a fresh assessment of Alan Richardson's varied contributions to the life of the church and the university; and it has therefore seemed best to let the rest of this foreword stand as it was originally written, apart from necessary changes of tense and the alteration of a few phrases.

The idea of a *Festschrift* was latent in the minds of several friends and colleagues but the one who first put it into words was Professor Anthony Hanson. Once expressed it was quickly acted on. It would have been possible to secure essays from scholarly admirers of Alan Richardson from all over the world, but the Editor opted for a more personal book from friends and colleagues of long standing who themselves have been active in some of the many fields in which Alan Richardson himself worked. With one exception all who were invited to contribute were able to accept, and they did so with great enthusiasm, and within the areas which were suggested to them. They were left quite free whether to draw on Alan Richardson's work or not, and if they did and wished to pay him the compliment of criticism they were to feel at liberty to do so. The range of study covered is itself a tribute to Alan Richardson's scholarly contribution to New Testament studies, the history of Christian doctrine, apologetic theology, the history of ideas, the contemporary expression of the Christian faith in society, and theology as an humanistic study in the university; and all of this in a profoundly ecumenical context. The only contributor who has not been a personal friend or colleague is Dr David Pailin. For some time he has been stimulated by Alan Richardson's long preoccupation with the critical philosophy of history and its importance for the Christian faith to work on the same problem, and as no one else was dealing with it he is glad to contribute to what remains an ongoing discussion of this central issue.

All the other contributors have had their own personal associations with Alan Richardson and their own special occasions of gratitude to and affection for him. Perhaps the Editor may be excused for mentioning his own. In 1934 I was a second-year undergraduate at the London School of Economics, having recently come back into the Christian faith after several years away from it, through the influence of the Student Christian Movement. I went to one of the summer conferences of the SCM at Swanwick in Derbyshire. On this occasion the main talks had been handed over to a team of young members of SCM staff and students. They did not speak to my condition at all. I had an enquiring and sceptical mind and at that point wanted something to stretch it; to me the talks seemed woolly and I was disappointed. But one of the 'parallel courses', as they were called, was given by Alan Richardson, on Christian doctrine. Here was certainly something to stretch my newly kindled and confused desire for Christian understanding, and delivered with beautiful clarity. This did speak to my condition. Subsequently the talks were published as *Creeds in the Making*, and after many reprints they are still on sale. It, and William Temple's *Christian Faith and Life*, were the first two Christian books on which I spent my own money; there was little of it at that time of economic depression, and parting with my own money for two *Christian* books was a major step for me, and an outward and visible sign of my recovered Christian commitment. Happily for me I was soon to get to know Alan Richardson personally, through his friend Arnold Nash who was then the SCM staff member whose field included LSE, and we were friends from that day forward.

Alan Richardson had great skill as an expositor and as a preacher. In the former role he saw it as his responsibility not only to produce the large, scholarly work, but the short popular one too. Several of these, notably *Preface to Bible Study*, have been reprinted many times and in the course of the last few decades have rendered an immense service to the churches.

He became Vicar of Cambo in Northumberland, a beautiful parish, large in area but thinly populated, which extended well towards the Scottish border. Here he was in the interesting position of having Sir Charles Trevelyan as his agnostic resident squire and patron. Sir Charles took pride in the prowess with the village cricket team of the Vicar he had appointed, and a love of cricket was a permanent characteristic of Alan Richardson; certainly the proximity of Trent Bridge made the later move to Nottingham an added attraction to him. At Cambo there was a fox terrier in the Richardson household, but that breed long since gave way to the golden retriever, and no visitor to the Deanery of York left it without his appreciation of those beautiful dogs being enhanced. What Mozart was to Karl Barth the golden retriever could be said to be to Alan Richardson.

From Cambo Alan Richardson became Study Secretary of the SCM, a job which I thought when I succeeded him in it in 1943, and looking back still think, was the most exciting 'church' job in the British Isles. Both of us were closely associated with and influenced by the SCM, and both of us had two spells of office on its staff. For a number of years now we were among the very large band of 'Senior Friends' who have been dismayed by its widespread collapse since 1969. This is not the occasion to explore why this has happened, nor can Senior Friends organize things for students. But student generations change rapidly and there are signs that the picture is already changing. Certainly it would be folly to look simply for a recovery of the past. Relevant expressions of Christian faith and life must arise out of the present situation in universities and other institutions of higher education. In recent years our main connection with the SCM has been through the Board of the SCM Press which is indirectly related to it, through its Trust Association. Alan Richardson was a member of the Board from 1940 to 1975 and its Chairman from 1957 to 1973. Apart from being one of its best-selling authors, he was a wise and far-sighted adviser, and a source of gentle support for a series of distinguished Editors under whom the Press has prospered, but who have in many ways a unique and therefore lonely job.

In the early days of the ecumenical movement Alan Richardson played a considerable part, notably in various stages of its study programme, as a member of the first three Assemblies of the World Council of Churches. Behind the scenes he and Dr John Bennett were personal assistants to Dr J. H. Oldham at the crucially important Oxford Conference of 1937 on 'Church, Community and State' (which I attended in the Youth Section).

Whilst Study Secretary of the SCM Alan Richardson took over from Arnold Nash the British agency of the quarterly journal of the Fellowship of Socialist Christians in the USA, edited by Reinhold Niebuhr. It was first called *Radical Religion* and subsequently *Christianity and Society*. In due course I took over the agency from him. The journal was congenial to us because it took a radical line in politics but did not derive the details of it *directly* from the Christian faith. We were opposed to various Christian Left or Christian Socialist or 'Christian Sociology' groups who in our opinion made too direct a link between socialism or some particular social order and the kingdom of God. That discussion has now gone round almost full circle and has to be continued today.

Alan Richardson went on to become a Canon Residentiary of Durham Cathedral, Professor of Christian Theology at Notting-ham University and then Dean of York. At Durham there were many informal links with the university (and close ones with St Hild's College), so that the eventual move to Nottingham was an appropriate one. Here Alan Richardson played a very full part in the life of the university. Theology was not tucked away in a corner but clearly seen to be an integral part of study in the humanities which itself is a key element in the over-all work of a university. His home was a centre of hospitality. He took care that the work of the Department of Theology influenced the whole region round about, and those with scholarly aptitudes were encouraged to relate to it and their studies thereby fostered, while young members of staff were encouraged and their progress gently and unobtrusively guided. His evenness of temper was invaluable in soothing agitated minds and calming ruffled feelings in the various issues that arose in the university community.

All this time at Nottingham and through the Durham years a steady stream of substantial theological work was produced, so that Alan Richardson became one of the most influential Anglican theologians of his time, and was read and listened to all over the English-speaking world, many parts of which he visited to lecture and preach. Writing on this scale was only accomplished by working well into the night for many years, for he never let up on his ongoing responsibilities during the day. Much of this period covered the dominance of what is often known as 'Biblical Theology', with which Alan Richardson's name is often connected, and whose demise in this country can be dated from the publication of Professor James Barr's *The Semantics of Biblical Language* in 1961. It has now entirely collapsed and questions which it pushed aside have come back again, and new questions with them. The time has not yet come to assess its contribution. No large-scale movement of theological thought is without its permanent legacy. As far as Alan Richardson's own work is concerned two things are clear, as essays in this volume bring out. One is that he was much more than a 'Biblical Theologian' *tout court*, and the other that in terms of actual exegetical work in the Bible he cannot be dismissed.

Eventually Alan Richardson became Dean of the Faculty of Arts at Nottingham, and he was holding that office when he was appointed to the Deanery of York. The effort to complete his period of office, finish his Bampton lectures and move to York all at the same time was undoubtedly the immediate cause of the severe heart attack he suffered soon after his arrival at York. Ever since then he had to come to terms with a slower pace of living, and to guard his energies carefully. He accepted this restriction with gentle grace and good humour and coped with this disability with the minimum of fuss. He might indeed have expected to continue academic work at York free from the multifarious duties of a professor in the post-war university. As everyone knows, however, no sooner had he got to York than the crisis at the Minster broke out, when it was discovered that the foundations were shifting owing to the lowering of the level of the water-table occasioned by the growth of York itself. Alan Richardson was inevitably at the centre of the task of renewing the building, not least that of raising the huge sum of money required, and uniquely among theologians his name will go down to history in connection with the saving of one of Europe's major church buildings. The renewal has been imaginatively completed, and in particular the opening up of the crypt with the many treasures on view is an outstanding feature of it. The award of a knighthood to Alan Richardson in 1973 was a fitting public recognition of the magnitude of the task accomplished.

In preparing this volume Alan Richardson's friends were greatly in his debt for his help with the Bibliography which otherwise could not have been completed in anything like its present form. They rejoiced in his friendship and were looking forward to honouring

~ 1 ~

After Liberalism:
Reflections on Four Decades

MICHAEL RAMSEY

I

Alan Richardson's path and mine first coincided near the end of the nineteen-twenties when as newly ordained men in the diocese of Liverpool we sat at the feet of Dr Charles Raven in his weekly seminar for the younger clergy; and we met again in the forties as friends and colleagues when we were both canons of Durham cathedral. Both of us have had periods in academic life and periods when involvement in other aspects of the church has diverted us from academic leisure and discipline. If both of us have cared greatly for the link between theology and the practical life of the church, this concern has been evoked not only by the pressure of circumstances but also by conviction. It is thus with kinship of experience as well as with feelings of grateful friendship that I take a small part in the tribute which this book offers.

Alan's first book was published in 1935, and my own first book a year later. To look at both of them now across the passing of four decades is to see that both were 'of their time' and both reflect what came to be called 'the reaction from liberalism'. Alan's book was *The Redemption of Modernism*, and its motive was the purging of liberal theology from dogmatic assumptions which he felt to be damaging to genuine theological freedom. My book was *The Gospel and the Catholic Church*, in which the biblical theology which I had learned chiefly from Sir Edwyn Hoskyns, with a whiff of influence from Karl Barth, was seen as the ground of the church's order and sacramental life. If Alan was setting English modernism under the searchlight of a larger theological scene, I was trying to set the doctrine of the church under the searchlight of biblical theology. Both of us had moved some distance from the kind of liberalism which Charles Raven used to discuss with the young clergy in the Liverpool chapter house.

The anti-liberal, or perhaps it would be fairer to say the post-liberal, trend which gained momentum in the nineteen-thirties had a number of ingredients, some of them coming from biblical scholarship and others from the crisis situation which began to replace the ideas of evolutionary progress at the time when the darkening skies were heralding the Second World War. There was the reaction of scholarship from the confident attempts to reconstruct the history of Jesus before and behind the theology of the apostolic age. There was a new emphasis upon the exposition of the biblical message in its own categories. There was the eclipse of the 'social gospel' by the catastrophic themes of eschatology. There was renewed interest in the classical Protestantism of the Reformers. Though the direct influence of Karl Barth in the English scene was small, those who disliked the new trends would use the term 'Barthian' to describe them, and those who shared in these trends might not be averse to being so described.

The recent biography of Charles Raven shows how a powerful exponent of liberal theology, with a special concern to relate an incarnational view of the world to the sciences, felt that a blight had descended. He grieved at 'how wide the gulf had become between the "liberal" whose eyes rejoiced to see the wonderful works of God manifested in nature and human personality, and the "reformed" who looked out on the world and saw God's judgements at work in the history of an apostate civilization'. Furthermore 'he was particularly distressed by the fact that the Student Christian Movement, which he had for more than twenty years regarded as the advance guard of the New Reformation, seemed to be selling out completely to Continental influences and to reactionary theology. He deplored the way in which the magazine *The Student Movement*, under the editorship of Alan Richardson, had swung far over to the neo-orthodox or anti-liberal position.'[1]

The emotions of that conflict, which was partly one of generations, as well as the sadness of a good deal of mutual non-comprehension, now seem far away. The so-called Barthians were sometimes blind to the achievement, and the still greater potential achievement, of those who were working out a concept of the evolution of nature and man with the incarnation and the cross as the key, a concept which was to have notable expression both in the writings of Teilhard de Chardin and in Raven's Gifford lectures, *Natural Religion and Christian Theology*. And liberals on their part failed to see that the so-called Barthians were not always engaged in a flight from reason but were exploring a deeper scientific exegesis of themes and words of the New Testament which concerned the contemporary world as a world under judgment. *Tempora mutantur, et nos mutamur in illis.* Time was to see the exponents of defined positions coming to be self-critical about their weaknesses. The 'neo-orthodox' phase was to see the recapturing of some of the concerns of liberalism against which it had reacted.

Alan Richardson's literary work, after some valuable pieces of 'popular' teaching, included some substantial pieces of New Testament scholarship which drew upon both the methods of form criticism and the lexicography of the *Wörterbuch*. *The Miracle Stories of the Gospels* (1941) brought a critical rigour and a theological interest to bear upon its subject. *An Introduction to the Theology of the New Testament* (1958) expounds words and themes in a way which is reminiscent of some of the older German works which treated biblical theology on systematic lines, while it is very English in its avoidance of rigid over-classification. But the wider context of theological concern was not being forgotten; and some of its issues had been discussed, in a simple way, in *Science, History and Faith* (1950) and were to be discussed again in *The Bible in the Age of Science* (1961). These interests, and more, were drawn together in the considerable work *Christian Apologetics* (1947). In this book the author gives a powerful criticism of liberal Protestant views of the relation of history and faith, parts company with both Barth and Aquinas on the understanding of revelation, and draws out with some fullness the concepts of 'general' and 'special' revelation, with much use of St Augustine's view of faith and reason. Old-fashioned enough to include a chapter on 'The Argument from Prophecy', the book is not old-fashioned in its treatment of the role of the prophets in discerning the divine pattern of salvation in the course of history. Those books were raising questions which were to be the theme of what is perhaps the most significant of his works, the Bampton Lectures for 1964 on *History Sacred and Profane*. The latter part of this essay will touch upon its theme, which may bear upon the needs of the seventies and after, even more than upon those of the sixties.

Though the writings so far mentioned include some which belong to the sixties, they are all of pre-*Honest to God* vintage, and none of them mentions the theological malaise and loss of nerve with which the sixties are associated. However, the years when the foundations of York Minster were found to be crumbling and its Dean was diverted from his study to the courageous leadership in saving it, were also the years when the rumblings of theological

4 Michael Ramsey

foundations were heard. To this new situation Alan Richardson contributed a paper-back work which diagnosed some of the problems and brought a remarkable weight of varied knowledge to bear upon them: *Religion in Contemporary Debate* (1966). He discusses the attacks made on 'religion' both by theologians and by rationalists and suggests that the answer to both lies in the 'Christianizing' of religion. He urges that the central issue between Christians and secularists lies not in the metaphysics of *theism* but in the need and fact of *grace*.

The real divergence between Christians and humanists does not lie in the area of shadow-boxing over the question of the existence of a metaphysical God, but in the very live issue of whether the inexorable demands of righteousness can be met out of human resources without the aid of an all-ruling and all-loving power by which the blessings of secularization have been previously attained and by which their promise for the future may in some measure be fulfilled (p. 47).

On religious atheism he warns his fellow Christians about the kind of dialogue with empiricism which adopts the empiricists' presuppositions to the extent of losing theology's own ground. Yet,

wherever there is a passionate atheist there is a failure of Christian charity or courage somewhere in the background ... Atheism in the modern world is an occasion of penitence for the Church (p. 62).

On cosmology and language he writes:

How far should we demythologize? For the most part, not at all, because the biblical writers have done the job for us already. It is we who have forgotten the art of poetic communication, and so we create a problem by our sophisticated literal-mindedness (p. 72).

On the new hermeneutics he writes:

What is lacking in Heidegger is any recognition of the connection between authentic words and the theme of righteousness. His hermeneutic is concerned with aesthetics and the numinous rather than with ethics and the biblical sense of the holy ... 'To hear' and 'to obey' are near synonyms in the Old Testament, and the knowledge of God comes by doing his will ... The obedient Son, whose actions authenticate his words, is most fittingly described in the New Testament as the Word of God – the 'word-event' which affects the course of all history, whether the individual man or of the world (pp. 98f.).

These quotations do not summarize the argument of the books from which they come, but they illustrate the thought of Alan Richardson about the problems which became pressing in the sixties, and they give a prophetic word for some of the problems now with us. A long journey has been made from *The Redemption of Modernism*, and yet that title still rings a bell. While Alan

Richardson's difference from liberalism remains, something reminiscent of liberalism appears in his insistence that morality is the key to theism and that it matters for Christianity that history is knowable and that history happened.

The Political Christ (1973) shows a mind at work in yet one more phase, the revolutionary activism now prominent in the ecumenical movement. It is interesting to note that the appeal is to the *historical Jesus*: what were his attitudes and actions in relation to the state, the problems of justice and the revolutionary movements of the time?

II

Through the four decades in which Alan Richardson was writing there are questions which recur. One of them is the question of history. What is the nature of history and its relations to Christian belief?

To the liberalism of the nineteen-twenties history was scarcely felt to be a problem, and the new tendency to treat it as a problem caused misgivings. Charles Raven's biography recalls:

> In the late nineteen-twenties echoes of these vigorous questionings about the nature of history began to be heard in England, particularly in the teaching of C.H. Dodd and Sir Edwyn Hoskyns, both of whom had studied in Germany and maintained close touch with German scholarship. But, to put it crudely, Charles found it difficult to understand what all the fuss was about. Had not the essential historical questions about the New Testament literature – documents, dates, authorship, context – been settled once for all through the magnificent labour of liberal scholars?[2]

The 'fuss' has in a sense existed ever since the scientific study of history was brought to bear upon the origins of Christianity a century and a half ago. What do we know about the life of Jesus of Nazareth? Do the gospels provide credible history, or do they obscure the history by importing into it the piety and doctrine of the early church? Is there a line of continuity between the teaching of Jesus and the teaching of the apostles? In the long story of this 'fuss' there have been times when something near to assured results seemed to be in the ascendant. One such time, at least in England, was the decade after the First World War when it seemed that the *literary* relations of the gospels were settled, with the establishment of the priority and primitive character of Mark's gospel and of a written source which lay behind Matthew and Luke. Here indeed was a sense of historical certainty in the view that Mark gives a

reliable historical outline of the ministry of Jesus and that much of
the teaching is corroborated in another primitive source. Into this
scene form criticism, imported from the Continent, brought a sense
of insecurity by its emphasis upon the hazards of oral tradition
which preceded the making of the written documents. In the event
there were scholars who showed that form criticism need not
produce or imply historical scepticism. But its best known
exponents on the Continent were drawing sceptical conclusions
from it; and many of those who devoted themselves to its methods
were more interested in asking questions about the theology of the
primitive church than questions about what Jesus actually did and
said.

Certainly form criticism brought into existence a new way of
reading the gospels. The older way had been to read them as
biographical memoirs of the life of Jesus, complicated indeed in
places by the intrusion of the church's teaching and piety but
yielding 'fact' which could be studied in contrast with 'interpretation'. The new way was to read the gospels in the context of
the preaching and teaching of the early church in which the
traditions were handed down, and to recognize that history and
interpretation are interwoven at every stage and the story of Jesus is
unknown apart from the preaching of it by the church. Amidst the
church's vivid belief in the continuing life of the risen Jesus there
might not always be clear distinction between Jesus as he was
before the crucifixion and Jesus as he is now as Lord, Teacher,
Saviour and Healer.

Does the scientific use of form criticism necessarily issue in
historical scepticism? Only, it would seem, if assumptions of a
philosophical or theological kind are allowed to influence the
treatment: such as an assumption that the early church was not
interested in 'the days of his flesh' or an assumption that the life of a
divine Saviour must be historically unverifiable. It is worth
recalling the method of investigation followed by C.H. Dodd in his
work *History and the Gospel*. He claimed to follow

... a method of criticism which promises a fresh approach to the problem of
historicity. It is a method which does not aim directly or in the main at
establishing a residuum of bare facts presumed to stand independently of any
meaning attached to them ... the aim is to recover the purest and most original
form of the tradition which inevitably includes both fact and interpretation.[3]

Using that method Dodd was able to draw a portrait of Jesus in
his relations to the various groups of his contemporaries, made
from the elements in the tradition which appear to be early and

widely attested in actions, sayings and parables. A similar method followed by D.E. Nineham in his *Commentary on St Mark* yielded similar results. Nineham goes so far as to say:

When we bear in mind the wonderfully retentive memory of the Oriental, who, being unable to read and write, had perforce to cultivate accuracy of memory, it will not seem surprising that we can often be virtually sure that what the tradition is offering us are the authentic deeds, and especially the authentic words, of the historic Jesus.[4]

Yet form criticism compels us to face the interrelation of fact and interpretation in a way that the older liberalism disallowed. Nor should we wish it to be otherwise. The Jesuit scholar Xavier Léon-Dufour well says in his work *Les Evangiles et l'histoire de Jésus*:

If the early Church had posessed only one authorized and authoritative life of Jesus the rationalist historian would probably never have realized what Jesus meant to his followers ... The disciples were concerned not only with remembering the teaching of Jesus like the pupils of a Rabbi, but with understanding and applying the spirit of his teaching.[5]

While, however, form criticism of itself lies within the realm of historical science and involves no disparagement of the role of history, it is a method which gives scope for interests other than historical; and some of its devotees have been concerned more for theology than for history, for *kerygma* than for event. Hence it has been important that its advance as a science synchronized with the existentialist phase in continental theology, and especially with the existentialist theology of Rudolf Bultmann. It was thus that there came about the situation of which Alan Richardson could write: 'The dominant schools in German theology have been engaged in a programme of disengagement from history.'[6]

This last phrase is a not unfair comment on Bultmann's presentation of the gospel as 'faith-event'. The event is, for Bultmann, Jesus as preached and believed in his encounter with the believers. The resurrection is not known as an event to which historical evidence is relevant, for it is the encounter of the crucified Jesus with the believer. To treat the resurrection as something which historical evidence could scrutinize or verify would be to descend from faith to the realm of secular *Historismus*. Not only has there been an immense influence of Bultmann upon those who follow his philosophy and his biblical method, but there has also been a more widely diffused movement from the kind of historical concern which was familiar to earlier generations.

Not surprisingly a reaction towards history has come. There have been those who have not been afraid of a new quest of an historical Jesus, so long as the errors of the earlier quest are kept at a distance. Amongst Bultmann's own disciples the return to history has been apparent, notably in the work of Günther Bornkamm. And Wolfhart Pannenberg has taught a view of revelation and history which breaks away not only from Bultmann's existentialism but from the concept, widely dominant in German theology, that the Word of God is the central concept for theological under-standing. To Pannenberg history is verifiable, and the mode of revelation is the inspiration given to prophets and apostles to interpret history in terms of God's acts and words. Revelation is seen as the divinely inspired interpretation of a divinely controlled course of events.

It is, however, impossible to judge rightly concerning these contrasted positions without probing into the nature of history itself. Here it seems to me that the analysis of the problems given in Alan Richardson's Bampton Lectures *History Sacred and Profane* comes into its own with sound criteria for the forming of judgments. His argument is in line with the 'post-liberals' in insisting that history is not bare fact divorced from interpretation, and that history cannot be in itself the ground of faith. Indeed history, so far from being in contrast with interpretation, is itself interpretation of the materials which evidence produces. But history is knowable, however mysterious its contents:

> There is only one history, and if it is incredible that the acts of God were worked in it, then the revelation in Christ cannot be salvaged by recourse to a *Heilsgeschichte* that runs parallel to secular history, never really intersecting it, and inaccessible save through some extra-historical perception known as faith.[7]

How does such an approach bear upon the resurrection of Jesus Christ? It is not only Bultmann who has refused to think of the resurrection in terms of verifiable history or of belief in the resurrection as grounded upon historical evidence. There are those who would say that the term 'historical event' cannot fairly be applied to something which was, on any showing, unobserved and outside any category of human experience. There are those who would say that, whether it be an event or no, belief in it was not and could not be founded on purely evidential processes apart from our attitude towards the claim and person of Jesus Christ. Thus Don Cupitt urges that 'ratiocination comes first, and vision second', and that 'the Easter faith was born by theological and existential reflection upon the completed life of Jesus'.[8] But, given the analysis of the concept of history which Richardson's Bampton Lectures provide, it seems to me reasonable to say that while belief in the resurrection has as one of its ingredients our attitude to God in Christ, the process of belief also includes the consideration that *something happened* to account for the survival, the faith and the witness of the church, and that the something was, as the apostles themselves claimed, the resurrection. Such is the view of Professor C.F.D. Moule, who, without emphasizing the empty tomb, says that is is 'not altogether easy to dismiss it as a late apologetic development',[9] and it is also the view of Professor G.W.H. Lampe, who (while rejecting the particular traditions of the empty tomb) holds the resurrection to be 'an event in the external world' and 'a fact attested by a series of events'.[10] Alan Richardson has written:

> Perhaps the strongest argument for the Resurrection of Jesus is the indubitable fact that the worship of the earliest Christian communities took the form of a re-enactment of the episode on the dreadful night in which the Master had been betrayed and arrested, when he broke the bread and blessed the cup. The celebration of the judicial murder of a dead leader would have provided no occasion of joy and *eucharistia* apart from the certainty that Jesus was risen from the dead.[11]

III

This essay has not provided, even in outline, a history of theological development through the four exciting decades, nor an adequate account of Alan Richardson's many-sided achievements through this period. It has attempted no more than a kind of *speculum* of trends which his work has both reflected and corrected. In retrospect one can be surprised at the over-confidence of liberalism that its evolutionary programme would continue amidst the catastrophic times which were coming, and its failure to see that some of the concerns of the neo-orthodox were deeply related both to scientific biblical study and to the agonies of the contemporary world. Conversely, it can be seen that neo-orthodoxy, in its blindness to some of the values which liberalism had cherished and in its self-chosen isolation from much of the world around it, could sometimes find itself unable to speak intelligibly. Meanwhile a new chapter is here which this retrospective essay scarcely touches upon; but we have seen that Alan Richardson's work contains some prophetic words about it.

One of those words has been about the need to take *history* seriously. If men can effect events, so can God; and he can inspire those who speak about the meaning of those events – some of which are as crucial for the present as for the past. Another of those words has been about the urgency of the issues of *grace* as well as the issues of reason for theology's speaking to the contemporary world. It is in the universal significance of the incarnation and the cross that grace and history together meet contemporary man, for in St Augustine's words, 'so low has human pride sunk us that only divine humility can raise us up'.

NOTES

1. F.W. Dillistone, *Charles Raven*, Hodder and Stoughton 1975, p. 288.
2. Ibid., p. 118.
3. C.H. Dodd, *History and the Gospel*, Nisbet 1938, p. 103.
4. D.E. Nineham, *St Mark*, Penguin Books 1963, pp. 50f.
5. Xavier Léon-Dufour, *The Gospels and the Jesus of History*, Eng. trs., Collins 1968, pp. 192, 199.
6. Alan Richardson, 'The Resurrection of Jesus Christ', *Theology* LXXIV, 1971, p. 152.
7. Alan Richardson, *History Sacred and Profane*, SCM Press 1964, p. 134.
8. Don Cupitt, *Christ and the Hiddenness of God*, Lutterworth 1971, ch. 10.
9. Cf. C.F.D. Moule and Don Cupitt, 'The Resurrection: a Disagreement', *Theology* LXXV, 1972, p. 509.
10. G.W.H. Lampe in *The Resurrection*, ed. W. Purcell, Mowbray 1966, pp. 30, 68.
11. Alan Richardson, *Theology* LXXIV, p. 148.

~ 2 ~

The Future Shape of Popular Theology

JOHN BOWDEN

Alan Richardson's great contribution as a writer was to what publishers and booksellers like to call popular theology. In his case it is certainly not a misnomer. If success is to be measured in terms of the size of an ongoing audience, he was extraordinarily successful. Many of his books, particularly those written in the decade beginning just before the Second World War, and including *Creeds in the Making, The Miracle Stories of the Gospels, Preface to Bible Study* and *Christian Apologetics*, have been reprinted in the region of ten times and are still available;[1] what is more, no newer books have appeared from elsewhere which really replace them. More recent works, *An Introduction to the Theology of the New Testament*, and the two larger volumes which Alan Richardson edited, *A Theological Word Book of the Bible* and *A Dictionary of Christian Theology*, have been equally successful.[2] He has not only been read throughout the English-speaking world, but his books have been translated at least into Chinese, Dutch, Finnish, French, German, Italian, Portuguese and Spanish.

Much of this writing came in a vintage period for popular British theology: at about the same time authors like C.H. Dodd, A.M. Hunter and William Barclay were also making known many of the findings and the consequences of modern scholarship, especially on the Bible, to a wide public. None of these, however, managed to· cover quite so wide a field as Alan Richardson. Few writers can not only have produced commentaries on both Genesis and the Fourth Gospel,[3] but have written books on subjects ranging from patristics and the Enlightenment to the latest developments in modern theology and the philosophy of history. All these books have been opportune: Alan Richardson had an unerring eye for the important issues, even if the answers he gave to particular questions were not always convincing.

What makes a writer popular is often difficult to analyse; and it is difficult for the writer himself to satisfy equally the demands of integrity and of a popular audience. Some of the secrets of Alan Richardson's success can, however, be singled out. The most characteristic feature was his assurance: that he identified the question and felt able to provide the answer. He seldom quoted other writers directly, but presented their ideas in his own terms and his own language, writing in a great sweep which could take in whole periods of history and whole movements in a single paragraph. This assurance was based on a firm conviction of the supremacy of the Bible at the heart of the Christian tradition and of the importance of a particular way of understanding it;[4] and it made possible a lucid style, conveying a reassuring message in a paternal way. The merits of these qualities go without saying; they also have their reverse side. Those more in sympathy with particular writers may feel that Alan Richardson's presentation can fail to do them justice; those not always happy with his perspective may feel that other points of view are sometimes crowded out; those aware of the many problems and unsolved questions may wonder whether the loose ends have not been tidied away too neatly, whether the solutions are not too magisterial. Revised editions of Alan Richardson's books were never produced[5] and his whole corpus indicates a remarkably consistent approach: what is written is written, and it is hard to imagine it being put otherwise.

A conversation recorded in the introduction to *Preface to Bible Study* is illuminating in this respect. It seemed, a friend remarked after reading some of the manuscript, that too much was assumed to begin with, that it presupposed that all its potential readers would already be convinced Christians who were seeking further instruction, rather than enquirers asking whether the Bible could give them any help with their search. Alan Richardson's reply is characteristic. Certainly the book was intended for enquirers, but he assumed that they wanted to know what Christians believe about the Bible, why they believe it and how they make use of the Bible.[6] That could be communicated and that was what the book was about.

Alan Richardson's achievement was substantial, but it is significant that no new generation of popular writers has appeared to carry on the work done by him and his contemporaries. That is not to say that no good books have been written for a wider audience. They have. But more recent authors have not been so prolific, and even with the growth of cheap paperback publishing, many good books have not reached so wide an audience. There are signs of a decline in good popular theological writing, and in an increasingly less favourable economic situation, we seem likely to enter a dark age unless precisely the right approach can be achieved. At present, the main danger seems to be a disturbing polarity around two extremes: on the one hand theological writing becomes denser and more specialist, accessible only to the professionals and increasingly sophisticated in its subject matter and argumentation; on the other there is an increasing resort by many Christians to simplistic books which avoid important questions and may probably be said to sit lightly to the question of truth, but which at least seem relevant and comprehensible. This is not a healthy situation, and it is a matter for real concern to see how it might be remedied. So what might be the shape of a future popular theology?

The contribution of the theologian is inevitably limited. Theologians seldom revive dying churches or lead crusades, nor are they often instrumental in creating belief. They are primarily the guardians of the church's integrity, looking critically at new developments to see whether they maintain the character of Christian belief, countering criticisms of Christianity which may arise from new discoveries or new social movements, or if necessary revising earlier viewpoints in the light of new insights. But they can also be guides to the treasures of a great living tradition, who with knowledge and enthusiasm can introduce newcomers to a world of which they might otherwise be ignorant, who can deepen the knowledge, correct the misconceptions and educate the sensibilities of those already within that tradition.

There is a great deal to engage the theologians' attention: the history of Judaism and Christianity, the Bible, the theological writings of the church, its life and thought and devotion, ethical issues and the many problems for religious belief in the modern world. But theological activity will always be pointless unless due attention is paid not only to the subject-matter but to the potential audience. Sometimes this does not seem to be fully realized, and the subject-matter and its minutest details seem to dominate all else.

Alan Richardson was not known for specialist articles. As we have seen, he wrote for the most part for an audience convinced of the basic truth of Christianity, but wishing to deepen its knowledge, ready to put into practice the insights gained in prayer, worship and daily living. Other popular theology continues to be written on this presupposition. One notable example, John

Macquarrie's *The Faith of the People of God*, is presented as lay theology: of the people of God, by the people of God, for the people of God.[7] It was well received by the church journals and obviously appeals to a particular public, but for one reviewer at least it raised two important questions which need to be asked of theology of its type.[8] Has it properly understood today's audience, and is it possible for professional theology and contemporary experience to be brought into a creative relationship?

To talk of 'the people of God', of 'the church' as a basis for theology may be a dangerous delusion. Doubtless there are churches which hold together as communities, which can honestly claim to share common beliefs and common styles of life, but experience shows that they may well be unrepresentative. Many churches find great difficulty in being a community of any kind; members may attend at irregular intervals, and even the most regular are likely to differ quite strongly among themselves in beliefs, practices and priorities. It is also well known that there is a large group of people with virtually no formal connection with the churches who are nevertheless interested in religious questions and whose lives show often impressive signs of commitment. These are often the more mobile, younger, better educated, who find the atmosphere of local churches stifling, unadventurous and undemanding, and the approach of even the best of traditional popular theology incomprehensible or irrelevant.

In present circumstances it would seem unrealistic to talk of a uniform, integrated Christian audience. Any popular literaure will have to cater for very varied readers. Indeed, for a period in the nineteen-sixties symbolized by the publication of J. A. T. Robinson's *Honest to God*, it appeared as though theologians might have to reckon with a public quite different from any before. There was now, it was being said, a fundamentally different type of modern, secular man who, as a result of increased knowledge and the influence of a world dominated by science and technology, no longer had a God-shaped gap in his make-up. The arguments and the controversies centred on 'secular Christianity' and the 'death of God' need not be described in any detail here, but one point is worth noting. Most of the writing which appeared was produced by theologians from the Christian tradition disillusioned with what had been handed on to them and intent on challenging old beliefs and knocking down old structures, with all the one-sidedness of the fervid reformer. Their arguments were contested from within the Christian churches. But after the novelty of the situation had worn off, the ensuing debate attracted less and less interest from those whose difficulty was precisely the opposite, who were not concerned with knocking down old beliefs and delighting in the freedom which they thought they had attained, but with discovering whether it was possible to find enough ground for even a modest religious faith.

No saitsfying evidence has yet been marshalled to demonstrate the existence of a new brand of 'secular man', and a great deal exists to indicate that human make-up has changed little over the centuries. Not only have sociologists called attention to the way in which a need for some sort of religious expression, if suppressed in one direction, may find expression in another, but novelists, writers, theatre producers and even philosophers – perhaps most strikingly Philip Toynbee in *Towards the Holy Spirit* – have indicated that this need is in fact a fundamental part of human make-up. Looking back over the past decade it is in fact interesting to note that while the most publicized theological controversy was pointing in one direction, much writing outside the theological field was showing signs of moving the opposite way, becoming more aware of the presence of a religious dimension in human affairs.[9]

The audience for this latter kind of writing is an important one. It is representative of many literate people, some still in the churches and some on the edge of religious belief. It is becoming increasingly better educated, as higher education and the opportunities for learning increase, but is by contrast remarkably ignorant about the dimensions of religious belief and the elements of the Christian tradition. One sign of this is the way in which gifted members of panels in television quiz programmes may show a breathtaking range of general knowledge but cannot answer the simplest questions about the Bible. In a similar vein, James Barr has pointed out that students engaged in studies to which the Bible might be relevant nevertheless consider it beyond the horizon of their work in a way in which they would not treat any other comparable body of material.[10]

The theologian may find a public among those who are simply looking for reassuring answers, for some clear cause to follow. It is significant that evangelical fundamentalism and the charismatic movements continue to attract many people in a way not dissimilar from the appeal of the occult and other abnormal phenomena. In a world in which computers and technological processes play such a large part, there is a disturbing recourse to a second, different world of ideas which stands quite apart. However, a majority seems likely to find this divorce too high a price to pay. There will be many who are prepared to make do with limited answers. They will be aware of the size of the world and the range of cultures within it; they will be aware of the relativities of history and of the inadequacies of human understanding; they will be aware of the differences in human psychological make-up and man's capacity for delusion. They may well be distrustful of absolutes, distrustful of rhetorical-sounding phrases which are difficult to interpret, but ready to listen to someone who can either communicate an infectious interest in his subject or give evidence of experience in realms to which ordinary people do not regularly go but which seem possible and worthwhile to explore.

Communicating with this audience, or even parts of it, will be extremely demanding. In attempting to satisfy everybody there is a risk of satisfying nobody; and the very nature of Christianity, in particular its roots in the past on the one hand and its concern for present and future on the other, makes matters more difficult.

Christianity is inevitably concerned with history, with events in Palestine and its surroundings for a period of over a thousand years, culminating in the life of Christ and the beginnings of the Christian church, and thereafter for almost another two thousand years over an increasing area of the globe. What happened, particularly at the crucial periods of this history, is a matter of the utmost importance for understanding the nature of Christianity; one recent study even went so far as to claim that, apart from the example of living Christians, for Christianity 'the past is all we have'.[11] Christianity has a stake in the doing of history and the doing of history well.

Now to be a good historian means to assess evidence, to think oneself back into the terms of the period under review, to understand the mentality and the social background of an age and see particular events against that background. This is difficult enough for the professional historian, and doubtless even more difficult for the theologian than he often seems to imagine. The work involved in coming to understand even a limited period may well take a lifetime. And even if this task has been achieved and its results communicated, the reader of the findings will still be left in the past, even if it is a religious past. It is possible to be as absorbed in the events of the exodus and the foundation of Israelite belief or in the circumstances of the birth of the Christian church as in the origins of the Thirty Years' War or the first stages of the Industrial Revolution – and still not connect one's interest in any way with present-day concerns. The good historian is unlikely to see part of his task as being the spelling out of the significance of his findings for the present. That approach is predominantly reserved for the historian writing from a particular ideological perspective. And by the generally accepted canons of history writing, when an ideological perspective dominates, the result is usually bad history writing, often made up of illegitimate projections of the present on the past. Much theological history writing has been of this kind, being based on impossible generalizations or unsubstantiated evidence. This is particularly evident in the historical surveys made use of by systematic theologians.

In writings on the Bible too, however, an over-hasty attempt to relate past to present has all too often produced an unsatisfactory mixture of history and theology, which is unsatisfactory in both directions.[12] Even a working New Testament theologian can complain that he finds very little material to help him share, or even understand for himself, everyday life in New Testament times. He is given either an abstract of ideas or an archivist's inventory. He complains of the tendency for theology either to present the Bible, itself a historical document, as though it were self-explanatory, with just the right background for anyone to understand it and no sign that it is material for an ongoing historical enquiry, or to give the finished products of a more or less critical interpretation with no indication of how it was reached.[13]

Attempt to do good history and you remain in the past; attempt to relate the Bible directly to today and you risk distorting it and failing to do justice to history. The dilemma is evident, and at the heart of Alan Richardson's writing can be seen an ongoing attempt to solve it. The book which he himself prized most highly, his Bampton Lectures *History Sacred and Profane*, is in fact an attempt to outline and justify a new, 'non-positivist' understanding of history, so manipulating the distinction between fact and interpretation that the biblical interpretation of events may both be taken as a legitimate historical perspective and have direct relevance for today.[14] However, the presentation of the theory is difficult and sometimes obscure, and it has found few supporters.[15]

It is in fact hard to see any solution to the dilemma. Both sides of the problem need to be held in tension. It is unthinkable that detailed historical criticism and exposition of the Bible and attempts to understand and describe the social, political and religious forces which shaped Christianity, should not be pursued with rigour, like any other history. It is no job of the theologian to attempt to redefine the historian's work for him. But he might well reconsider how the results of the historian's work are to be applied. Not only has history (whether certain things happened or did not, precisely what the nature of past religious practices were) become something of an obsession with Christian apologists, but historical results have often been taken over in a naive and simplistic way.

Two brief illustrations may substantiate the point. In modern critical work on the Bible, the emphasis has been on illuminating the historical circumstances of the Bible and rendering its text in a clear modern version to the exclusion of all else. But for most of Christian history the Bible has been used without historical criticism, and much of it is not in fact historical. Has there been sufficient investigation of the way in which myth, allegory, aesthetic beauty make an effect on the hearer or reader? Is there not something to be said for the situation where a familiar version of the biblical text gradually grows on a person in the same way as happens with great poetry and prose, gathering associations and significance with the passage of time? Is the person who longs for some at least of the Bible in the Authorized Version misguided, and is someone who has made his own many parts of the Bible in that form less well equipped than someone with a thorough knowledge of critical problems and no firm memory of the text? In this area there are many questions to be asked, let alone answered.

Secondly, in liturgy, and in the public and private use of the Bible for worship and devotion, the problem is particularly acute. In public reading of the Bible, passages are over-used and their appeal is blunted by excessive repetition, or all too brief and discontinuous sections are presented, out of context, to an audience which no longer has a background against which to set them. Or devotional guides insist on imposing a moral, rather than providing just sufficient guidance to allow a passage to speak in its own terms, if at all. When even the familiar resonance is removed, and all is left to conscious reasoning, the result can verge on the absurd. What happens if historical criticism and a new view of the composition of the Bible seems to indicate that certain parts of the Bible have no plausible relevance for today?

Without pleading for a reactionary conservatism which goes to the other extreme and ignores all critical questions, it is surely reasonable to argue that the time has come when greater attention needs to be paid to the non-historical elements in Christianity. Some historical knowledge is, of course, helpful in understanding a poem, a play, a piece of music, but once that has been assimilated, understanding has to be guided into other dimensions. And again, in liturgy, must the form of services be so governed by what Christians have done in the past, be dictated by traditionalists concerned with the exact verbal reflection of the conclusions of past theological struggles? Is there not also a case for starting from the present and the wealth of means for expressing worship, provided that liturgical constructions have some organic links with the past?

Churchmen often seem to have only a primitive aesthetic sense, and theologians are hardly better. The number of theological books which are attractive to read as books are few, and the domination of abstract argumentation can be oppressive where the writer, like the poet, should really be struggling for evocative words. What is all too rare is writing which can present, say, the Bible in such a way as to make it more meaningful than it was before, without seeking to over-edify, or apply too direct a moral, or provide all the answers, merely arousing a sense of expectation and interest and enthusiasm over what might be found by those with sufficient interest to look.

Might not greater strides be made in understanding the Bible and Christian tradition if more attention were diverted in this direction, in place of the constant retreading of the well-worn tracks, many of which increasingly look as if they are going to lead nowhere? For biblical criticism and the understanding of doctrine are not without their crises, and one of the problems facing the would-be popularizer of the findings of the professional theologians is that there are fewer 'assured results' to be presented than there seemed to be a generation ago. As the reviewer mentioned above suggested, it may be that the time has gone when the task of the popularizer is to mediate the findings of scholarship to a wider audience; instead, he may need to reflect the questionings of the audience back to theologians, indicating the new tasks which they need to undertake.

Through Alan Richardson's writing also runs the assumption, embodied most clearly in the *Theological Word Book of the Bible* which he edited, that a prior claim on anyone concerned with Christianity is to understand the specifically biblical concepts in their specifically biblical sense. In this, his view is not unrelated to that of Karl Barth, though its context is different and its logic less rigorous. But for reasons which cannot be enumerated here,[16] matters have proved rather more complicated than that. No simple answer in these terms would seem to be viable. The Bible cannot be treated in isolation from its own culture, from the questions of philosophers, from the relativities of historical understanding, in a safe haven of 'biblical theology'.

By contrast, more recently the theologian has been portrayed as a cartographer, attempting to draw an outline map of the universe in order to construct an interpretative scheme within which men may plot and make sense of their own thought, actions and experiences.[17] He may stand in the Christian tradition, but he is involved in the consideration of the religions of the world and religious experience in general, of morality and the basis of moral judgment, of human make-up and human emotions, of historical experience, of nature, of aesthetics. In one sense there is nothing that is alien to him, though at the same time he must allow each of these areas its own independence, without becoming an imperialist and trying to bring each of them under his own rule. For if God is the God of the Christian faith, with the character that the enlightened Christian tradition has come to give him, it is reasonable to expect that while freedom was given to men and the universe, sufficient indications of the divine presence would be left to be realized and followed by a wide variety of people.

It must certainly be held against a great deal of theological writing that its authors do not seem quite to be real people, that their proposed programmes have not been tested out in real life under the conditions in which most people have to live it. They often do not reflect the world of the ordinary man's experiences and emotions, his personal dilemmas and failings and glimpses of something greater. Often they do not even reflect much knowledge of the ordinary person's interests and affections, the enlargement of a personal world that can be offered by novels and plays, music and painting, television and travel, friendship and work. In some respects theology must surely be a discipline which resists specialization, for specialization can be seen not only as the deepened knowledge of one area of the world but as the inevitable and accompanying restriction of knowledge in a great many others – and there is no evidence that the most profound knowledge of God is to be found by digging deeper and deeper into one particular burrow.

After all, theology must be related to a faith by which it is possible to live; it is for people on a journey, and no traveller can make sensible use of more than a certain amount of luggage. He needs his perception to be sharpened, his eyes to be opened to make sense of what he sees, to recognize his route, to interpret the scenery, to enjoy or to tolerate what he can.

There is no knowing quite what will prove relevant to acquiring this kind of perception. But it does seem as though the demand to be made on a future popular theology *is* a training in vision rather than a communication of facts, findings and theories; a stimulus for the imagination and an indication of new discoveries to be made rather than supposedly cut-and-dried solutions. After all, we surely expect to grow, to be on our way, rather than to have arrived.

In this respect, it is encouraging that there are signs that some theological writing is beginning to move in this direction. It would be good to think that for example John Taylor's book *The Go-Between God* received the extremely wide readership and the acclaim that it did precisely because its subject-matter was so diverse, because it was related to so many areas of human experience, because there were both passages with which it was possible to identify and passages indicating the shape of new potential experience to come and to be sought after.[18]

Similarly, the recent interest shown in analysing works of fantasy is a healthy one.[19] There is considerable pressure upon us, given the kind of world in which we live, to be too literalistic, or to pass off deeper issues with a joke or a shrug of the shoulders. But this can be indicative of all too narrow an outlook, and fantasy can play a part not only in making sense of our own personalities, with which we have to live, but also in seeing other dimensions to our world which we might otherwise miss.

Music, too, can be relevant, even though it is too difficult to analyse its significance in words. Its truth in expressing emotion has been pointed out: precisely because it is ambivalent in a way words cannot be, it can be an instrument in conveying feelings, a means of therapy and restoring wholeness, even a vehicle for a sense of the transcendent.[20]

This whole realm of fantasy, of aesthetics, of the arts, is particularly important as training for worship. Men's emotions are moved and their hearts are stirred by many things, which is one reason at least why worship should be as diverse as possible.[21] And in a new age, worship may often prove easier outside the church than in. Men may be moved to it perhaps through some sense of what has been called the holy, the numinous, standing apart from and over the everyday world: in the theatre, the concert hall, the opera house, the country, as well as in church or cathedral. And it may equally well appear in every-day life, in human relationships, in humdrum incidents, for those who have the eyes to see.[22] Theology will need to look at this experience, analyse it and attempt to evaluate its significance, trying to distinguish the real from the spurious, the healthy from the unhealthy.

However, there will be an insistent pressure on any theology which attempts to dwell too long on an aesthetic dimension, pressure from our knowledge of the world and the need for commitment to remedy its wrongs. The popular theology of the last generation was written in the shadow of a world war, but some of it at any rate shows remarkably few traces of that. Since then, consciousness of the fragile checks and balances which keep the world habitable, of social and international unrest and inequality, of all the factors with which we are so well familiar, has developed greatly. Indeed, serious commitment to a sacrificial life-style and a concern for the remedying of injustice in the name of reconciliation and love is in no way an exclusively Christian or religious prerogative. Men of many ideologies or none at all have a common concern for the welfare of man and his planet, and one thing the theologian might have to learn is to be content to look in the name of humanity for developments to which he might want to give a more specifically religious motivation. Where the theologian need not bring in his theology, it might well be that he would do better to keep silent. But his concern is with God and his activity, with the transcendent, and unless he can talk meaningfully about that he has no contribution to make at all. He cannot be so dominated by the concepts and claims of sociology, psychology, ecology and so on that he has little tangible to contribute *qua* theologian.

One contribution which he might regularly be expected to make is an emphasis on the person and claims of Jesus of Nazareth. It is noticeable how at a time when belief in God has seemed more problematical, books about, references and appeals to Jesus have become more widespread. But a great deal of this talk about Jesus, like the references to Jesus in popular devotion, is often rooted only loosely in the basic documents of the Christian tradition. Often talk of Jesus is no more than the ideals of a particular age projected on to Jesus as a lay figure, or perhaps no more than phraseology meaningful to a small group, striking an emotional chord with a few others, but to the majority just meaningless rhetoric.

There are manifestly those for whose religious belief a picture of Jesus, even the biblical record of him, has paramount meaning. To question the veracity of their impressions may produce angry and hostile reactions. But it is a fact that modern criticism has raised many questions about our possible knowledge of his life, death and resurrection, and there is no simple answer to those who are inclined to be more sceptical, particularly those who have been especially closely involved in a study of the gospel tradition. Indeed, it should be recognized that there may well be Christians who, while feeling at home in the Christian tradition, while believing that within it is to be found more of the truth than anywhere else they know, while recognizing the magnitude of the events focused on Jesus Christ and the church's claims for him, nevertheless cannot avoid placing a question-mark over his figure. For them, other figures from the Christian tradition elsewhere or even people of their own acquaintance may sometimes hint as meaningfully at the nature of Christianity. They may feel sufficiently agnostic to leave on one side many of the questions of fact or fiction, truth or falsehood, orthodoxy or heresy, which bother other Christians, trusting that if they live by what light they see and look for the grace and forgiveness of which the Christian tradition speaks, the God whom they believe that they can glimpse, at least dimly, in the Christian tradition and even outside it, will not abandon them.

It is depressing that an attempt at a statement of Christian belief in terms similar to this has recently been put forward and has been greeted with horror, dismay, protest and abuse.[23] It may be open to question in many respects, but its positive side has been ignored and it has largely been compared with a 'fuller', more 'orthodox' doctrinal system. Much popular theology which may appear in coming years may well meet with the same reaction in some quarters. There is still a deep-seated feeling that Christian faith must be all or nothing, that even the slightest deviation from the norm will open the floodgates for doubt, despair, moral collapse and anarchy. The feelings of those who react in this way must be understood. But theology cannot progress without risk. Even in the days of classical theological expressions of doctrines, distinctions between 'orthodox' and 'heretics' could only be made after the event. At a more difficult time like our own, it may well prove better to venture on new paths which might possibly provide a better way forward, even at the risk of failure or disaster, than to put up the shutters and attempt to sit out the storm.

NOTES

1. Details are: *Creeds in the Making* (1935), 11th impression; *The Miracle Stories of the Gospels* (1941), 10th impression; *Preface to Bible Study* (1943), 8th impression; *Christian Apologetics* (1947), 8th impression. All published by SCM Press.
2. *An Introduction to the Theology of the New Testament* (1958), 6th impression; *A Theological Word Book of the Bible* (1950), 12th impression; *A Dictionary of Christian Theology* (1969), 3rd impression.

3. *Genesis 1-11*, Torch Bible Commentaries (1953), 8th impression; *The Gospel according to Saint John*, Torch Bible Commentaries (1959), 5th impression.

4. For a brief summary of his views see *The Bible in the Age of Science*, SCM Press 1961, pp. 174-86.

5. Compare the work of A.M. Hunter, whose *Introducing the New Testament* and *The Work and Words of Jesus* have each been revised at least once.

6. *Preface to Bible Study*, SCM Press 1943, pp. 7f.

7. John Macquarrie, *The Faith of the People of God*, SCM Press 1972, especially pp. 5f.

8. Anonymous review, *The Times Literary Supplement*, 20 October 1972.

9. Philip Toynbee, *Towards the Holy Spirit*, SCM Press 1973, especially pp.24ff.; as two examples among many see Bernard Levin, *The Pendulum Years*, Cape 1970, especially chapters 1 and 21; Peter Brook, *The Empty Space*, Penguin Books 1972, chapter 2, 'The Holy Theatre'.

10. James Barr, *The Bible in the Modern World*, SCM Press 1973, p. 61.

11. F. Gerald Downing, *The Past is All We Have*, SCM Press 1975.

12. Compare works like Siegfried Herrmann, *A History of Israel in Old Testament Times*, SCM Press 1975, and Martin Hengel, *Judaism and Hellenism*, SCM Press 1974, and their sound historical method, with works like John Bright, *A History of Israel*, revised edition SCM Press 1972, or Floyd V. Filson, *A New Testament History*, SCM Press 1965. As one example of bad history writing by a systematic theologian, Harvey Cox, *The Secular City*, SCM Press 1965, may be cited.

13. F. Gerald Downing, *The Past is All We Have*, pp.25f., 20.

14. See especially *History Sacred and Profane*, SCM Press 1964, pp.184ff. A serious problem is posed by the concept of 'real' history, which appears e.g. on p. 249.

15. See Van A. Harvey, *The Historian and the Believer*, SCM Press 1967, esp. pp.231ff.

16. For a summary see Brevard S. Childs, *Biblical Theology in Crisis*, Westminster Press, Philadelphia 1973; James Barr, *The Bible in the Modern World*, SCM Press 1973.

17. See James Richmond, *Theology and Metaphysics*, SCM Press 1970, pp.92ff., for an elaboration of this point made by Ian Ramsey.

18. John V. Taylor, *The Go-Between God*, SCM Press 1972.

19. See e.g. Gunnar Urang, *Shadows of Heaven*, SCM Press 1971; Sallie TeSelle, *Speaking in Parables*, SCM Press 1975.

20. See e.g. Suzanne Langer, *Philosophy in a New Key*, Mentor Books, New York 1964, p. 206; Bryan Magee, *Aspects of Wagner*, Panther Books 1972, pp.66f.; Deryck Cooke, *The Language of Music*, Oxford University Press 1959, p. 272.

21. See John Killinger, *Leave it to the Spirit*, SCM Press 1971.

22. See J.G. Davies, *Every Day God*, SCM Press 1973.

23. Maurice Wiles, *The Remaking of Christian Doctrine*, SCM Press 1974.

~ 3 ~

Alan Richardson and his Critics in the Area of Hermeneutics

ANTHONY HANSON

Presumably hermeneutics meant originally the attempts to answer the question how one should interpret the Bible. This question became acute when a large number of educated Christians began to realize during the last two hundred years that traditional Christian theology had not always interpreted the Bible correctly. Robert Morgan in a recent book has expressed this clearly when he says that the problem of hermeneutics has arisen because of the modern doubt as to whether traditional Christian theology was really biblical.[1] From this doubt would arise an attempt to write a theology of the Old Testament or of the New Testament which should give an account of what the Bible really teaches. This has been attempted on a considerable scale ever since the last century; and this is undoubtedly what Alan Richardson was doing in his *Introduction to the Theology of the New Testament.* Indeed he is the only English theologian to have done so with any serious intent. This sort of attempt must, of course, be distinguished from the old, pre-critical treatment of the New Testament, which would simply consist in arranging texts in order so as to show how they supported traditional doctrines.

But Alan Richardson's attempt had its own difficulties, as he was fully aware: in the first place there was the danger that traditional belief might exercise too great an influence on the writer's judgment; and in the second place there was the danger that he might impose on his material a pattern which did not really belong to it. Thus Alan Richardson could write that for many modern scholars

New Testament theology means either an attempt to unify dogmatically the varieties of New Testament thought (which they rightly disapprove) or simply the evolutionist tracing of the development of the Christian religion from its antecedents in the ministry of Jesus to its proliferation in Hellenized second-century Catholicism.[2]

There is, however, a more fundamental difficulty than the danger of orthodox or other dogmatic interpretations: what if the New Testament does not present any one theology? Suppose that there is in fact no intrinsic theological unity about the New Testament at all, then obviously the very conception of 'New Testament theology' is futile. This is in fact the doubt which has been increasing all through this century, particularly since the last war, with the result that in some quarters the era in which a 'New Testament theology' could be written seems already past. Thus James Barr can write in a recent book that the various attempts to write a theology of the Old Testament or of the New Testament were useful indeed and not by any means hopeless enterprises; but he obviously regards them as phenomena of the past.[3] In much the same vein Käsemann can accuse the ecumenical movement of seeking to impose an artificial unity on the New Testament:

> The ecumenical movement furthers the tendency to stress what binds rather than what divides, and looks for the same disposition in the New Testament.[4]

Thus, because it is doubted whether the New Testament has one consistent message, the question of hermeneutics has had to be put one stage farther back. Instead of asking 'How should one interpret the Bible?', we have to ask, 'What was the original Christianity?'

I

When we turn to those who have attempted to answer this question, we find that they fall into two main groups: there are those who believe that there is an essential continuity between what Jesus taught and what claims he made on the one hand and the preaching of the early church on the other; and there are those who deny any such continuity. Within these two groups there are wide divergencies of outlook, but the great divide falls between these two groups. I think the recognition of this divide would have clarified the various estimates which representatives of the two groups have made of each other, and perhaps obviated some of the criticisms which have been levelled against Alan Richardson's *Introduction to the Theology of the New Testament*. It may help to put Alan Richardson's work in its right context if we look at representatives of each of these two groups among modern scholars. It will at least serve to show that Alan Richardson was no Anglo-Saxon reactionary, intent on maintaining a position which has been abandoned by all reputable scholars on the continent.

We begin with E. Stauffer, who is himself among the number of those who have published a *New Testament Theology* within the last forty years. The nineteenth century, he says, had ended by saying that a biography of Jesus was impossible. Instead we are offered by Bultmann Jesus' proclamation, the words and works of Jesus by K.L. Schmidt, by Dibelius the miraculous theophany of Jesus. But the New Testament offers the way of Jesus; Jesus speaks of the way of the Son of man, the way of suffering.[5] In effect therefore Stauffer sees the Son of man concept as the link between the Jesus of history and the christology of the early church. He writes: 'The coming of Christ is God's answer to the questions raised by human history' (p. 103). Stauffer therefore aligns himself with those who see salvation history as the key to the early church's proclamation. He believes that Jesus described his 'significance for the theology of history' by means of the title 'Son of man' (p. 108) and that Paul's Second Adam christology corresponds to Jesus' Son of man christology 'Son of God' he associates with the messianic title, which he certainly thinks Jesus claimed, albeit with a difference (pp. 113-5). Stauffer can be legitimately described as a conservative scholar, and he wrote before the publication of the Qumran material. But he had a very extensive knowledge of the Judaism which was contemporary with the birth of Christianity, and he cannot be merely ignored as if he were outdated by later scholarship.

Oscar Cullmann is, of course, the great champion of salvation history as the bridge which joins the Jesus of history to the Christ of faith. He says very clearly that 'as scholars we simply cannot neglect to take Jesus' own self-consciousness into consideration'. And he adds: 'In his teaching and life Jesus accomplished something new from which the first Christians had to proceed in their attempt to explain his person and work.'[6] In an interesting critique of Bultmann he says that we can hardly 'have the same faith as the early Church if we accept its Christological views, but still assert that Jesus himself had "no self-consciousness" of being what we confess him to be'. A little later on he writes: 'The early Church believed in Christ's Messiahship only because it believed that Jesus believed himself to be the Messiah' (p. 8). He sums it up very clearly on p. 9 when he writes: 'There emerges in the thinking of early Christianity one total picture of the Christ-event from the pre-existence to eschatology. It is not as if the New Testament were a series of monographs like Kittel's theological word-book.'

Salvation history is here taken not only as the bridge which links the historical Jesus to the early church but also as the feature which gives unity to the New Testament itself. Another distinguished modern champion of the salvation-history approach is W.G. Kümmel, who writes that what Jesus, Paul and John have in common is 'belief in God's saving eschatological action in Jesus'.[7]

Alan Richardson himself certainly belonged to the school of theologians who interpreted the New Testament according to the schema of salvation history. He maintained that Jesus himself thought out his own vocation and taught it to his disciples. He wrote:

> The assumption that Jesus himself thought out (humanly speaking) the problem of his own existence and taught the answer to his disciples makes far better sense of the historical evidence than all the attempts of the liberal critics to explain the evidence away.[8]

In another work he claims that the theology of the New Testament is 'the Spirit-guided working out of the clues suggested by Jesus'.[9] He expressed the same view when he wrote elsewhere: 'The theology of the New Testament as a whole is based primarily upon Jesus' own interpretation of his mission and person in the light of the understanding of the Old Testament.'[10]

These quotations in themselves would not perhaps point to salvation history as such, but only to a strong and definite link between the historical Jesus and the proclamation of the early church. But Alan Richardson was also much more specific. In his *Introduction to the Theology of the New Testament* he held, for instance, that Jesus did identify himself with the figure of the Son of man (p. 57), that this figure was inspired by the book of Daniel (p. 87), and that this figure meant to him 'a Messiah who suffers according to the Scriptures' (p. 134). Moreover, 'Jesus conceived of himself as establishing by his self-oblation a new covenant between God and a new Israel', and 'he thought of himself as a new Moses' (p. 86). Alan Richardson assumed that Jesus did think of himself as Messiah (p. 128). He had also a unique filial consciousness: 'Jesus . . . is conscious of having been assigned a special mission and task by God.' This is defined in corporate terms, for Alan Richardson added: 'It is as the New Israel that Jesus is to be understood as Son of God' (pp. 149f.).

The last three scholars whom we have mentioned, including Alan Richardson himself, can be said to belong to the same school, those who hold the theory of 'salvation history'. The next one we consider, Wolfhart Pannenberg, stands with those three in that he holds that there is an essential continuity between the Jesus of history and the Christ proclaimed by the early church. But Pannenberg cannot accurately be described as a disciple of the 'salvation-history school'. He writes as follows about the historical Jesus:

> Only if the history of Jesus – understood in its original historical context, and not as an isolated event by itself – has its meaning in itself will one be able to show, positively, how and to what extent the inherent meaning of the event itself has been unfolded in the various forms of the kerygma and in the language of each new situation in the history of the transmission of tradition in primitive Christianity.[11]

This implies that the Jesus of history does provide sufficient historical basis for the christology of the church. This implication is made explicit two pages later, when he writes: 'The Christ-event is not value-neutral in itself; it does not just have to be clothed with this or that meaning by a kerygma different from itself.'

For more specific details about what the historical Jesus provides us with, we must turn to Pannenberg's book on the incarnation, *Jesus – God and Man*. Here we learn that he specifically rejects the thesis (which goes back to Kähler) that christology must begin with the proclamation of the early community and not with the historical Jesus.[12] And later on we read: 'Christology must start from Jesus of Nazareth, not from his significance for us' (p. 48). But Pannenberg is much more sceptical about what can be known of Jesus' own consciousness of his vocation than is any of the salvation-history school. Pannenberg thinks that Jesus probably expressly rejected the title of Messiah (p. 31). Indeed, on a later page it is implied that we cannot be certain whether Jesus claimed any title at all, even that of Son of man (pp. 251f). Pannenberg does, of course, lay very great emphasis on Jesus as the final revelation of God, but this revelation is only made known at Jesus' resurrection. Israelite tradition expected God to manifest himself at the end of the age, and this is what happened in Jesus (p. 70). In the resurrection we understand the historical career: 'The Easter event reveals Jesus' activity and fate as a unified complex of meaning' (p. 115). But as far as Jesus' own vocation is concerned, Pannenberg limits himself to the sole element of filial consciousness. He argues that Jesus' historical obedience to the Father must reflect an ontological Father-Son relationship (p. 159), and this means that Jesus must in some sense have been conscious of his unity with God (p. 326). And in a passage already referred to (pp. 251), Pannenberg says that Jesus claimed an authority which really transcended that of Moses, and to that extent justified the Jews' accusation recorded in such passages as John 5.18.

Thus Pannenberg cannot be described as defending a salvation-history scheme, since he does not commit himself to the view that Jesus claimed any titles that would lead from Jesus' own vocation to the christology of the early church. The solitary plank left in his bridge is Jesus' filial self-consciousness, on which Pannenberg's entire christology is built. However, he does bridge the gap, albeit precariously, and must therefore be counted among the number of those who believe that there is an essential continuity between the Jesus of history and the Jesus of faith, and who use this continuity as a key to the interpretation of the New Testament.

II

In contrast to the group of scholars so far considered there is, of course, a very influential school who in effect deny any real continuity between the Jesus of history and the Christ proclaimed by the early church. Among living theologians who belong to this school Rudolf Bultmann is still by far the most famous. He states in so many words: 'The theology of the New Testament begins with the kerygma of the earliest Church and not before.'[13] Bultmann would agree with Pannenberg that none of the titles given to Jesus in the New Testament can be confidently traced back to Jesus himself; but he would make no use at all of Jesus' filial consciousness. Indeed he would hold that we can know nothing about it. Thus Bultmann poses very acutely the problem of continuity. But he has his own answer to it: according to Bultmann, what is common between the original teaching of Jesus, the proclamation of the early church, the christology of Paul and of John, and the message of authentic Christianity in this and every age is the element of existential demand which Christian preaching makes upon the individual. This, and nothing else, is what is essential to Christianity. By this means Bultmann has bridged, to his own satisfaction, the 'two gaps' of which Pannenberg writes,[14] the gap between the Jesus of history and the Jesus of faith, and the gap between the language and concepts in which the New Testament message is presented and our way of thinking today.[15] Consequently Bultmann is not really concerned about the unity of the New Testament, or whether the original Christianity is correctly reproduced in the New Testament or not. He believes that he can show how the original message of Jesus developed under the influence of various external forces until it reached the form of early

Catholicism; and he has a clue which enables him to distil one and the same message under all the forms of Christianity from Jesus to Irenaeus: all present the same existential challenge. In this respect he is quite different from one of his most distinguished disciples, whose work we must presently consider.

The problem of the second gap, that between New Testament man and modern man, has provoked an entire literature of its own, at the heart of which lies Bultmann's concept of demythologizing the New Testament. Pannenberg acutely observes that Lessing's famous remark about the 'ugly ditch' which he could not cross was provoked by exactly this problem.[16] For eighteenth-century idealism the gap between eternal truths of reason and contingent facts of history (represented by the New Testament message) was too wide. Pannenberg accuses Bultmann of being actuated by a fear that the Christian faith is not grounded in an actual past event.[17] Professor Barr in his most recent book has shown that this desire to free the Christian message from its rootage in history is not confined to Bultmann and his school. It can be found among English scholars also: those who, like D.E. Nineham, emphasize strongly what Barr calls 'cultural relativism', in the sense that each culture can only be understood by those who actually live in it, can hardly be reconciled with those who, on the other hand, emphasize the literary qualities of the Bible and try to help us to appreciate these by an act of empathy with the writers to the Bible: 'The argument for cultural relativism is deeply in contradiction with the appeal to literary appreciation.'[18] Barr himself believes that this second gap can be bridged through the life of the church and the church's use of the Bible:

> The relation between the man of the Bible and his situation and the man of today with his modern situation is provided by two things: that they are in the continuity of the one people of God and that their faith is related to the biblical model of understanding (p. 141).

Bultmann's way of bridging the first gap has inevitably led us into a discussion of the second gap, because he uses the same method for bridging both. It is important, I believe, that English scholars at least should keep the two gaps as quite separate questions, even though both come under the heading of what the Germans call hermeneutics. This is because very few English scholars, if any, accept the existentialist philosophy which is still so popular on the continent, and also because Alan Richardson's most acute critic, Käsemann, does not accept it either. If one does not accept Heidegger's philosophical presuppositions, then the various modifications of Heidegger proposed by Bultmann, or Fuchs, or Ebeling, or any other of Bultmann's disciples, simply do not concern one. As a matter of fact Alan Richardson considered these various modifications in a chapter called 'The New Hermeneutics' in a fairly recent book.[19] It is very remarkable that nowhere in that chapter did he make any link with the other problem, the gap between the Jesus of history and the Christ proclaimed by the church. But a solution to the problem of the second gap depends on finding a solution to the problem of the first: if you cannot show that there is a dominant message in the New Testament, there is no point in discussing how to translate the message into modern terms. Alan Richardson's contribution to the problem of hermeneutics, for better or for worse, lies in the area of the link between Jesus and the early church. It is in this field that his critics attacked him. No one, as far as I know, has felt moved to discuss his chapter on 'The New Hermeneutics'.

Hans Conzelmann, one of the most distinguished of Bultmann's disciples, wrote an introduction to the theology of the New Testament in 1968. He shows himself well aware of the disintegrating effect of modern biblical criticism when he writes of the danger 'that the New Testament tends to break up into a more or less fortuitous accumulation of "conceptions", types or "theologies" '.[20] For Conzelmann,

> The basic problem of the New Testament theology is not, how did the proclaimer, Jesus of Nazareth, become the proclaimed Messiah, Son of God, Lord? It is rather, why did faith maintain the identity of the Exalted One with Jesus of Nazareth after the resurrection appearances?

He thus agrees with Bultmann that the titles came only after the resurrection. His aim is 'the understanding of the message in the texts' (p. 7). And indeed he also adopts Bultmann's philosophical framework, for he assumes that there is one message in the texts and that it must be demythologized. Käsemann says of him that he regards 'the confessional formulae as the objectification of the Christian self-understanding, which in the subsequent process of interpretation is partly elucidated, partly made more uniform, and partly distorted'.[21] Conzelmann is therefore interesting from the point of view of our study because he is a disciple of Bultmann who has realized the danger that the New Testament material will simply disintegrate if there is no real christological link between Jesus' message and the proclamation of the early church, or no underlying philosophy to supply the deficiency.

Pannenberg has claimed that modern criticism of the Bible really sprang from the Reformers' conviction that the Bible could be understood from itself without referring to the tradition of the church. But when advancing criticism did away with the traditional doctrine of the inspiration of scripture, the very unity of scripture on which the Reformers depended so much was shattered.[22] Thus from the Reformation onwards the disintegration of the New Testament was always a possibility. This possibility was usually obscured by the presuppositions of the critics: throughout the nineteenth century the search for the Jesus of history seemed to supply the necessary key to the message of the New Testament, even though this involved writing off a great deal of New Testament material. At the turn of the century the 'history of religions' school diverted attention from the question of *message* altogether, since they appeared to have resolved the New Testament into a casebook of oriental religion. Karl Barth introduced the question of faith and therefore of theology again, and Bultmann was sufficiently in sympathy with Barth to see the need to supply a unifying system of thought, even though what he offered was existentialist philosophy and not neo-orthodox theology.[23] But now that we are living in a post-Barthian epoch, and since we Anglo-Saxons at least do not feel the overwhelming attraction of existentialism, the possibility of there being no unifying theme in the New Testament must be honestly faced. Significantly enough, the person who faces it most starkly today is himself a German scholar and a disciple of Bultmann, Ernst Käsemann.

In a recent article, representing a presidential address originally delivered to the *Societas Novi Testamenti Studiorum*, he has expressed very clearly the doubt which he entertains about the unity of the New Testament. He begins by quoting Wrede to the effect that 'the New Testament is not an intrinsic unity and indeed is no more than one surviving component of Christian origins'.[24] We may note *en passant* that the language here is very much that of the history-of-religions school, and not that of a theologian. Käsemann goes on to claim that 'a relatively complete history of early Christianity cannot be reconstructed', and 'the liberal notion of an organic development is now as bankrupt as the idealist unfolding of the divine Spirit in dialectical movement'. He adds that to concentrate on the theology of Paul and John may be to miss the 'community-faith' which is better represented in Matthew, Luke, the Catholic Epistles and the Pastorals. He criticizes those whom he calls conservatives, specifically including Alan Richardson in this

category, on the ground that they have imposed an *a priori* pattern
on the material. We must examine this criticism in detail later. For
the moment it is sufficient to note it, and to observe that Käsemann
goes on to say that Braun has discredited Bultmann's fundamentally anthropological interpretation of the New Testament by claiming that there is no one anthropology common to all
the writers of the New Testament. The New Testament, he
continues, has no internal coherence; the appearance of coherence
is given by 'an early catholicizing and more or less orthodox
Church's interest in normative doctrine'. Towards the end of the
article Käsemann does indicate that clues do exist which may help us
eventually to see the New Testament as some sort of unity: 'All the
documents are designed to witness to the Lordship of Christ ... The
identity of the Nazarene is defined by the cross more than by
anything else.' These are interesting evidences of Käsemann's less
negative conclusions, which we must examine later.[25]

Here, then, is a scholar who has come very close indeed to the
conclusion that there can be no hermeneutics at all because the
material is too diverse and fragmentary for us to be able to put any
one adequate interpretation upon it. Since he can hardly support
the absurd conclusion that there was no original Christianity, he
must mean to imply that we do not have the evidence to tell us what
the original Christianity was. In Käsemann in fact we seem to have
come almost to the bottom of a descending scale: at the top is
traditional pre-critical orthodoxy, which believed it knew exactly
what the message of the New Testament was, and was prepared to
fit every part of the Bible into an orthodox theological system by
means of deliberate harmonization. Next come the salvation-history
school, who claim that they can find leading themes which
integrally connect the Jesus of history with the Christ of the early
kerygma, and which also run all through the New Testament, till
they appear (considerably altered it may be) in the creeds of
catholic Christendom. One stage below the salvation-history school
comes Pannenberg, with his one essential christological link (Jesus'
filial consciousness) between Jesus and the early church. Pannenberg is, however, still to be numbered among those who believe
that from the Jesus of history to the traditional christology of
the church there is a succession to be traced such that one can
legitimately claim that the church rightly interprets Jesus' message
and mission. Below Pannenberg on the scale we find Bultmann,
and all those who deny the continuity between the Jesus of history
and the kerygma of the early church, but who mend the gap by

means of existential philosophy. For these at least there is a theology of the New Testament and a legitimate hermeneutics, however achieved. Then at the very bottom of the scale comes Käsemann, who questions the assumptions of all those who are above him in the scale, and who is on the very verge of denying the possibility of hermeneutics altogether. If we are to understand Alan Richardson's contribution to hermeneutics in its true perspective, it is essential that we place him in some such context as the foregoing. In this field he is no solitary Kierkegaard.

Before we pass to consider Alan Richardson's most positive contribution to hermeneutics, it may be well to glace at two recent British contributors to this subject, both of whom we have already had occasion to quote, Professor James Barr and Dr Robert Morgan. Barr is not explicitly dealing with exactly our problem in his latest book, though he has much to say that is relevant to it. At one point he mentions two demands which an adequate Christian theology must meet: it must give a central place to Jesus of Nazareth, and its God must be the God who was already known in Israel.[26] This sounds like a very modest claim, but in fact it implies a great deal. The fact that Barr puts Jesus of Nazareth at the centre and not the Christ of faith implies that according to him the gap between the two can be bridged, though he does not indicate how. His demand that theology's God should be the God who was already known to Israel is equally far-reaching. It involves at least two theological assumptions: the first is that God has revealed himself. It is true that elsewhere in this book (and even more in his previous work *Old and New in Interpretation*)[27] Professor Barr avoids the category of revelation, primarily perhaps for philosophical reasons. But in fact I cannot see how one can avoid the concept, if not the word, if one is going to talk about God being 'known'. The other theological assumption is that Jesus of Nazareth must somehow be related to the God of Israel. Unless Professor Barr is prepared to have a totally disintegrated theology, he must presumably relate his two explicit principles to each other. This implies some sort of a considered christology. Thus what at first sight might seem a minimum or reductionist theology of the New Testament has proved to stand perhaps between the salvation-history school and Pannenberg.

Dr Robert Morgan's suggested solution to our problem is somewhat different. He does, it is true, at first appear to align himself with a more traditional point of view, for he insists that the Christian theologian is not free to interpret the tradition any way he likes. If he is a Christian theologian he must show himself to be in line with Christian tradition.[28] A little later on, however, he amplifies this in a long footnote, in which he sets out what he believes to be constant in Christianity.[29] He writes:

> A similar means of controlling the modern form of critical interpretation would be to look for 'constants' in the tradition and argue that no interpretation of the tradition is Christian if it lacks these. They can be written into one's definition of Christianity.

He then quotes Schleiermacher's definition by way of example, and goes on to give his own:

> The man from Nazareth, the assumption that he is decisive for human existence, and something about the positive way in which he is decisive.

We must bear in mind that this is only a suggestion, not a carefully thought out position. All the same, it is rather startling. For one thing, it seems to have no reference to God; the 'death-of-God' theology would apparently fit this definition quite well. But also it insists on 'the man from Nazareth'. If God were subsequently to be brought into the scheme, this detail would imply that the first gap had somehow been bridged. The reference to human existence may be an indication that existentialism is hovering in the background, or it may merely be a rudimentary doctrine of redemption. We may reasonably conclude that it is impossible to define the minimum content necessary for a Christian theology without implicitly committing oneself one way or the other on the question of hermeneutics; and also that those who believe that they are limiting themselves to the very minimum of theology have often found themselves making claims which implicitly carry them much further than might appear at first sight.

III

So far as we have confined ourselves to placing Alan Richardson in his context in the field of hermeneutics. Now we must examine his main positive contribution to the theory of hermeneutics, as opposed to his solution to the problem posed by the 'first gap'. This will lead us straight into a consideration of the main criticism that has been made of his work. Alan Richardson believes that there is no such thing as scientifically 'objective' historical criticism; the critic's correlations will be influenced by the presuppositions which he brings to his work. Thus he can suggest that it was the positivist assumptions of the form critics that led them astray;[30] and he criticizes Bultmann in particular. Bultmann's denial that Jesus had any messianic consciousness is, he says, 'based on modern existentialist philosophy rather than on scholarly consideration of historical evidence';[31] he accuses him elsewhere of re-introducing Ritschlian liberal theology, substituting for Ritschl's 'value judgement' the conception of 'significance for man';[32] he also says that Bultmann and others treat dogmatic presuppositions about Jesus as unhistorical, but accept liberal presuppositions as 'scientific'.[33] Alan Richardson is fond of quoting Reinhold Niebuhr's dictum: 'It is impossible to interpret history at all without a principle of interpretation which history as such does not yield.'[34] He concludes, therefore, that to rule out the possibility of God acting in history is arbitrary: 'There is no *scientific* presupposition of historical method which requires historians to rule out the possibility of divine action in history.'[35] Alan Richardson can thus claim that his theory about the relation of the Jesus of history to the proclamation of the early church is true because it is the hypothesis which best fits the facts. We assume, he says, that the apostolic church possessed a common theology and then test the hypothesis by reference to the text of the New Testament 'in the light of all available critical and historical knowledge'.[36] The only right methodology is to frame various hypotheses (not.labelling them 'conservative' or 'radical') and then to decide which best satisfies the New Testament evidence.[37] Elsewhere he writes: 'The principle of interpretation here employed is that of historic Christian faith' (a notable phrase, one which would perhaps incur the criticism of Käsemann). The ultimate criterion, he adds, is that of coherence; liberalism, positivism, or existentialism do not provide a satisfyingly coherent explanation.[38] Alan Richardson therefore prefers a 'coherence' theory of truth to a 'correspondence' theory. William Temple has said that revelation consisted in the coincidence of the event and the minds able to interpret it. But Alan Richardson would modify this by adding that there are no 'objective' events; we can only recognize an event when there is an element of subjectivity.[39]

Alan Richardson was never a disciple of Barth, but he was sufficiently influenced by him to insist that faith is a necessary element in hermeneutics. As early as 1947 he wrote that only in the church can we apprehend special revelation by faith.[40] The Bible, he says, is the church's book.[41] He claims that the interpretation of history 'necessitates the personal involvement of the historian in an act of decision, a judgement of faith',[42] but he also writes: 'But to say that Christian truth cannot be attained by historical enquiry apart from the insight of faith is a very different thing from saying that the historical facts which criticism can investigate are irrelevant to Christian belief.'[43] His idea seems to be that the prophets interpreted the events of Israel's history. If we, by reading the Bible, put ourselves in their place (or perhaps in the place of the apostles), we can by faith understand and accept essentially the same interpretation. We encounter God there. But he insists that faith was created by events and not *vice versa*. It was their experience of deliverance at the Red Sea that inspired Israel's faith in Yahweh. It was the resurrection that inspired the faith of the first Christians, and not *vice versa*.[44] Alan Richardson goes very far along with Oscar Cullmann in calling for a new theology in the light of salvation history, expressed in terms of action rather than substance. This may perhaps be a tentative step towards bridging Pannenberg's 'second gap', that between the world of the New Testament and the modern world. But he did not pursue this clue, and it is not clear whether he realized how far the New Testament writers themselves are already committed to something like a 'substance' christology at least. Alan Richardson does refer to 'the gap which has opened up between the biblical exegete and the dogmatic theologian', which seems to correspond to Pannenberg's second gap. He believes it has now been closed, but does not indicate exactly how.[45]

In thus emphasizing the place which faith must play in hermeneutics, Alan Richardson stands in a very distinguished tradition which goes back at least to the early years of this century. We have already noted that Karl Barth re-introduced the element of faith into the interpretation of the scriptures. Barth insisted that historico-traditional criticism and history-of-religions criticism were .only the prolegomena to interpretation, not interpretation itself, which must be carried out by faith.[46] Alan Richardson is entirely justified when he accuses the history-of-religions school of believing that they could 'as a matter of "objective" history trace the evolution ... of Christianity from its beginnings as a simple Jewish ethical pietism through its obscuration under layers of apocalyptic fanaticism and Hellenistic mysticism to its final emergence into the full-blown "Gnostic Catholicism" of the second-century Church'.[47] This arrogant belief in his ability to compile 'objective' history is certainly a characteristic of Wrede, one of the founders of the history-of-religions school. Robert Morgan, in his illuminating introduction to Wrede's work published in 1897, 'The Task and Methods of "New Testament

Theology'", admits this.[48] But even before Barth, Adolf Schlatter had made exactly this criticism of the history-of-religions school. In the same volume with Wrede's essay Morgan also includes a long essay by Schlatter called 'The Theology of the New Testament and Dogmatics', published in 1909, where this point is made again and again. Schlatter writes:

> It is therefore clear that the historian's objectivity is self-deception, and that the convictions which influence him have a dominating influence upon his work.[49]

And Schlatter also has the thought which we found in Alan Richardson that the church cannot fail to be an element in the interpretation of the Bible (p. 132). Schlatter's insistence on the place of faith in interpretation is well expressed in the following passage:

> Sharp opposition to biblical dogmatics is expressed in the judgment that New Testament theology is a misguided undertaking because the New Testament does not contain theology but religion. But this judgment also applies to people who are still unclear about the inner difference between that form of knowledge which we call science and the word directed to us by the New Testament ... Because through God's relationship with us knowledge of God comes to relate us to him, the New Testament is consciously and irreconcilably opposed to every form of thought which is only meant to produce a religious concept (pp. 161f.).

Alan Richardson, however, does not merely stand in a distinguished tradition of the past in rejecting the misguided claim to 'objectivity' made by Wrede and others and in insisting on the importance in hermeneutics of faith; both these features are found in the work of a German theologian who came into prominence just after Alan Richardson had completed the works from which we have quoted in this essay. In *Basic Questions in Theology* I and II[50] Wolfhart Pannenberg has in fact reproduced very much Alan Richardson's positive contributions to the problem of her-meneutics, but he has enshrined them in a more fully articulat-ed philosophy of religion. Thus he insists on the part which faith must play in interpretation; but for him faith is not purely subjective: 'Faith is not something like a compensation of subjective conviction to make up for defective knowledge' (I, pp. 64f.). Later he insists that the faith-interpretation is not something that is added by the believer to a series of pure facts, in such a way that someone else could just as reasonably add a different interpretation. The interpretation of faith is part of the facts, and is in the last analysis the only correct interpretation. But in order to apprehend it you must refer to the whole 'in view of the universal connection of all events' (II, pp. 30f.). Pannenberg rejects the Kantian tendency to divide being and value; in history this means separating an event from its meaning. The meaning, he claims, is part of the event (I, p. 86). This remind us very much of the passage from Alan Richardson's *Christian Apologetics* (p. 147) already referred to, where he modifies William Temple in saying that there are no 'objective' events. We can only recognize an event when there is an element of subjectivity. Pannenberg also seems to be approximating to Alan Richardson's demand that we should put ourselves in the place of the apostles when he writes that all historical research can only understand past events in so far as in some way it relates them to its own understanding of life (I, p. 100). Thus the past is not dead and there is no such thing as an historian losing himself in the past. For example, the sort of things we today want to know about the New Testament period are not the same things as mediaeval scholars would want to know about it. We find an echo of Alan Richardson's suggestion that we must test various hypotheses to see which best coheres with the fact when Pannenberg writes: 'Testing the multiplicity of interpretations that have appeared is exactly what theology is all about' (I, p. 139). Last of all we may refer to Pannenberg's account of what it means to apprehend an act of God in history. It does not mean, he says, apprehending the act and then superimposing the God-interpretation. Nor does it mean supposing that God is the author of the act in the apprehensible way in which we suppose a human person to be the author of an act. It means 'the moment in which we grasp, by means of a single event, the totality of the reality in which we live and round which our lives circulate' (I, p. 229). We may well suggest that this is a clear account of what Alan Richardson meant when he wrote about events as the media of revelation.

It may seem surprising that Pannenberg seems quite unaware of his agreement with Alan Richardson in the area of hermeneutics, except that one does not nowadays expect German theologians to take notice of more than a very select number of their English counterparts. But it has been worthwhile demonstrating that Alan Richardson's basic position has been vindicated by so eminent a theologian as Pannenberg, since we must now consider Alan Richardson's most formidable critic.

IV

Ernst Käsemann's criticism is contained in an article in *New Testament Studies* already referred to. He is discussing the difficulties involved in composing a theology of the New Testament, and writes as follows:

> More conservative scholarship of course had fewer difficulties, as is shown in their different ways by Meinertz, Bonsirven, Richardson and the still unfinished work of K.H. Schelkle (1968). Tribute is paid to historical criticism, at least to the extent that distinctions are drawn between different periods and persons. But this does not amount to much when everything remains subsumed under the term 'apostolic tradition'. For in this case it is possible either to go on putting to each document the same dogmatically predetermined questions or, making use of its key-words, to orientate the exposition towards a specific church tradition or conception of *Heilsgeschichte*. The result is from the very start a harmonisation within which there is room only for developing or at best for complementing given perspectives. A world which at its beginning is already ecclesiastically pure and whole knows no serious conflicts, contesting parties, or even heresies of any theological relevance.[51]

Part of the difficulty of this critique lies in the fact that Käsemann lumps together Alan Richardson with others who do not by any means share his position. For example, it is unfair to put Alan Richardson with one who is so totally unaware of the 'two gaps' as is Bonsirven. One is therefore not quite sure which of Käsemann's descriptions applies to Alan Richardson. Most of them seem more appropriate to Roman Catholic scholars. Does he, for example, mean the criticism about 'apostolic tradition' to apply to Alan Richardson? I cannot think of any passage in which Alan Richardson appeals to 'apostolic tradition' as a predetermined or unimpeachable criterion of authenticity. In one place, it is true, Alan Richardson writes: 'The principle of interpretation here employed is that of historic Christian faith'; but this is not the same as 'apostolic tradition' and is further discussed in our next section.[52] The only criticism which I clearly recognize as applying to Alan Richardson is that concerning salvation history.

If we wish to know why Käsemann objects to 'salvation history' as a solution to the problems connected with the New Testament that concern us here, we must turn to his book *Perspectives on Paul*, where they are very fully set out. The whole passage from p. 49 to p. 76 ought to be read, but we must restrict ourselves to the minimum necessary for understanding Käsemann's position. His first contention is that for Paul what is essential is the preaching of the cross, rather than 'the facts of redemption'. He writes:

> This means that for Paul the 'facts of redemption' cannot be separated from the Word of Christian preaching; nor can they be played off against it. They are undoubtedly the basis of preaching, but without preaching we cannot have them at all (p. 50).

Thus Käsemann rejects a theology of events in favour of a theology of the preached word (it is remarkable that here the English translator has preserved the capital that would be used in German anyway). Now we may observe about this thesis that, whether it be true to Paul or not, it is a decidedly Lutheran one. Indeed one suspects that it is more Lutheran than Pauline. The evidence Käsemann gives for attributing this view to Paul is not by any means overwhelming. Thus far, therefore, I take it that what Käsemann really objects to about Alan Richardson is not so much that he is a conservative as that he is not a Lutheran.

However, later on in his essay Käsemann gives much fuller reasons for his rejection of salvation history as a clue to the christology of the New Testament. They seem to be three in number, as follows:

(*a*) The concept may lead to a theory of development. He writes:

> I have nothing against the phrase salvation history although it is often used in what seem to me questionable ways; I would even say that it is impossible to understand the Bible in general or Paul in particular without the perspective of salvation history. On the other hand, we should not isolate the phrase from the problems associated with it and, like all dangerous phrases, it should be defined as closely as possible. In no case should what we call the divine plan of salvation be absorbed by an immanent evolutionary process whose meaning can be grasped on earth, or which we can control and calculate (p. 63).

As far as this objection is concerned, we can surely plead 'not guilty' on behalf of Alan Richardson. The charge may apply to Oscar Cullmann or Pierre Teilhard de Chardin, but not to him.

(*b*) The conception is capable of being used 'in a secularized and political form' and was so used by the Nazis (p. 64). This is an argument *ad hominem*, and the *homo* is not Alan Richardson but the Christian theologian in Germany today. Just as British theologians are under no obligation to embrace existentialism, so they are under no obligation to boycott thought-forms which they have not abused. One might perhaps draw a useful historical analogy here. It might be plausibly argued that because of St Augustine of Hippo's unfortunate sexual experiences the Western church was saddled for a millennium with a most unfortunate and one-sided theology of marriage. We do not want the Western church today to be inhibited from using what may be a fruitful and biblical conception just because of the unfortunate experience of the German church under the Nazis. Incidentally I note with interest that Alan Richardson himself made a somewhat similar remark in his last work, where he said of Käsemann's book *Jesus Means Freedom* that it 'deals chiefly with a church quarrel in Germany'.[53]

(c) Justification by faith, and not salvation history, is 'the centre, the beginning, and the end of salvation history' (p. 76). Käsemann does not abandon salvation history in favour of justification by faith, he subordinates it. Salvation history is the 'sphere' in which justification takes place. Käsemann argues this with great depth and passion. To deal with his arguments would far exceed the scope of this essay. But in fact the place which he gives to salvation history is by no means necessarily incompatible with Alan Richardson's position. Indeed it seems rather absurd that Käsemann should so scornfully reject a salvation-history solution to the problem of the New Testament when it is offered by Alan Richardson, seeing that he himself has already given it such a significant place in his own account of New Testament christology. One cannot help suspecting that *odium theologicum* has crept in. Alan Richardson's real fault is that he is not a Lutheran.

On the other hand, Professor Käsemann's objection to Alan Richardson's version of salvation history may be more fundamental still. Perhaps he objects to salvation history as a solution to the problem of the 'first gap' just because it is a solution. After all, the rest of his article in *New Testament Studies* from which we have quoted does very strongly suggest that there is no solution to the problem of New Testament theology, or at least that the evidence does not exist for providing a solution. Here, I must say, it seems to me that Käsemann can claim no particular advantage. He does in his article (p. 238) write about those who 'go on putting to each document the same dogmatically predetermined questions', which presumably refers to Alan Richardson as well as to the Roman Catholic scholars whom he includes under the category 'more conservative scholarship'. But we are entitled to ask where Käsemann gets the questions which he puts to the document. Is he free of predetermined dogma? Robert Morgan has pointed out that Käsemann's own exposition of the New Testament is based upon Luther's dictum *crux sola nostra theologia* (indeed we have noted traces of this ourselves already).[54] This would seem to contain quite as much predetermined dogma as Alan Richardson's approach. It is also worth observing that R.S. Barbour has recently made a very

acute analysis of Käsemann's own approach to the Jesus of history,
giving good reason to believe that Käsemann himself is not free of
quite definite presuppositions about how he believes the Jesus of
history should make his impact upon us today.[55] Indeed Käsemann
himself is far too good a disciple of 'the dialectical theology' to deny
that we all come to our study of the New Testament with
presuppositions. He himself writes of 'the entanglement of all
exegesis in systematic prejudices which we can diminish but never
entirely rid ourselves of'.[56] What I find objectionable in his
treatment of Alan Richardson at least is his assumption that
Richardson is conditioned by dogmatic presuppositions, while
Käsemann himself, because he asks more radical questions, has got
some sort of a moral advantage. The sentences which follow the
long quotation from his article which we have given above represent
Käsemann as rejecting Alan Richardson's solution with
superiority. He writes of himself and those who agree with him
thus:

> Will he not be inclined – with a mild melancholy or scorn, according to his
> temperament – to make a break with this projection into early Christianity of an
> ideal ecumenism, and to acknowledge with realism the existence of historical and
> theological confusion even in the beginnings?

Now this seems to me to be claiming a moral superiority for his
position. Note the 'mild melancholy or scorn', the claim to be more
realistic than those who offer a solution to the problem. There is
also of course a great deal in *Perspectives on Paul* about the
advantages of 'radical Protestantism' over any other approach to
the New Testament. It all adds up to an extraordinarily arrogant
attitude, remarkably inappropriate to one who writes much about
the theology of the cross. I cannot see myself that Käsemann has
any grounds for this claim to superiority, at least as far as Alan
Richardson is concerned. What Alan Richardson has done is to put
forward an hypothesis, based on salvation history, which explains
how the Jesus of history is integrally linked with the Christ
proclaimed by the early church, and how that proclamation
developed into the creed of the second-century church. Alan
Richardson does not claim that this hypothesis is logically
demonstrable, only that it is the one which best explains the facts.
Käsemann rejects this hypothesis without himself offering any clear
alternative. This does not, of course, mean that Käsemann is
necessarily wrong, but it does not give him any necessary
advantage either. Indeed I would say of Alan Richardson's solution

that it does at least make sense of the facts and offer an explanation of the origin of the Christian church.[57] It would be different if Alan Richardson's solution were based on a crude refusal to face critical questions, such as was exhibited for example by Pius X's Biblical Commission in its attempt to answer the questions put by the 'Modernists'. But it would be absurd to accuse Alan Richardson of adopting so obscurantist a position. The difference between him and Käsemann is primarily that he has put forward an hypothesis which claims to make sense of the evidence, whereas Käsemann is not certain whether any such hypothesis can be satisfactorily framed. I do not see that this gives Käsemann the right to use the scornful and arrogant language which he has employed.

A very similar issue has recently been discussed in the pages of *Theology* by Professor C.F.D. Moule and Dr H. Willmer.[58] The issue is that of the distinctiveness of Christ. Dr Willmer, commenting on the case which Professor Moule has put forward for Christ's distinctiveness, says in effect that it cannot be proved from history. He writes:

> Professor Moule is explicitly concerned with the *claims* made by the earliest Christianity, claims which could be stated only as a result of a selective treatment of source material, by a process of idealization or withdrawal from the openness of history. The conceptual claim, Jesus-Israel-Man, is dependent on history, at least in that it was in historical Israel that it became possible for 'Israel' to be read as 'Man', and yet it also involves a break from historical Israel, since Judaism from the first would not allow that Jesus was true Israel.

In other words, in the interpretation of the New Testament historical considerations will take you a certain distance, but an element of faith must come in. This, as I understand it, is Alan Richardson's position, and this is why, in the deepest sense, only the church is competent to interpret the Bible. Much the same point is made by Professor Barr when he insists that the Bible has to be interpreted by a theology.[59] If we want a solution, we must form a hypothesis.

V

Last of all we must pay attention to a criticism of Alan Richardson's work which is to be found in Robert Morgan's book already referred to.[60] He criticizes Alan Richardson as an interpreter of New Testament theology on three grounds. First Morgan is surprised that Alan Richardson should describe Gore's theology of the New Testament as 'orthodox' and Bultmann's as 'heretical'. In a historical work, he says, such categories should not enter. Very similar to this is Professor Barr's rejection of the notion of orthodoxy as a criterion for interpreting the Bible. In 'the biblical scene', he says, there is 'no picture of a fixed and standard orthodoxy to which the biblical writers uniformly conformed'.[61] This statement is disputable: we do find the biblical writers on their guard against what they regarded as false teaching. However difficult it may be to decide what exactly was the teaching of Paul's opponents as reflected in II Corinthians, for example, there can be no doubt that Paul is arguing against it. Very much the same can be said of Galatians, different though his opponents were. In other words, Paul believed he had a gospel to preach which was *the* gospel and which could be, and was, misrepresented. This is even more obvious in Colossians, where he is consciously arguing against false teaching. The question at issue, it might be said, is whether any other biblical writer would have acknowledged Paul's standard of orthodoxy. Certainly the author of the Pastoral Epistles believed that he did, though we may well doubt whether he really understood Paul. In the Fourth Gospel and the Johannine epistles also there can be little doubt that at certain points what is regarded as false teaching is being opposed. And we do not normally regard the Johannine writings as a likely place to look for opposition to 'Paulinism'. Thus the concept of orthodoxy and heresy is appropriate to the New Testament, however much dispute there may be about its content; consequently Alan Richardson cannot justly be criticized merely because he brings this criterion into his discussion of New Testament theology.

In any case, it is misleading to represent Alan Richardson as a champion of traditional orthodoxy. Though he does, as we have seen, claim to employ 'the historic Christian faith' as a principle of interpretation, this phrase must be taken in a fairly broad sense. For example, he does not regard the picture of Jesus which we find in the Fourth Gospel as one which is true to history.[62] This in itself implies some sort of a modification of traditional christology, which is very largely based on the acceptance of the Jesus of the Fourth Gospel as an actual historical figure. Indeed, amusingly enough, while Morgan criticizes Alan Richardson for passing judgments in the name of orthodoxy, Navone criticizes him for not being quite orthodox enough.[63]

Secondly, Morgan questions whether Alan Richardson's work 'keeps within the bounds of historically allowable interpretation'. This presumably means that according to Dr Morgan, Alan

Richardson's interpretation of the New Testament can be shown to be wrong by historical methods. This seems a daring claim to make. Where, we may ask, does Alan Richardson's historical technique palpably fail? One can only guess, but no doubt it would be in that area where there is most controversy, the question of Jesus' consciousness of his own vocation. We might well concede that Alan Richardson's treatment of the question of the Son of man now looks a little old-fashioned. Few would probably defend T.W. Manson's 'corporate' interpretation as Alan Richardson does.[64] On the other hand, the conclusion that Jesus claimed to be neither the Son of man nor the Messiah has nothing like a consensus of scholars behind it. Quite the reverse; weighty testimony can be cited for the view that Jesus did in some sense claim both titles. Indeed, considering the state of complete disintegration in which scholarly opinion now finds itself concerning the meaning of the title 'Son of man' (not to mention the astonishing inability of scholars to established agreed criteria for distinguishing authentic material about Jesus from creations of the early church), it would seem very rash indeed to say of anyone as well versed in the question as Alan Richardson that he has transgressed the bounds of historically allowable interpretation.

Thirdly, Morgan accuses Alan Richardson of reverting to the old-fashioned method of producing biblical dogmatics. He objects to a phrase used by Alan Richardson, 'the underlying theology of the New Testament documents'. Morgan writes as follows:

> It is one thing to speak of an underlying unity and quite another to find this in a particular theology which can be spelled out like a textbook of dogmatics. In fact Richardson's work looks in some ways like a return to the pre-modern, unhistorical textbooks of biblical dogmatics which failed to distinguish between the theologies of different authors.

His final scathing comment is:

> That many people have found Richardson's work so helpful is an indication that a genuinely historical understanding of the New Testament is not widespread.

Presumably the 'underlying theology' to which Alan Richardson refers is the salvation-history schema which, Richardson believes, makes best sense of the New Testament evidence. Strictly speaking one would be safer in talking about an 'underlying theology' than about an underlying christology, since presumably all the writers of the New Testament begin from the conception of God found in the Judaism of the day. But if the phrase here does refer to salvation history, and if this is what Morgan refers to, then Morgan is hardly justified in his severe strictures. He may not agree that salvation history is the key to the problem of New Testament theology, but the salvation-history solution is still a perfectly reasonable one, supported by a number of distinguished scholars. The suggestion that Alan Richardson's *Introduction to the Theology of the New Testament* is really little better than the old-fashioned dogmatic text-books is unfair, as a glance at such a work as Bonsirven's will prove[65] (and even Bonsirven's book is by no means identical with the old-fashioned textbooks). One suspects that Morgan's real objection to Alan Richardson is that he does offer a solution to the problem. Morgan's use of the phrase 'a genuinely historical understanding of the New Testament' is reminiscent of the history-of-religions school. Is such an understanding possible? Or rather, when one has reached such an understanding, is that all that is necessary in order to interpret the New Testament? If one is to judge by the essay of Adolf Schlatter which Morgan edits, and indeed by his own introduction, the answer to this question should be No. In short, Morgan does not seem to allow Alan Richardson that element of faith in the matter of hermeneutics which Richardson's own theoretical approach requires and which Morgan himself appears to approve elsewhere in his book.

It would indeed be unrealistic to claim that there were no points at which Alan Richardson's work is open to justifiable criticism. In so large a volume of fairly detailed work weaknesses are inevitable. He is, for example, too optimistic about the extent to which the historical reliability of the traditions about Jesus would be vindicated by the scholarship of his day. Writing in 1963, he says: 'More recent scholarship has found it possible to discover a very much greater measure of historical reliability in the tradition of the apostolic church as it is recorded in the New Testament.'[66] That was an over-optimistic statement at the time and has certainly not been confirmed since. Indeed when Alan Richardson was writing his major works, though Bultmann had of course given an example of very far-reaching scepticism about the historical basis of the gospels, the suggestion that there may not in fact be any underlying unity in the New Testament at all had not come very much to the fore. In other words, Alan Richardson was not prepared for Käsemann's approach to New Testament theology. He would no doubt have replied that there was no reason why he should be: each man can only be expected to encounter the scholars of his own day. In the same way one could say that Alan Richardson put rather too much reliance on the possibilities of a new understanding of typology. He wrote: 'It was the failure to understand St Luke's typological scheme which led the source-critics to postulate the document Q.'[67] In fact this sort of treatment of the sources is a form of *Redaktionsgeschichte*; and *Redaktionsgeschichte*, far from establishing the historical reliability of the gospels, tends to lead in an exactly opposite direction.

Alan Richardson is also vulnerable to criticism from the point of view of Professor James Barr on two counts. First of all, Richardson, as a disciple of the salvation-history school, finds the divine disclosure in events. For example, he claims that faith was created by events and not *vice versa*: it was their experience ·of deliverance at the Red Sea that inspired Israel's faith in Yahweh.[68] But, as Barr has emphasized in his last two books, very often what Israel's writers described as events turn out not to be events at all; they disappear into the mists of legend. Hence, what Alan Richardson is asking us to accept as the locus of revelation is very often not historical events but Israel's faith. However, it is quite possible that he is aware of this difficulty, for by revelatory events he always means events as interpreted by faith.[69] In the second place Alan Richardson would no doubt come under censure from Barr for the stark contrast which he so often makes between Hebrew and Greek thought and for the way in which he claims that the writers of the New Testament almost invariably manifest the influence of Hebrew thought rather than Greek. An example of this might be found in his article in *The Cambridge History of the Bible*, where he claims that the passage in II Timothy 3.16 does not imply the Greek doctrine of inspiration.[70] I would maintain that on the contrary, it does,[71] and so do two other passages in the Catholic Epistles.

But, when every justifiable criticism of Alan Richardson's work has been taken into consideration, such criticism will only apply to this or that detail. To describe his work as a whole as reactionary or tendentious is grossly unfair. He was not a *parti pris* conservative. His position as far as concerns the interpretation of the New Testament was not hopelessly out of date. On the contrary, it was an eminently reasonable approach well evidenced and supported by a number of distinguished scholars.

I suspect that the essential difference between Alan Richardson and his critics (as well as those whom he criticized himself) was the difference between those who believe that one can, and should, make sense of Christianity as it has developed in history and those who believe that one can go back directly over the centuries to the biblical or pre-biblical sources and distil a form of Christianity out of them. In other words, Alan Richardson's approach to hermeneutics represented, in the deepest sense, the catholic tradition, whereas that of his critics belongs to the tradition which goes back to the radical strain in Luther. This is not to say either that Alan Richardson was prepared to defend everything that has ever gone under the name catholic, or that he had nothing to learn from the radicals. But the distinction is still worth making. So far the task of interpreting the New Testament in the light of modern critical and historical methods has been left very largely in the hands of Protestants, because the Catholics on the whole have been afraid of the new techniques. The situation is now changed: more and more Roman Catholic scholars are accepting the challenge. A scholar such as Schnackenburg is an indication of what is to come. When the catholic wing of Christianity does fully enter into the debate about hermeneutics, finally abandoning its former claim to a superior knowledge in virtue of its catholicism, the deepest issues can be faced. Existentialist philosophy, which is really a distraction, will, one may hope, be left on one side. When this takes place, I believe that the Anglican tradition in interpretation, which, beginning with the great trio Lightfoot, Westcott, and Hort, has always held that catholic Christianity need not be afraid of modern methods of study, will be in some sense vindicated. Then Alan Richardson will be seen in his true context as an Anglican interpreter who strove both faithfully and successfully to show that the traditional Christian understanding of the Bible was not incompatible with the critical and historical approach, even in the middle of the twentieth century.

NOTES

1. Robert Morgan, *The Nature of New Testament Theology* (Studies in Biblical Theology 2.25), SCM Press 1973, p. 25.

2. Alan Richardson, *History Sacred and Profane*, SCM Press 1964, p. 234.

3. James Barr, *The Bible in the Modern World*, SCM Press 1973, p. 159.

4. E. Käsemann, *Perspectives on Paul*, Eng. trs., SCM Press 1971, p. 64.

5. E. Stauffer, *New Testament Theology*, Eng. trs., SCM Press 1955, p. 25.

6. O. Cullmann, *The Christology of the New Testament*, Eng. trs., 2nd ed., SCM Press 1963, p. 5.

7. W.G. Kümmel, *The Theology of the New Testament*, Eng. trs., SCM Press 1974, p. 329.

8. Alan Richardson, *An Introduction to the Theology of the New Testament*, SCM Press 1958, p. 125.

9. Alan Richardson, *The Bible in the Age of Science*, SCM Press 1961, p. 108.
10. Alan Richardson, *History Sacred and Profane*, p. 141.
11. W. Pannenberg, *Basic Questions in Theology* I, Eng. trs., SCM Press 1970, p. 196; see also p. 155: 'The peculiarity of the New Testament texts as witnesses to Jesus can be traced back to the peculiarities of the history and person of Jesus himself.'
12. W. Pannenberg, *Jesus – God and Man*, SCM Press 1968, p. 22.
13. R. Bultmann, *Theology of the New Testament* I, Eng. trs., SCM Press 1952, p. 3.
14. Pannenberg, *Basic Questions in Theology* I, p. 197.
15. See W.G. Kümmel, *The New Testament: the History of the Investigation of its Problems*, Eng. trs., SCM Press 1973, p. 372, where there is a clear exposition of how Bultmann makes existentialist philosophy provide him with a method of crossing both these gaps.
16. *Basic Questions in Theology* I, p. 142.
17. Ibid., p. 56.
18. Barr, *The Bible in the Modern World*, pp. 38, 73.
19. Alan Richardson, *Religion in Contemporary Debate*, SCM Press 1966.
20. H. Conzelmann, *An Outline of the Theology of the New Testament*, Eng., trs., SCM Press 1969. For this and the next quotation see pp. xiii, xviii.
21. See E. Käsemann, 'The Problem of a New Testament Theology', *New Testament Studies* 19, April 1973, p. 241.
22. Pannenberg, *Basic Questions in Theology* I, pp. 191, 194.
23. With such reflections compare Kümmel, op. cit. (n. 15 above), pp. 284f., 366f.; Conzelmann, op. cit., pp. 5f.; Morgan, op. cit. (n. 1 above), pp. 13, 21, 28, 41.
24. This and all the subsequent quotations in this paragraph are taken from Käsemann's article (n. 21 above), pp. 237-44.
25. See also Käsemann's essay, 'The Problem of the Historical Jesus', in his *Essays on New Testament Themes* (Studies in Biblical Theology 41), SCM Press 1964, pp. 19-47, where this conclusion is also indicated, though only generally outlined.
26. Barr, *The Bible in the Modern World*, p. 114.
27. James Barr, *Old and New in Interpretation*, SCM Press 1966.
28. Morgan, *The Nature of New Testament Theology*, p. 41.
29. Ibid., p. 175 n. 101.
30. Richardson, *History Sacred and Profane*, p. 129.
31. Richardson, *An Introduction to the Theology of the New Testament*, p. 135.
32. Richardson, *The Bible in the Age of Science*, p. 112.
33. See *History Sacred and Profane*, p. 141.
34. Quoted by Richardson in *Christian Apologetics*, SCM Press 1947, p. 99, and in *History Sacred and Profane*, p. 247; cf. also *An Introduction to the Theology of the New Testament*, p. 11: 'Science (including historical science) cannot evaluate the principles of interpretation by which it itself proceeds.'
35. *History Sacred and Profane*, p. 153.
36. *An Introduction to the Theology of the New Testament*, p. 9.
37. *History Sacred and Profane*, p. 142.
38. *An Introduction to the Theology of the New Testament*, p. 13.
39. See *Christian Apologetics*, pp. 144, 147.
40. Ibid., p. 137.
41. *The Bible in the Age of Science*, p. 154. Cf. also this sentence: 'The Bible is the Church's book, and apart from the Church's faith and worship its meaning cannot

be understood from the inside, or as it is in its essential character.' See the article, 'The Rise of Modern Biblical Scholarship and Recent Discussion of the Authority of the Bible', in *The Cambridge History of the Bible: the West from the Reformation to the Present Day*, ed. S.L. Greenslade, Cambridge University Press 1963, p. 333.

42. *History Sacred and Profane*, p. 259; cf. also 'Scripture, Doctrine of Holy', in *A Dictionary of Christian Theology*, ed. A. Richardson, SCM Press 1969, p. 309: 'The Scriptures are the gift of God and are incomprehensible without his gift of faith.'

43. *History Sacred and Profane*, pp. 138f.

44. For all this see *The Bible in the Age of Science*, pp. 168, 173.

45. See his article 'Hermeneutics', in *A Dictionary of Christian Theology*, p. 154.

46. See Kümmel, op. cit. (n. 15 above), p. 366.

47. *An Introduction to the Theology of the New Testament*, pp. 12f.

48. See Wrede's entire essay (*The Nature of New Testament Theology*, pp. 67-116), and Morgan's comment, p. 21.

49. Ibid., p. 124; see also pp. 126f.

50. Wolfhart Pannenberg, *Basic Questions in Theology* I and II, Eng. trs., SCM Press 1970 and 1971.

51. Käsemann, art. cit. (n. 21 above), pp. 238f.

52. See *An Introduction to the Theology of the New Testament*, p. 13.

53. See Alan Richardson, *The Political Christ*, SCM Press 1973, p. 115.

54. Morgan, op. cit., p. 52.

55. R.S. Barbour, *Traditio-historical Criticism of the Gospels*, SPCK 1972, pp. 36-42.

56. Käsemann, *Perspectives on Paul*, p. 65.

57. Cf. J.J. Navone, *History and Faith in the Thought of Alan Richardson*, SCM Press 1966, p. 66: 'The existence of the Church and its faith offers abundant historical evidence which demands historical explanation. Positivism, rationalism, and absolute relativism preclude the possibility of an explanation for the historical existence of the Christian Church and its faith; they imply that the evidence is inexplicable, and can therefore be discredited on historical grounds alone.'

58. C.F.D. Moule, 'The Distinctiveness of Christ', *Theology* LXXVI, November 1973, pp. 562ff., and H. Willmer, 'A Comment', ibid., pp. 573ff.

59. Barr, *The Bible in the Modern World*, p. 133.

60. Morgan, *The Nature of New Testament Theology*, pp. 57f.

61. Barr, op. cit., p. 147.

62. Alan Richardson, *The Gospel according to Saint John* (Torch Bible Commentaries), SCM Press 1959, p. 26.

63. Navone, op. cit. (n. 57 above), pp. 143, 145f.

64. See e.g. *An Introduction to the Theology of the New Testament*, p. 87.

65. J. Bonsirven, *Theology of the New Testament*, Eng. trs., Burns and Oates 1963.

66. See 'The Rise of Modern Biblical Scholarship and Recent Discussion of the Authority of the Bible' (n. 41 above), p. 331.

67. Ibid., pp. 335f.

68. See *The Bible in the Age of Science*, p. 173.

69. Navone, op. cit., p. 112.

70. Art. cit. (n. 41 above), p. 313.

71. See my *Studies in the Pastoral Epistles*, SPCK 1968, pp. 42-55.

Recent Studies on the Resurrection of Jesus

ROBERT LEANEY

This essay will deal with only one aspect of its subject, contrasting in its limitation with the peculiarly synoptic and balanced outlook of the scholar to whom it is dedicated, whose range and lucidity were matched only by his modesty. The aspect is some work on the historical character of the New Testament accounts of the resurrection of Christ, mostly published from 1970 onwards, although one book was first published in 1956.

It was both as New Testament scholar and as philosophical theologian that Alan Richardson himself wrote an article on 'The Resurrection of Jesus Christ'.[1] In it he quoted Bultmann's phrase, 'Christ is risen in the preaching', acknowledging that 'there is a sense in which this slogan of Bultmann's is profoundly true'; but Bultmann says of Christ that he 'meets us in the word of preaching and nowhere else'. Emphasis on the existential significance of Christ's death takes the place of emphasis on the living Christ. The next step, Richardson fears, is the 'death of God' theology. Bornkamm, Fuchs, Ebeling and Käsemann nevertheless speak of Christ's resurrection as constitutive of Christian faith, and Richardson sums up (p.148): 'The resurrection of Christ ... created the Church by calling faith into being', adding his conviction that the strongest argument for the resurrection of Jesus is that the earliest Christian worship was a re-enactment of his arrest and death. Such a celebration could not have been the joyful act it was without conviction that he was alive.

Richardson is sympathetic to Pannenberg in his rejection of the over-emphasis of both Barth and Bultmann 'that the key category of theological interpretation is the Word of God' (p. 151). Pannenberg is sure there must be an objective something or an event to interpret: words are about history and the prophet sees meaning in it; but the prophetic word is not the only form of the word of God who 'speaks', i.e. his word is efficacious in nature and in history, a view more congenial than Bultmann's to a long line of British theologians: Lightfoot, Westcott, Hort, William Temple and John Baillie.

Willi Marxsen insists on a truth, that the living and permanent presence of Jesus is the essence of Easter faith, which would be welcomed by very many who would not agree to his further statement that the resurrection of Jesus is a first-century Jewish apocalyptic notion which we cannot share. Somewhat surprisingly for so late in the twentieth century, Althaus, von Campenhausen and Pannenberg support the truth of the tradition of the empty tomb: the claim could not have been maintained in Jerusalem for a day if the authorities could have shown this to be untrue. We shall see that this argument may be seriously weakened by the possibility that the empty tomb tradition arose too late for demonstration either way; but for the moment we can make Richardson's conclusion (p. 153) our starting-point:

> For my part I am convinced that the origins of the Christian Church cannot be accounted for by any other historical explanation that that Jesus did in fact rise from the dead.

It is with the examination of this fact, as recorded in scripture, by three very important studies, that this essay is concerned.[2]

Hans Grass, *Ostergeschehen und Osterberichte*, was first published in 1956 and reached a fourth edition in 1970. R.H. Fuller refers to it as the only full recent study of the subject; we must therefore begin by giving some account of it. It has two great attractions: it pursues the neglected task of seeking the historical fact or facts behind the varied and puzzling accounts of the resurrection appearances by means of a sufficiently ruthless critical analysis, and it never loses sight of the consequences for believers of the conclusions reached.

A basic opinion of Grass is that the twelve (or eleven) returned to Galilee at the time of the crucifixion (Mark 14.50 must be taken seriously) and there received the first appearances, the very first being to Peter, which changed not only the course of their lives but that of history. He insists that such an experience was necessary, justifiably using the simple argument that public deception involves self-deception, and no self-deception could survive the rough and painful tests involved in the work and witness which the apostles gave (pp. 14, 29-32, 127). This is not to argue for the appearances as simple objective facts which would have been observed by anyone who might have been present, but that they were not self-generated. This difficult psychological problem is dealt with later; for the moment we are concerned with the Galilee appearances. Their establishment as facts is one result of a systematic examination of the relevant passages, beginning with Mark. Grass believes that the lost ending was erased after Mark's death by a community whose motive is not easy to guess, but it may be that the later tradition of a third-day appearance in Jerusalem conflicted with an appearance in Galilee which had therefore to be expunged. Their objection could not be to the first appearance being to Peter if they accepted the gospel of Mark at all, and Mark 16.7, with its implication of just such an appearance in Galilee, is left intact. Curiously, the original form may be represented in John 21.1ff., in a manner characteristic of that gospel. Indeed, the whole of John 21, an appendix by a different author, contains a Galilaean tradition clearly older than the theologically weighted tradition of John 20 (p. 74).

Passing on to Matthew, Grass emphasizes the legendary character of 27.62-66 and that it belongs to a quite late stage in the development of controversy, being directed against Jewish denial of a third-day resurrection no less than of the empty tomb. The unhistorical character of Matthew's additions is shown completely by the continuation of the narrative in 28.4, 11-15: the angel's activity is dovetailed into the Marcan material in an unsatisfactory manner and this suggests that Matthew took over an already existing legend also present in the *Gospel of Peter*. Grass aptly points out that (as in later apocryphal works) a proof of the resurrection to non-believers is involved here, for the chief priests and elders evidently believe the guard's story, to say nothing of the guards themselves. This, he remarks, is an advance upon the tradition that the Lord revealed himself as alive after his crucifixion only to his own chosen ones, a tradition surviving in Acts 10.41 in a specific and accurate form (p. 25).

The elaborate parousia-like scene in Matt. 28.16-20, legendary as it is, contains a striking historical element: it takes place in Galilee. Matthew preserves this element which Luke 24.6 transforms by a transparent manipulation of Mark 16.7. Moreover, Matt. 28.17 summarizes a well-attested motif in the tradition, the doubt of some disciples even at an appearance, which must reflect a real fact. Grass thus gives some support to the theory of a possible historical element to which too little attention has been paid by scholars (with Trocmé as a notable exception): the probability of the persistence of local traditions about Jesus. Mark reflects more Galilaean traditions than those concerned with the resurrection, and Matthew, if it is a Syrian gospel, is naturally less anxious to suppress them. Nevertheless, Matthew adds no historical material – that the Lord appeared to the eleven in Galilee could have been obtained (and surely was) from Mark 16.7. Before passing on to consider Luke and John, Grass notes the rise of the question about the manner in which a commission to build up a community and to engage in mission is founded in encounter with the risen one (p. 32). Grass does not discuss the possibility, which perhaps did not occur to him, that the appearances can be distinguished by whether they constituted a summons to community or church construction, or to mission. Such a possibility is more than a possibility to Fuller, as we shall see, but it remains open how far it is legitimate to make such a distinction among such ancient and overlaid material.

Grass does not add anything original or significant to the usual critical verdict on the historicity of the Emmaus pericope in Luke, and discusses Luke 24.34 with less firmness than it deserves. Does it not connect with the call of Peter which has come down to us in the form of a call in Galilee but during the earthly ministry? But he rightly observes that 24.36ff. is not well united with what goes before, for all the eleven, perhaps including Cleopas and his companion and certainly including Peter to whom the Lord has already appeared, are terrified and doubtful, which makes no sense if some had recently had a reassuring experience of a private appearance. The entire narrative is full of obvious apologetic and Grass thinks it can hardly parallel the appearance of I Cor.15.5b to the twelve. Without going into the problems connected with the end of Luke and the beginning of Acts in any detail Grass is surely right to maintain that the narrative of the Easter and post-Easter events offer no sure ground for an analysis seeking to establish whether there are any traces of historical tradition lying behind them: the ascension and the forty days' converse of the Lord with the twelve (or eleven?) are clear examples of post-Pauline theology attempting to answer the question how the appearances, now thought of as far more naturalistic and nearer to verifiable public events than they were, had ceased and were no part of the church's later experience (p. 50).

The resurrection narratives of John 20, closely related as they obviously are to those of Luke, offer no clue to historical events, but John 21, as already noted, is different. Grass sees clearly that the historical tradition underlying the narrative in this chapter is shared with Luke 5.1-11, and John 21.1-14 is a more developed form than Luke's. Against Bultmann, Grass rightly sees that the original story concerned Peter, not the beloved disciple, and that it was apparently preserved in the *Gospel of Peter* 58-60 where only the beginning of the story is extant; Grass is probably right in supposing that in its complete form the original story was of the

Lord's first appearance specially to Peter, accepting his penitence and restoring him to his apostolic task and status. His hesitation in linking this with I Cor. 15.5 is unnecessary, but he rightly stresses the significance of the survival of an account of an appearance in Galilee among the obviously later church traditions, an appearance which implied that the disciples had returned to their ordinary occupations; the later overwhelming tendency was to reduce almost to nothing the time between the crucifixion of Jesus and his first appearance as risen Lord. The question of place is important to Grass in his quest for a historical core; we should ask, however, not so much, 'Where did the Lord appear?' as 'Where were the disciples when they received the appearance?' This is a proper and important historical question, whereas the other implies that there is significance in the place of appearance for him who had passed beyond the limitations of space. He insists that Mark 14.27 is a remarkable testimony, overlaid by later tradition, to the scattering of Jesus' followers when he was arrested; their retreat to Galilee would be natural. Valiant efforts have been made by Lohmeyer and especially von Campenhausen to provide an explanation of a sequence of events in which appearances in Galilee followed an original beginning of Easter faith in Jerusalem, but their arguments are submitted to a thorough and devastating criticism. Grass seems to be right in this and to strike a sensible balance with regard to the importance of Galilee; he does not doubt that there were early flourishing Christian communities there (perhaps it might be more accurate to say that there were communities of followers of Jesus), but there is absolutely no evidence (*pace* Lohmeyer, and, we may add, others who have written about 'Galilaean Christianity') for a mission centre there second only to Jerusalem. In fact, it seems that the other centre was Antioch, and that the following of Jesus which began in Galilee moved, as he had frequently done, northwards. Grass thinks that the appearance to more than five hundred was probably in Jerusalem, and may well have followed the return of the twelve there after the first appearances in Galilee to Peter and to the twelve (pp. 122-5).

Apart from this insistence on the probability of appearances in Galilee, Grass, perhaps with an emphasis not altogether consistent, in discussing the relation of the Pauline list (I Cor. 15.3-10) to the stories of the evangelists, characterizes the latter as 'stark legendär', no longer giving a genuine picture of the events. If this seems a little harsh after his own successful analysis of the gospel accounts had located the earliest historically reliable appearance in Galilee, he is no doubt right to say in concert with the vast majority of scholars that I Cor. 15.3-10 is the oldest and most reliable tradition on the resurrection in the New Testament (pp. 106-7). He regards as 'generally accepted' the view that the kerygma taken over by Paul contained only the two first appearances, those to Peter and to the twelve; vv. 3b-5 were not formulated by Paul but originally Aramaic, perhaps obtained by the apostle from Damascus even before he met Peter and James; while the tradition in vv. 6f. Paul may well have received from the two 'pillars' (Gal. 1.18f.). Grass does not believe that this or any analysis is correctly used to argue that there are two rival Easter traditions put together by Paul: that would be characteristic of a later age. In the passage in question (15. 3-10) Paul is giving plain historical statements, and the core of them was formulated very early after the crucifixion and resurrection. James and the other brethren were (in spite of Acts 1.14) relatively late in adhering to the believing community and their conversion is a strong argument for the reality of the resurrection. Grass ventures the summary that Peter and the twelve received appearances in Galilee, James and 'all the apostles' (not necessarily an exact definition of the group) in Jerusalem, and while this last was before Paul's conversion, some considerable time may well have elapsed since the first appearances (to Peter and the twelve); the third in Paul's list, that to the 'more than five hundred', required some little time after the first appearances but could be earlier than that to James (p. 101). Grass does not make the distinction which seems to be a special mark of Fuller (pp. 47-50), between eschatological revelation and appearance, the place of the former being irrelevant; we have indeed already seen that place is important to Grass, and specially so with regard to the earliest of these experiences.

At no point is Grass's analysis more radical than with regard to the 'third day' and the empty tomb, which to some extent he discusses together. He notes with justice that 'on the third day' shows precision contrasting with the vagueness of the intervals between the appearances; its fixed position in the earliest tradition might be explained by claiming that the empty tomb was discovered on the third day, and that this is the only explanation possible if it be accepted that the appearance stories in their present form are quite late and unreliable as history. But the close connection of the empty tomb with 'the third day' would not establish that the resurrection took place on that day. This precise 'dating' may well be historically secondary, arising from early Christian use of Judaism's current interpretation of Hos. 6.2 in forming belief about the general resurrection (p. 134).

The question of the empty tomb is given a thorough discussion and in the process of subjecting its historicity to very radical criticism Grass produces what is perhaps the most valuable part of the book, an exposition of Paul's understanding of resurrection and eternal life as it arose from the ideas of his day, with a lead towards what is possible for twentieth-century man. First it is argued that archaeology cannot really establish the identity of any ancient tomb with that of Jesus – a point which should not need making but is important in these days when the popularity of travel to the 'holy land' has encouraged the pious and naive to draw a veneer of godliness over a tour by describing it as a 'pilgrimage'. The Church of the Holy Sepulchre would be better called by its original name, the Church of the Resurrection, and has little claim to be regarded as occupying the site of the tomb of Jesus. To return to Grass; he adds that the passages about the resurrection in Acts, including those in the early chapters where the disciples witness to the resurrection, give no help to those who would argue that the empty tomb is part of the most ancient traditions. Far from being primary, it is part of a quite late development; and its doctrinal significance is clear. It arises from the necessity to regard the earthly body of the Lord as preserved from corruption and as having ascended into heaven (pp. 45f.).

It is with this in mind that Grass discusses Paul's teaching about the resurrection of those in Christ and especially II Cor. 5.1-10, specifically with a view to establishing the significance or otherwise of the empty tomb for his understanding of Christ's resurrection. He argues that the II Corinthians passage is best explained against the background of gnosis and gnostic-influenced Jewish-Christian apocalyptic, not the apocalyptic of late Judaism such as is found in the Apocalypse of Baruch, I Enoch and IV Ezra; the 'house from heaven' to be bestowed on that ill-defined centre of our being left when the earthly body is lost in death is the garment of glory found in the Ascension of Isaiah and the Slavonic Enoch, a garment 'laid up in heaven' and preserved there for the righteous. Thus in Paul's view those who rise from the dead do not need their old bodies in any form. The tomb of Jesus does not need to be empty. Such an interpretation of Paul is not difficult when I Corinthians is studied in its light. See for example I Cor. 15.49 and cf. I Cor. 15.53 with II Cor. 5.1. Grass therefore concludes that Paul is not interested in the empty tomb and his 'and was buried' in I Cor. 15.4 does nothing more than emphasize the Lord's death. The body of the resurrection is not the earthly body but the body of glory. This exposition is satisfactory indeed, but unfortunately does not succeed in separating the third day from the earliest tradition, a separation which would seem to be almost necessary for his view that this article of belief was connected closely with the empty tomb. The sequence: resurrection, search of scripture in its light and in the light of other half-conscious feelings, the consequent addition of 'on the third day', followed obviously very quickly on the actual event of the resurrection. If the empty tomb arose as naturally out of the same need as prompted 'on the third day' (non-corruption of the Lord's body as well as merely scriptural ratification), then it may have arisen as early.

It is however true that, as Grass claims, at no point does Paul rely on the empty tomb as part of his argument; indeed, he does not envisage its use at all, as seems clear from a glance at I Cor. 15.13, 'If there be no resurrection, then Christ was not raised.' For Paul, as II Cor. 5 shows, resurrection did not necessitate the transformation of the body which was buried, but its replacement by a glorious body. Grass concludes that there is no unconditionally convincing argument for the historicity of the empty tomb. It may have become important in a later development than the first primitive kerygma through two factors: increased emphasis on the physical character of the resurrection (as in the end of Luke and the opening of Acts) and the need to combat Jewish denials; both these rise against a background of a revulsion against two intolerable thoughts – the almost total desertion of Jesus by his followers and the corruption of his physical body (p. 184).

The appearances are often classed among visionary and ecstatic phenomena. Grass discusses the latter and concludes that while the appearances are not to be so described, yet those who experienced the appearances belonged to a circle in which such phenomena occurred, and the factual connection between them must be considered. Paul's Damascus road experience had inner and exterior aspects, but there is no evidence in Paul's own allusions to his conversion that this was a subjective vision only; rather does he testify to the unexpected and 'reversing' character of the experience. Strangely, Grass does not contrast the Acts accounts with Paul. The former are theophanies in the form of christophanies, with increasing emphasis on the presence of the glory (or *shekinah*) of God, while nothing that Paul himself says attributes his conversion specifically to an appearance, even though I Cor. 9.1 and 15.8 claim an appearance specially to himself. Grass is in fact content to argue that .it is difficult if not impossible to distinguish other visionary experiences from appearances by any other means than their content: they were of the risen and exalted Lord and summoned the recipient to witness to him as such, not merely to witness to his 'survival'. Christ appeared always in his *sōma doxēs* or *sōma pneumatikon*, in spite of Lucan attempts to argue the resurrection of the earthly body (p. 232).

Visionary does not mean subjective: 'That a psychic gift in certain disciples caused visionary experience of the exalted Lord is not more probable than the reverse supposition, that "enthusiast" phenomena were the result of encounter with the risen one' (p. 238). Grass is knowingly led back constantly to the 'visionary' experiences of the disciples and finds it inevitable and proper to claim that in these divine authority was at work, an activity preceded by and resting on divine working in Christ (p. 247).

Grass does not mention Dodd, but in discussing the words of the risen Christ in the appearances emphasizes the constant theme of commissioning which he believes may well represent the original nucleus of historic fact, however much the form of words in each case has been embroidered by the formation of the early kerygma. Almost as constant is the promise either of his presence or of the Holy Spirit, not seldom including a warning of impending suffering. Other motifs are the use of scripture, reminder of words spoken by the earthly Jesus and 'institutional' sayings. With Brun, Grass regards the motif of exaltation and 'the eschatological motif' as playing a comparatively slight role, promise of an early return being a feature remarkably conspicuous by its absence. Grass thinks that it should be concluded that the form of words which we now have is relatively late. The commissioning element he regards as very old and 'original', but this does not mean authentic, for it is useless to ask which sayings are authentic (pp. 252f.). It may, however, be urged that the absence of the eschatological motif in such important sayings occurring within a sphere where this motif was so pervasive suggests the memory of what had actually been said at least on some occasions, without making the extravagant claim that we have the *ipsissima verba*.

Wilckens' treatment of the evidence is a similarly radical analysis but with very different results. He dwells on the possible *Sitz im Leben* of the portions of available material. I Cor. 15.5-7 may be catechetical and is distinguished by its brief sentences and by the names Peter, James and Paul, specially mentioned because called as special instruments to be given missionary power and authority. Other appearances, to unnamed and collective groups (vv. 6-7), are additions to the original list (pp. 28ff.). Equally ancient is the pre-

Marcan Easter story which is now the closing portion of Mark's passion narrative; it influenced Paul as well as Mark. These are conjectures, but intriguing conjectures, made by one well versed in the kind of literature which he thinks to be the forerunner of Mark, late Judaistic literature with late Judaism's interpretation of the Old Testament and apocryphal literature, apocalyptic and other. Wilckens' striking claim for very early material in Mark is supported by insistence that Paul's mention of the burial must have a full significance – it does not simply emphasize Christ's death. It is probably connected with the empty tomb tradition of the evangelists who have emphasized the exact place of the tomb being known (Mark 15.47 probably originally followed by 16.2). The *Sitz im Leben* of this story may be liturgical. Perhaps there was a ceremony at Jesus' grave in the Jerusalem community which we should link with Rom. 6.3f. The 'third day' can be explained only from the tradition which preceded Mark and which he wrote down in 16.1-8. The 'more than five hundred' he also connects with the Jerusalem *Urgemeinde*; they may have been followers of Jesus who renewed their discipleship after the appearances to Peter and to the twelve, and were thus established as the eschatological divine redemption-community. Paul refers to them as though well known because they held an honoured place in that community. Thus Wilckens trusts more the narrative behind Mark and does not feel the need to place the first appearances in Galilee. Mark himself knew only the fact of the appearances to Peter and to the twelve as in I Cor. 15. 3-10, not the manner. The women at the tomb story was originally independent of the appearances tradition. Their telling no one was due to their knowing Jesus had told people not to tell others of his miracles and not to proclaim him till he was raised from the dead. Now that he was so raised, proclamation was the disciples' task and not theirs. The story was first connected with the other tradition, of appearances to the disciples, by Mark (pp. 50ff.).

Wilckens makes out a good case for the notion that the passion narrative, with its story of the Messiah delivered over to rough ill-treatment and death and himself despairing of God's intervention, comes to a climax with the story of the women at the tomb learning from a divine messenger, 'He is not here, he is risen!' The whole course of the story corresponds to the main Old Testament conception of the suffering one. The connection between Mark 15.24 and Ps. 22.19, and between Mark 15.29 and Ps. 22.8f., is familiar, but Wilckens suggests a considerable number of other such parallels. He also makes almost the same point as

Richardson: the ruthless emphasis on the stark unmitigated loneliness of unrelieved suffering on the part of God's representative and chosen one is a story told by Christians. For them to have constructed it in part on the basis of appropriate Old Testament passages but without any hint until the end of the story that the sufferer was to be vindicated, they must have been convinced of the truth of his resurrection. Its form remains unknown; the empty tomb story is not a proof of his bodily resurrection but a declaration made by an angel that Jesus is with God (p. 50).

Matthew according to this interpretation takes further the combining process started by Mark. He combines the angelic message to the women with the appearances. The appearance to the disciples is now an articulated and specific commissioning (28.16-end) (pp. 53f.).

Enough has been said to show the special outlook of Wilckens with regard to the historicity of the resurrection stories. He agrees with others that we cannot describe the resurrection nor the actual quality of the appearances (or experiences which have come to be so described); but he claims the empty tomb and the event as happening on the third day as part of the earliest tradition. The most important contribution of Wilckens arises from his sense of the oneness of these early Christian traditions with the pre-Christian literature and ways of thought to which they were assimilated so naturally. In tune with this ability he makes an interesting point concerning both the heavenly being and the place of the risen Christ. The Lord appears as a heavenly being, and no question arises in the gospels as to whither he goes because it is understood that it is to heaven. It is therefore natural that such revelations as the appearances – of the heavenly son of God – should be complemented by those acts of revelation in the Bible which show to a privileged person secrets of heaven, that is, hidden facts or future events. Thus in Rev. 1.9ff. John on Patmos sees a vision of the heavenly Christ and receives further heavenly revelations. The risen one does not come to him but he is granted, like Stephen, a sight of the risen one in glory. Both these further examples and those specifically connected with the resurrection imply that being raised by God from the dead and exaltation belong inseparably together (Rom. 8.34; Eph. 1.19ff.; Col. 1.18ff.; Heb. 1.3; 13.20f.; see pp. 91ff.).

Thus both Grass and Wilckens see the appearances in the context of a range of supranormal events, Grass dwelling more on the way in which they were experienced by the recipients, Wilckens tending to stress rather the apocalyptic stamp given to them in the New Testament. Both make balanced judgments, but Grass is more explicit that God acted in this milieu and ambience, Wilckens giving the impression that the thought-style of the first century is for him a more difficult barrier than it is for Grass.

Fuller's already widely-read and influential work consists of a critical study of the resurrection narratives, taking account of the previous work of scholars in this field, including Grass and Wilckens, and rather more comprehensively than they had done. His method is 'to reconstruct the history of the tradition from its earliest recoverable form ...' (p. 7) rather than like Grass to seek the historical nucleus underlying the tradition. He anticipates his results by saying (p. 8): 'Resurrection faith then becomes not a matter of believing in the historical accuracy of the narratives but of believing the proclamation which these narratives, for all their differences, enshrine', but before embarking on his analytical task he interjects an assertion that the resurrection was meta-historical and not a 'historical' event: 'What took place between God and Jesus took place at the boundary between history and meta-history ...' (p. 23). It is doubtful whether such terms advance our understanding. Since few know what is meant by 'meta-history' it makes the boundary between it and history shadowy indeed. It might be better to stick to New Testament terms such as mystery and briefly to indicate what is meant by them. Fortunately he comes down to earth by avouching that the resurrection event 'can be known ... only by indirect revelatory disclosure within history'. It is good that Fuller thus acknowledges the occurrence of revelatory disclosure within history and thus far adheres to his British heritage, even if it was perhaps Pannenberg who pointed him to it.

Fuller's analytical work is more probing even than that of his forerunners. He begins with I Cor. 15.3-8, material which he believes may combine Damascus and Jerusalem traditions. He accepts a suggestion of Goguel that ' "on the third day" is not a chronological datum but a dogmatic assertion: Christ's resurrection marked the dawn of the end-time ...' (p. 27). The list of appearances is a catena of Jerusalem traditions acquired by Paul from Peter and James (Gal. 1. 18-19) and collected by him on his own initiative. He thus used them as evidence for the resurrection whereas until then they had been individual and unconnected examples of kerygmatic assertion. Barth was right: Paul's purpose was to claim by identity of the preaching (v. 11) to be as much an apostle as the others; but Bultmann is also right in seeing that Paul thereby initiated the process of 'proving' the resurrection (p. 29). The appearances are in reality self-disclosures or revelations of God to his chosen recipients of events belonging to the eschatological age disclosed through this-worldly events. It is not quite clear whether for Fuller the latter are – or could have been – public and in principle verifiable, but an interesting and persuasive study of the earliest traditions suggests once again that the appearances to Peter and to the twelve, the very earliest, are historical events of such a character. It is a particlar point of Fuller's (p. 35) that these appearances to Peter and the twelve have a special function, the founding of the eschatological community, and those to James and the apostles that of inaugurating a mission (at first only in the Jewish Diaspora). The difficulty of maintaining this distinction is great and it is hard to believe that the apostles could have made it.

Certainly, Fuller's delving into the earliest traditions leads to some suggestions which are too conjectural; he believes that the earliest tradition about the burial is that represented by Acts 13.29 which makes it a hostile action (pp. 54ff.). If this were so, a common grave for Jesus and other condemned men such as the two 'bandits' crucified with him is extremely likely; yet Fuller includes Mary Magdalene's discovery of the stone rolled away and the tomb empty among the earliest traditions, a story consistent only with a single and easily identifiable grave.

Fuller regards the location of the two primary appearances in Galilee as being Marcan rather than as primitive and authentic (pp. 57f.); and he tends to regard Mary's (or the women's) finding the tomb empty as early Palestinian and apocalyptic tradition (rather than Hellenistic materialism) and believes the disciples may have received the report as 'a vehicle for the proclamation of the Easter faith which they already held as a result of the appearances' (p. 70). On the tendencies in Matthew his most important reflections are that the angelophany in Mark has in Matthew become a Christophany in Galilee (both being to the women): 'The earlier tradition of primary Christophanies in Galilee is beginning to react upon the originally quite separate story of the empty tomb with which only the women were originally associated (Mark 16.1f.)' (p. 78). 'The Christophany of Matt. 28.11-17 is the first instance we have of materialization of the appearances' (p. 79). He shares with Grass the important point that 'the final scene in Matthew's Gospel adds only one fresh point to our knowledge of the resurrection appearances as they actually occurred, viz., that some of the disciples doubted' (p. 91). Important for Fuller's own special view are his assertions that Matthew has re-interpreted the tradition in Mark 16.7, which was concerned with the founding of the eschatological community, as the inauguration of mission; and that the narratives as distinct from lists still do not exist at this time (pp. 91f.).

With regard to Luke, Fuller thinks that although Luke's concern is with salvation history he is nearer to actual history with his picture of a diffusion from Jerusalem, and asks where the evidence is for 'spontaneous combustion' Christianity 'in places like Joppa, Lydda, or Damascus or even Galilee?' (p. 212). The question seems to be addressed partly to myself: it is certainly worth consideration. Wilckens' view that Galilee was a centre of mission we have rejected, but the presence of Christians in the places named is known from Acts and rabbinic writings. It raises the question whether they are the result of the earthly Jesus' missions or, like the apostolic church in Jerusalem, of appearances and resultant missionary activity. It seems unlikely that followers of Jesus in the areas where Mark says he was active existed only after the resurrection. A possible and natural explanation might be that they are due to the resurrection restoring faith to communities originally the result of Jesus' own earthly mission in Galilee, the Decapolis and Syria. The appearance to more than five hundred need not have been in Jerusalem. Perhaps, like the community or communities envisaged in the Johannine epistles, they are the result of pentecostal experiences. As Fuller notes, 'In the missionary charges of the earthly ministry the conferral of the Spirit or of authority takes place simultaneously with the sending forth of the missionaries' (p. 118). He compares John 20.21 for a post-resurrection charge. John summarized and perhaps telescoped what Luke separates out into resurrection, appearances, ascension, and Pentecost; but the Pentecost of Acts 2.1ff. is neither the only nor the most credible of such experiences in the New Testament. On the other hand, the *Pseudo-Clementine Recognitions* afford evidence for preferring Christian leaders whose authority was not wholly post-resurrectional and earlier church disputes were often about authority. Luke sees to it that pre-resurrectional authority is given to Peter (5.1-11), Paul believes post-resurrectional authority is entirely sufficient (although he is not worthy to be called an apostle), John makes the authority the Spirit received by all who have the *chrisma*. Other views have been suppressed or otherwise lost. Mark, for example, as Trocmé has shown, may well have been arguing that true and brave discipleship was essential to the permanence of authority.

Ultimate authority resides in the risen Lord and in discussing the Johannine writings Fuller makes the excellent point that the appearances in John emphasize that the faith or belief engendered is not factual (he *did* rise) but christological (since it is he, alive, he is my Lord and my God) (pp. 143f.). This is the belief aroused in the beloved disciple who saw the tomb was empty and 'saw and believed'.

Fuller adds his voice to the many who rightly insist that an Easter event is necessary to explain the rise of the church, as when saying, 'The resurrection does not mean that the earthly Jesus is relegated to past history but has as its consequence the extension of the word and work of the earthly Jesus into the present life of the community' (p. 173). Again, 'Faith seeks the earthly Jesus not as a dead teacher, but as the living Lord whose word and work were not merely accomplished once upon a time, but are now made ever present in the community' (p. 174). This says excellently what Grass in the final part of his book says equally well as he seeks to describe the relation of our own Easter faith to that of the apostles who received the original revelation of the risen Christ. The apostles themselves learnt not wholly from their Easter experiences, but from obedience and suffering, what faith in God who had 'justified' the crucified Jesus really meant. This was even more true of those who had no Easter experiences of their own but built on the tradition of the first generation, believing their witness and committing their lives as individuals and congregations to unity with and in the living Lord; and gradually developing from scripture and their traditions of the Lord's own teaching a theology embracing his life, death and resurrection. Such is indeed the faith of the church in every age.

NOTES

1. Alan Richardson, 'The Resurrection of Jesus Christ', *Theology* LXXIV, 1971, pp. 146-54.
2. H. Grass, *Ostergeschehen und Osterberichte*, 4th ed., Vandenhoeck & Ruprecht, Göttingen, 1970; U. Wilckens, *Auferstehung*, Kreuz Verlag, Stuttgart, 1970; R.H. Fuller, *The Formation of the Resurrection Narratives*, SPCK 1972.

~ 5 ~

The Absurdity of God's Non-Existence:
St Anselm and the Study of Religion

JAMES RICHMOND

Those of us who worked with Alan Richardson and knew him well are aware that among his many interests was the problem of relating a theological department to the structure and syllabus of a modern university, and that he made a persuasive contribution to the view that the exploration of theology and religion enriches in an unparalleled way that *humanitas* to which all universities have always rightly directed so much attention, a thoughtful contribution which has stimulated considerable discussion of the. complex issues involved. I should here like to make my own contribution to the discussion of one aspect of this many-sided subject – namely, to the question of the incorporation into a modern university of a large, diversified department devoted to what many in our culture would regard as an inappropriate enquiry, that is, into the Transcendent and man's relation to it. I say 'inappropriate' deliberately, because in many contemporary universities questions such as these are often vigorously discussed: Is the question of God any more an intellectually respectable one? Is it not time to agree that (in the light of modern philosophy, science, psychology, sociology, etc.) the question of God and its ancillaries ought to be dropped from serious academic syllabuses? Ought we not therefore to concentrate our attention (abilities, time, resources, man-power, etc.) on intellectually more respectable enquiries?

In the light of the attention which has been given to such questions in senior common-rooms in recent times, it is interesting (and, for some, alarming) that in 1967 the three-year-old University of Lancaster founded (after much controversy, internal and external) a brand-new Department of Religious Studies, a department which would indulge in open-ended, full-scale research into and teaching about the question of the Transcendent. This was interesting because the university regarded itself in many ways as *avante garde*, having instituted departments such as Systems Engineering, Marketing, Behaviour in Organizations, Operational Research and the like. The questions are therefore: Can the institution of such a department be any more intellectually justified? Do we need an entire large department (together with expensive complementary research, library and administrative facilities) in order to investigate a topic of such a kind? (Of course, the department is not exclusively concerned with the Transcendent; it also describes, explores and evaluates the non-transcendental manifestations and history of religion in its widest possible aspect.)

Clearly, one justification could be mounted by attacking English provincialism, by describing how such departments have for long been the rule in North American liberal arts colleges and in universities, and how such departments are springing up in Australasia. But I want to elaborate here a much more weighty justification which is derived from my teaching and research. This is, briefly, that the question of God (or the Transcendent) is so many-sided and complex that it can *only* be *fully* and *adequately* explored in the context of a large, multi-disciplinary and poly-methodic enquiry, such as is pursued within (typically) a university department. I now wish to elaborate upon what this means.

A convenient and helpful starting-point is to be found in a brief consideration of the views of St Anselm of Canterbury, with special reference to his *Proslogion* and his ontological arguments for the existence of God. When we consider St Anselm, the main thing to be dealt with and explained is the perennial fascination with the notion of God's necessary existence, as this has been so subtly argued for by St Anselm and his disciples. Why cannot we agree with the proposition (defended within much Western philosophy from Kant to Wittgenstein) that 'existence is not a predicate', and drop the whole thing? There are, I think, two main answers to this question. The first has to do, naturally, with modern work on the ontological argument associated with the names of Norman Malcolm, Charles Hartshorne and others, which may conveniently be examined in John Hick's and Arthur McGill's symposium *The Many-faced Argument*.[1] The second is this. The more we read the *Proslogion* and meditate upon St Anselm's words, the more suggestive the whole thing becomes. Whether or not his ontological arguments are thought to be logically valid, the *Proslogion* throughout its long history has suggested many different things to many different people. For example, some have derived from the *Proslogion* a set of semantic rules which apply to theistic discourse, informing us when we are using the word 'God' correctly and when we are using it incorrectly. (Indeed, if many of the fashionable 'death-of-God' and other theologians of the last couple of decades had pondered the words of the subtle doctor, they could not possibly have perpetrated much of the nonsense for which they are now rightly notorious.) Others have found in the *Proslogion* (taken together with, for example, the *Cur Deus Homo*?) a brilliant and original enquiry into the relationship of faith to reason, how one may interpenetrate the other, or how the two may overlap, or how one may blend into the other. Indeed, as the Hick-McGill symposium demonstrates, St Anselm's *Proslogion* is in every generation not unlike an undug mine.

This brings me to what I think about the *Proslogion* and what I have learned from pondering it and teaching from it. I have learned two things. The first closely concerns my fascination with the thoroughly Anselmian notion that the proposition 'God does not exist' is (and here I re-interpret) an absurd, unacceptable, even a ludicrous or fantastic one. I agree with Hartshorne that every generation returns to Anselm in order to answer the extraordinarily difficult question whether Anselm (*a*) committed a colossal philosophical error (in assuming that existence is some kind of property or defining attribute) or (*b*) made a fantastically important discovery in the history of Western philosophy. At any rate, Anselm's teaching has led me to formulate an argument in the following terms. If we understand (grasp, gain insight into, wrestle with, study, prosecute research into, ponder, meditate upon, etc.) the concept of the notion 'God' we come eventually to see (intuit, became aware, become convinced, have revealed to us, etc.) that the proposition 'God does not exist' is an absurd (fantastic, ludicrous, unacceptable, shocking, contradictory, anxiety-provoking) one. The question which we shall have to tackle presently is: Can sense be made out of this argument? I think that it can. And I believe, moreover, that it can cast a great deal of light on why so many are attracted in every generation to such a notion as God's necessary existence. The second thing that I have learned is rooted in the *Proslogion's* firm insistence that the concept of God is conceptually a quite unique one. That is, that it is in the strictest possible sense *incomparable*. This entails that the logic which applies to God and his existence applies to God alone; that it is in connection with God and *with no other* (an echo of Deutero-Isaiah?) that there arises the mysterious notion of necessary existence. This means that it will not do to try to refute the argument sketched above by pointing to other things to which (it might be suggested) the logic of the argument applies with equal validity. It is only of this one and uniquely incomparable concept that we may say that the notion of non-existence does not aptly or happily apply. Can sense be made of this second Anselmian insight also?

But first we must try to elaborate and fill out the Anselmian notion that to grasp or explore the concept of God leads somehow to the conviction that he must exist, and that the glib acceptability of his non-existence is the result of not adequately grasping the notion of God in the first place. To do so, I want to argue that we can predicate three attributes of the notion of God, as this notion has played a part in human thought and experience; the three attributes are *length, breadth* and *height*. But before doing that I want to broaden and thus to strengthen my argument by expanding the concept of God into the concept of the Transcendent (or the Supernatural). To adapt the words of a recent writer, I want to suggest that belief in the Transcendent (as the factor common to all religion) is 'the belief (implicit or explicit) that man's environment is other and greater than it seems, that interpenetrating the natural, but extending behind or above or beyond it, is the Supernatural (the Transcendent) as a larger environment to which men must relate themselves through the activities prescribed by their cult'.[2]

I now wish to explore these three attributes in turn, beginning with the attribute of *length*. I intend the word length in terms of time, for the notion of the Transcendent is clearly a staggeringly *old* one. Even if we go back to the mists of antiquity to contemplate the most rudimentary animism, we can by no means be certain that we have got to its historical roots. And the concept is still with us. Or is it? A great many in our transatlantic culture would argue that there are clear signs that in modern secular (and secularist) societies the concept is doomed, that it is a moribund one. Now here I want to underline that the answer to the question whether or not the concept of the Transcendent is doomed depends on the results of an extremely demanding intellectual enquiry about the place of 'transcendence' in the modern world. What should not be overlooked here is the staggering persistence (survival-value) of the idea of the Divine, even in our modern world. One way of ensuring that it is not overlooked is to note, however briefly, some of those onslaughts which the notion of the Transcendent has wondrously survived. We might note and study, for instance, the revulsion from religion which occurred in the second half of the seventeenth century, the attack on the notion of God by rationalism and empiricism during the European *Aufklärung*, the critique of theism formulated by nineteenth-century positivism, materialism and evolutionary naturalism; there was also the critique of theism produced by Marx and Engels, the later one produced by Freud, and the attempt to eliminate from human speech all talk of the Transcendent by twentieth-century logical positivism and empiricism. Now it is clear that during these developments the notion of God as some kind of pseudo-scientific explanation of the natural world was rightly discredited, and rendered disreputable within intellectual circles. Nevertheless the notion has survived and, it might be argued, due to intellectual honing and polishing, has survived in qualitatively higher forms.

Again, while considering the notion's persistence, it is worth considering whether the reason why the notion of the Transcendent is not entertained so seriously or widely today is because there is something fundamentally *wrong* or *sick* in our Western civilization. After all, the twentieth century has had no lack of rather pessimistic, if misunderstood, prophets and thinkers like Martin Buber, whose message has been that the notion of the Transcendent has been progressively eclipsed because of a deadly malaise which has infected modern man. But there are many other possibilities which might be taken up and explored. For example, we might listen to those who argue that Western society may be moving into a stage where the return of the awareness of the Transcendent will be through the return of transcendent moral absolutes, apparent perhaps in the refusal of many of our contemporaries to tolerate certain political, social and economic systems and ideologies.

Clearly, all of this needs to be thrashed out and considered in a contemporary discussion which will of necessity be very complex. But what I am aiming at here is the following. When one contemplates (meditates upon, ponders, explores, etc.) the Transcendent under the category of its incomparable *length*, and the number and severity of the onslaughts which it has survived, one can only be staggered and overawed by what I have called its survival-value, by its incomparably unique persistence. And that is one reason why the notion of non-existence is an extremely hard one to swallow when it is glibly, superficially or unthinkingly applied to the Transcendent.

Second, I deal with the category of *breadth*. The concept of the Transcendent is an incomparably *broad* one. Perhaps the description of *all-pervasiveness* is not inept here. I am using the concept 'broad' in two quite distinct senses. First, I intend it in a geographical sense. Awareness of the Transcendent is most broad because it is found in the west and in the east, in the north and in the south. It is not too much to say that awareness of the Transcendent has been and still is *global* in scope. We can perhaps sense something of what this means by reading right through a work like Ninian Smart's *The Religious Experience of Mankind*.[3] We find there an impressive wealth of description, referring to the Indian experience, the Chinese and Japanese experience, the Jewish experience, the Christian experience, the Muslim experience, and so on. The more one reads about, studies and explores these experiences the more one is impressed by the *broad* pervasiveness of the awareness of the Transcendent and, I would argue, the more one feels distinctly anxious about the notion of non-existence as unreflectively applied to it. Second, I intend the term *breadth* in a different sense, namely *logical*. The notion of the Transcendent is incomparably broad in the sense that it occurs in or is generated in a very broad range of logically diverse and distinct areas. The concept arises from contemplation of and meditation upon (*inter alia*) history, moral experience, religious experience, human existence, mystical experience, the natural world; some have claimed to 'see' or 'perceive' God configured in the world; others have appealed strongly to the category of revelation. Here again, I suggest that the term 'all-pervasiveness' is not inappropriate. The scholarly elucidation and exploration of this awareness is found within the tradition from, say, F.D.E. Schleiermacher to Edmund Husserl and Rudolf Otto. Within this tradition we find expressions such as 'the idea of the uninduced pressure exerted by the Holy', or Schleiermacher's 'interpenetration of the finite by the infinite, of the temporal by the eternal', and so on. But once again the main point I wish to make is that extended study of and meditation upon the notion of the Transcendent under this category of *breadth* leads, the more one indulges in it, to a distinct feeling of uneasiness when the notion of non-existence is cavalierly or unreflectively applied to it.

Third, I deal briefly with the category of *height*. By using this word (I might also have used the word *depth*) I want to suggest that we find awareness of the transcendent firmly integrated into every stratum of human existence, so that we might say that it pervades 'every sort and condition of men'. Let me begin at the bottom: it is certainly true that we find awareness of the Transcendent within the most primitive and superstitious groups, in the most grotesque forms. It is undeniably true that it is evident in distorted forms in the emotionally immature and sexually disturbed. I should not want to quarrel with the Freudian over this. Nor should I want to quarrel with the historian or sociologist who argues that the symbols of the Transcendent are occasionally used as crude generators of very dubious social or national value-systems (the weirdly religious and pseudo-Christian atmosphere generated by the McCarthyites in the post-war Communist witch-hunt in the USA is a case in point). In an English context we might think of the dubious exegesis and theology made to support a doctrine like the Divine Right of Kings. Nor would I care to deny that often false anxiety for the Transcendent is whipped up in order to justify the cohesion and continuance of a group dedicated to prolonging a dubious *status quo* (but it is instructive to consider philosophically in this regard the not uncommon misuse for political and social purposes of ethical symbols in a not dissimilar way, e.g. honour, truth, justice, freedom, etc.).

But, on the other hand, this is only a small part of the story. The awareness of the Transcendent is not limited to superstitious primitivity; it is also to be found amongst the most intellectual and sophisticated of men. After all, could we undertake a package-tour of Western and Eastern university libraries, we might well find that more books had been written about the Transcendent than about any other subject. Nor indeed is such awareness confined to the emotionally immature or the disturbed; it is to be found among the most sane, balanced and integrated of personalities. That is simply part of our experience. Nor again is the concept of the Transcendent tied exclusively to the maintenance of dubious social values or systems. If we take symbolic figures such as Kierkegaard or Karl Barth and others, we find there that social, ecclesiastical and political systems and groups are attacked in the name of the Transcendent. That is, that symbols of the Transcendent are being utilized in an anti-social direction. (Such an analysis as this is necessary in order to understand the contemporary stance of certain Latin-American churches in the context of social and· political ethics.)

At any rate, for the third time the point I wish to underscore is that the more we study and analyse the notion of the Transcendent under this category of *height*, the more we realize its insertion into all kinds of human endeavour and activity – into thought, contemplation, activity, passivity, revolution and counter-revolution, within layer upon layer of the human species and its experiences. The more we contemplate and meditate upon the notion of the Transcendent under this category of *height*, the more we are led to a distinct deepening of our feeling of anxiety when non-existence is flippantly or glibly applied to it.

I want to turn now to the second thing which I claim to have learned from St Anselm; namely, that the concept of God or of the Transcendent is conceptually quite unique, strictly speaking quite incomparable. This means that it is *only* of this concept that we may say that the notion of non-existence applies only very unhappily or inappropriately. (It ought to be remarked in passing that certain philosophers and theologians of an idealistic turn of mind would want to argue that they feel philosophically anxious about the application of non-existence to certain derivative ethical, aesthetic and personalistic concepts – but such an argument would necessarily be very technical and extremely difficult.) Self-evidently, the main way of opposing the argument outlined above is to bring forward other notions, concepts or beliefs to which the logic of the argument is applied in an attempt to effect a *reductio ad absurdum*. We might think here of notions such as a flat earth, fairies, witches, vampires, or whatever, which have undeniably influenced human conduct and changed expectations about the world. It might be argued that these constitute widespread beliefs which have gradually been undermined and eroded by human thought and experience. Confronted by such an argument, I should want to concede that *if* indeed we can apply the three categories of length, breadth and height to these *in quite the same way and to quite the same extent* that we can to the Transcendent, then of course my argument must work with these also and to that extent the argument is indeed discredited by enabling us to prove the absurd. But only a little reflection enables us to see that the three categories do not apply *in anything like the same way* to, say, beliefs in fairies or in witches. This brings me to another point: the difference between the concept of the Transcendent and, say, the concept of witches (or the like) can be brought out sharply by affirming that arduous and rigorous analysis of what is involved in the former makes it undeniably clear that the former (the Transcendent) is *incomparable* because it is uniquely *important*, of quite unique existential or anthropological *significance*, quite uniquely *pervasive*, quite uniquely *persistent* in the face of unique opposition, a quite uniquely weighty and massive concept – a unique *incomparability* which is brought home to us in direct proportion to the amount of time, energy and rigour that we give to its study, contemplation and meditation. (Is it not curious to recall that a logician of the stature of St Anselm is alleged to have committed the blunder of supposing that existence is some kind of predicate-in-general? Surely the argument of the *Proslogion* as a whole is that clearly existence is not a predicate except in the one incomparable case of the uniquely incomparable concept of the '*Aliquid quo maius cogitari nequit*'? And it is interesting to compare with this one of the main discoveries of recent post-analytic philosophy of religion, that theistic talk is 'logically very odd'.)

Is it possible now to reach some tentative conclusion? There are two issues of particular significance here. The first is that it is too often assumed, I suspect, that the problem of God or of religious belief is that that the existence of unbelief is an almost intractable problem for religious believers. Indeed, I have sympathy with those who say this is so. But, on the basis of what we have been exploring, I should also want to argue that the problem of persistent and pervasive *belief* (sophisticated as well as crude) is a serious and difficult problem for religious unbelievers. Hence my argument that the problem of belief versus unbelief (or, crudely, that of a naturalistic versus a supernaturalistic interpretation of our environment) is one that demands the utmost that we can give it in terms of scholarship, patient effort, intellect and the rest. The second has to do with the question of justifying the existence of an entire university department given over to (amongst other things) the study of the Transcendent and its manifestations. Can a justification be given for a polymethodic and inter-disciplinary department of this kind? If what I have said makes sense, the question of the Transcendent is one that can only be adequately handled in terms of some familiarity with (*inter alia*) mediaeval thought (Anselm and others), the history of religions, the history of philosophy (Hume, Kant, Husserl and others), the geography of religion, the phenomenology of religion, the psychology of religion (Freud and others), the sociology of religion and the history of religious thought (Aquinas, Kierkegaard, Barth and others). And perhaps the framework of length, breadth and height which I have crudely sketched above would provide a useful model for arranging and interrelating the various items and pieces of which such an over-all enquiry would ideally be composed. It follows that if it is true that to study religion involves us necessarily in so many disciplines, how can it be disputed that to engage in it can do other than to give a most rigorous and enriching training to the human mind? I close with a vivid recollection of Karl Barth being asked in seminar whether theology might still be labelled 'the Queen of the Sciences': his answer was that indeed it might, because no other subject of his acquaintance required the mastery of so many *Hilfswissenschaften*.

NOTES

1. John Hick and A.C. McGill, eds., *The Many-faced Argument: Recent Studies on the Ontological Argument for the Existence of God*, Macmillan 1968.
2. John Hick, *Faith and Knowledge*, Macmillan 1967, p. 137.
3. Ninian Smart, *The Religious Experience of Mankind*, Fontana 1971.

~ 6 ~

Lessing's Ditch Revisited:
The Problem of Faith and History

DAVID PAILIN

In a recent 'appreciation and review' of Ian Ramsey, Bishop of
Durham, Alan Richardson both pays tribute to Ramsey's work and
yet questions 'whether the real battle for faith can be waged in the
terms of epistemological philosophy'. According to Richardson:

> Much more decisive for the issue is the almost forgotten area of the critical
> philosophy of history. (Note the word 'critical' in this sentence; what is intended is
> the critical study of historical method, not 'philosophy of history' in the sense of,
> say, Hegel). This is far more important for an historical religion which bases its
> truth-claim upon historical testimony to events which have actually passed before
> the eyes of men. It is the existential significance of history, as the living and
> challenging past, upon which the Christian faith stands, not upon whether
> abstract concepts like 'God' can have any meaning for subjective empiricists.[1]

The historical character of the Christian faith has been
persistently affirmed by Alan Richardson. In his *Christian Apologetics*
he describes Christianity as 'an historical religion in the sense that
it arises out of a prophetic interpretation of certain events in
history',[2] while in his Bampton Lectures, *History Sacred and Profane*,
he puts it that 'the affirmations of the Christian creeds are
historical, not metaphysical, in character, and Christian theology
itself is a matter of the interpretation of history'.[3]

Such statements are not surprising in view of the various ways in
which traditional Christian self-understanding refers to certain
past events as being of crucial significance for its faith. This faith is
largely formed by the biblical interpretation of certain events in
Jewish and early Christian history – God is the one who called
Abraham, brought the people out of Egypt, made a covenant with
them, sent them into exile and brought them back, spoke by the
prophets, guided the apostles and sent his Spirit to establish the
church. At the heart of the Christian faith as traditionally

understood are doctrines of incarnation and atonement which maintain that in the events of the life and death of a particular historical person, Jesus of Nazareth, the nature of God was normatively revealed and man's salvation established. From the earliest days Christian theologians have claimed that their faith is not a matter of abstract theories and speculative ideals but is grounded in what really happened and still does happen.[4]

In view of this deep-seated and widespread understanding of the Christian faith, it may seem that any properly 'Christian' theology must see the Christian faith as depending upon the 'happenedness' of certain events. If this is so, doubts may arise about the adequacy of Maurice Wiles' *The Remaking of Christian Doctrine* since it denies the need for a doctrine of 'the unique incarnation of God in Jesus Christ' and speaks of Jesus Christ as 'the central figure within history who focuses for us the recognition and the realization' of the purposes of God for the world.[5] It may seem that such a 'focusing' role gives Jesus Christ the status of a useful illustration rather than that of the actual ground of Christian truth. If such doubts are possible about Wiles, they arise more strongly in the case of Van Harvey's *The Historian and the Believer*. In this fundamental study, Van Harvey concludes that 'the content of faith can as well be mediated through a historically false story *of a certain kind* as through a true one, through a myth as well as through history'. For Harvey 'no remote historical event . . . can, as such, be the basis for a religious confidence about the present'. Faith refers to 'one's confidence in God', involving 'trust and commitment'. It has 'no clear relation to any particular set of historical beliefs at all' and must find its basis 'in one's present experience'. The significance of 'Jesus Christ' is that this figure provides 'the key image in a parable which the Christian uses' to find the meaning of reality.[6] It is too easy, however, to dismiss the conclusions of Wiles' use of the criteria of economy and coherence or of Harvey's penetrating investigation of the 'morality' of historical understanding as inadequate or unacceptable because they do not conform to the way Christian believers and theologians have apparently understood their faith. It may be that the common self-understanding is a misunderstanding. What has traditionally been maintained and what is widely maintained are not safe criteria for truth – as the history of Christian thought itself illustrates with the cases of Athanasius and Galileo! – but neither should such evidence be discarded lightly. To be persistently out of step with the majority can be the mark of a madman! A useful – if not the least controversial – way forward is to examine the principles involved in the general question of the relation between faith and history. In this paper I want to outline one way of doing this, namely, through considering various ways in which the relation of events to faith may be understood.

The fundamental question of the relation between faith and history was classically posed by Lessing in the eighteenth century.[7] In its most challenging form it has been studiously avoided by most theologians ever since! They have been able to slip by on the other side partly because they have been concerned with other questions and partly because Lessing's remarks do not clearly distinguish between at least two distinct issues. Theologians have consequently been able to consider that they have dealt with Lessing's problem when they have dealt to their own satisfaction with one of these issues, not realizing or not admitting that another, much more critical, issue remains unsolved. Both issues, however, are important and we shall consider them in turn. They are to be found in Lessing's pamphlet 'On the Proof of the Spirit and of Power'.

In this pamphlet Lessing begins by discussing the attempts to prove Christianity by miracles and by fulfilled prophecies. These were the dominant arguments used by Christian apologists, especially in the early part of the eighteenth century, against those who were unwilling to accept more than what they supposed to be universally ascertainable natural theology. It was argued that by performing miracles and both by fulfilling prophecies and by making prophecies that were fulfilled at a later time Christ is shown to be divinely attested and, hence, that his teaching is to be accepted as a revelation from God. Lessing first accepts the argument in principle but argues that it has force only for those who actually witness the miracles and the fulfilment of prophecies. Unfortunately these things no longer occur: 'I live in the eighteenth century, in which miracles no longer happen.' Consequently the proof of the Christian religion is not in events that happen 'before my eyes' but in reports of the occurrences of such events in the past. The difference is crucial. Lessing does not deny 'that the reports which we have of these miracles and prophecies are as reliable as historical truths ever can be'. He simply maintains that they are only that reliable – and that means that they can never be demonstrated. The inescapable probability of all historical judgments – and its range in different cases according to the material under review – is now generally recognized. Lessing, however, applies the logical principle that a conclusion cannot be stronger than its premises to this characteristic of historical judgments, to reach his famous conclusion:

> If no historical truth can be demonstrated, then nothing can be demonstrated by means of historical truths. That is: *accidental truths of history can never become the proof of necessary truths of reason.*[8]

Lessing, of course, is primarily referring to the 'proofs' of miracles and prophecy: he is maintaining that as the evidences for the truths of Christianity can only be known as probable, the truth of Christianity cannot thereby be shown to be more than probable. His conclusion can, however, be generalized. It need not refer only to the two 'proofs' of the Christian revelation from miracle and prophecy; indeed by 1777 those proofs had lost much of their prestige among the more percipient apologists for Christianity.[9] What Lessing maintains is equally applicable to any attempt to find the grounds or content of the Christian faith in past events: as so structured that faith can be given no higher epistemological status than that of the historical knowledge of those events. It is in this generalized form that Lessing's problem is significant. Lessing, of course, is applying to history and faith respectively Leibniz's distinction between contingent truths of fact and necessary truths of reason,[10] though in Leibniz's own work the view that there is a 'sufficient reason' for each contingent truth of fact somewhat diminishes the significance of the distinction.

Christian theologians have not been over-troubled by this conclusion of Lessing. It ceases to be an insuperable objection to the validity of the Christian faith once it is allowed (*pace* the understanding of theology in the Leibniz-Wolff tradition) that 'faith' is not the entertainment of rationally demonstrated truths but is a matter of commitment in the face of recognized uncertainty. Macquarrie, for instance, puts it that 'we cannot abolish faith to replace it by certitude, for our destiny as finite beings . . . is that we have to commit ourselves in one way or another without conclusive proof'.[11] If this is the nature of faith in general, no problems of principle are created by the essentially probable character of historical judgments when faith is supposedly grounded on them.

Some theologians have, indeed, emphasized, even almost absolutized, the non-demonstrable character of faith's understanding rather than treated it as a problem to be overcome, by showing that this understanding of the character of faith can nevertheless be significantly supported by rational arguments.

Following Kierkegaard, they maintain not just that 'without risk there is no faith' but that 'instead of the objective uncertainty, there is here a certainty, namely, that objectively it is absurd; and this absurdity, held fast in the passion of inwardness, is faith'.[12] Here, then, the accidental character and probable status of the historical judgments about the past events on which faith is held to be grounded are considered to be virtues rather than problems, since they help to show that faith is not a rationally indicated assent. One product of this kind of theology has been the development of a scepticism which casts doubt on the possibility of reaching any historical knowledge of those past events. Thus it is in accord with Bultmann's epistemological application of the doctrine that salvation is by faith and not by works (and hence that attempts to verify faith's understanding deny the faith that they intend to support), that he finds no difficulty with that 'critical radicalism' which concludes that the Jesus of history is practically unknowable by us:

> I calmly let the fire burn, for I see that what is consumed is only the fanciful portraits of Life-of-Jesus theology, and that means nothing other than 'Christ after the flesh' ... But the 'Christ after the flesh' is no concern of ours. How things looked in the heart of Jesus I do not know and do not want to know.[13]

He does not need to know these things because 'the ground of faith is solely the Word of proclamation (Rom. 10.17)' and 'no other validation can be demanded for the Word and no other basis created it for it than the Word itself'.[14]

Historians without a theological axe to grind frequently seem to be amazed at the historical uncertainties contained in such views and to criticize them as the products of unrealistic demands for conclusiveness in historical judgments. To the extent that their criticism concerns the generally accepted criteria for historical judgments about such periods, it is entirely valid. What it may fail to recognize, however, is that the scepticism about historical judgments in matters of faith is not simply a result of historical investigation. It is, rather, the result of a combination of a severely critical historical approach (probably a justifiable reaction to the far from critical approach to our knowledge of past events that has frequently marked the use of history by believers) and a theological understanding of faith that finds little or no significance for faith in the knowledge of past events. The response to it must, therefore, be theological as well as historical.

Where this scepticism arises from the difference in logical type between historical judgments and the understanding of faith, it will be discussed later in this essay. So far, however, as it arises from the view that faith is not rationally justifiable, it can be argued theologically that this view of faith is unacceptable because it takes away any personal responsibility in man for his faith and makes mockery of his existence as a rational being created 'in the image of God'. A coherent theology where God is puppeteer and men are his puppets, where faith does not in any way involve considered acts of choice and will, may be possible but it is not the only possibility. Since such a theology implies the depersonalization and de-rationalization of man at the fundamental level of his being, it is at least theologically possible to reject it in favour of a theology which sees the purpose and gracious activity of God as seeking to en-hance, *inter alia,* the personal and rational character of man. These, though, are questions which concern the basic un-derstanding of the purposes of God and his relationship to man. They are not questions which we can pursue further in this essay once the point has been made that it is far from theologically necessary to understand faith as antipathetic to the historical knowledge of its supposedly historical grounds.[15] Furthermore, in so far as the scepticism is a product of a radical historical criticism, it is far from obvious that sound historical methods must lead to such a conclusion. As has already been suggested, some historians at least hold that it is quite possible, within the limits of all historical understanding, to reach some fairly sure conclusions about the past events on which faith sees itself as founded.

The general theological response, however, to Lessing's initial distinction between the accidental truths of history and necessary truths of reason has not been to make a virtue of the historical uncertainty but to maintain that faith is a deliberate assent on the basis of what is recognized to be evidence that can at best lead to only probable conclusions. Since, then, faith is not a matter of the entertainment of (or perhaps one should say submission to) irresistibly demonstrated truths, there is in principle no problem here in holding that some parts of faith are based on past events. Furthermore, if attention is paid not to the mode of entertaining the truths of faith but to the mode of those truths themselves, and if it is allowed (as seems possible) that natural and historical reality constitute a single, all-embracing whole, it does not seem unreasonable to expect that some of the necessary truths of ultimate reality will be discernible in and confirmed by (though not, in the strict sense of the term, demonstrable from) the events of history so far as those events depend upon that reality, and also to expect that incorrect understandings of that reality may be shown to be such by the course of actual events. The problem that remains for the believer and the theologian seems, therefore, to be the practical one of deciding whether what actually happened in the past, so far as it is historically ascertainable, does in fact agree with or even verify faith's understanding that is based upon it. In this respect Lessing's initial formulation of the problem receives an answer, although at the price of admitting in principle the vulnerability of faith to historical investigations.

While this response to Lessing has some justification, it may also be asked whether the theologians who adopt it are really and not just professedly prepared to take seriously the corollary that faith might be disconfirmed instead of confirmed by historical investigations. Although to some it has seemed, as Voltaire puts it, that 'Sacred history is a series of divine and miraculous operations, by which it has pleased God formerly to direct and govern the Jewish nation and, in the present day, to try our faith',[16] believers have shown a surprising ability to overlook the discrepancies between faith's references to and use of past events and the apparent import of the evidence about the character of those events. David, for example, still manages to survive as a kind of hero of faith in spite of the way in which historical critics from Bayle onwards have pointed to the embarrassing aspects of his activities. More disturbing, perhaps, is the way in which presentations of Jesus as the Christ for contemporary men still manage to slide round the apocalyptic and eschatological elements in Jesus' understanding, at least as presented by the New Testament. These elements may make him a remote figure for contemporary men. They may even suggest that on basic points he was mistaken about the historical context of his teaching and about the consequences of his activity for the near future. They may even suggest that he was more than simply mistaken about the cosmic timetable, but misunderstood the nature of God by regarding him as one who would introduce his kingdom by fiat rather than through the lure of love. As such these elements may, therefore, be held to tend to disconfirm some of faith's understanding of Jesus as the Christ. Those who hold that the conclusions of certain historical investigations are significant for faith can only be taken seriously if their response is not to sweep apparently offending material under the carpet but to consider its application seriously and, where appropriate, allow it to modify their faith. Nevertheless, while those who hold that the Christian faith is partly grounded on historical knowledge of past events cannot in principle exclude the possibility that future research may show that 'the historical form of Jesus' does not provide such grounding, there is no reason for them to hold that the possibility will ever be actualized. Pannenberg, for one, is confident enough to state that 'I see no occasion for apprehension that such a position of research should emerge in the foreseeable future'.[17] In any case, whether the events of the past as historically determined confirm or disconfirm the understanding of faith that is grounded upon them, Lessing's objection that the accidental character of truths of history prevents them from being used as a basis for faith is overcome as long as faith is admitted to be an assent guided by probabilities, not the acceptance of truths proved with the rigour and indisputability of geometrical demonstrations.

The objection that probable premises cannot by themselves be the ground of inescapable demonstrations of necessary truths is the easier of Lessing's problems concerning history and faith to answer. Though the fact is less widely recognized, his pamphlet 'On the Proof of the Spirit and of Power' goes on to raise a much more difficult problem. The presentation of this second problem is mixed up with comments that reflect the first question. Nevertheless, whether or not Lessing recognized it at the time, his remarks express a quite different – and much more disturbing – doubt about the possibility in principle of grounding faith's understanding on past events. Basically Lessing's objection is that faith's understanding and past events (or the reports of past events – the distinction is not very significant at this point) belong to two distinct logical orders so that there is no logically valid way of deriving the former from the latter. He arrives at this objection through considering the significance of accepting as historically true four reports about past events. The first is the conquests of Alexander. Lessing suggests that no one would be likely to 'risk anything of great, permanent worth' upon the acceptance of the historical accuracy of reports about Alexander. Nor, his remarks hint, would there be any important loss for us if it were discovered that the stories about Alexander are fictitious. The discovery would only make us revise what we could reasonably regard as having happened in the past. Beyond a few changes in our views about the past, then, the discovery would have no significance for our current way of life – unless we were a student of ancient history whose reputation rested upon published researches into the life and times

of Alexander! The crucial point, though, is that the faith by which
a man lives is not determined by whether or not events like the
conquests of Alexander occurred. This point is true in the case of
most reports of past events. The question is whether it is true of all.
Christian believers, for instance, would presumably want to
maintain that unlike those of Alexander's career, the events of
Christ's life are not neutral for faith. Lessing challenges this view
by considering three reports about Christ, reports that 'Christ
raised to life a dead man', that 'this Christ himself rose from the
dead' and that he 'declared himself to be the Son of God' and was
believed to be such by his disciples. If the historical truth of these
three events is seen to be neutral for faith, then it would seem to be
reasonable to infer that the Christian faith does not ultimately
depend upon the simple happenedness and historical determination of any past event or series of past events. Lessing's case
for the neutrality of these past events in relation to faith is made
by accepting the reports about them as true, as reports of
what actually occurred (and so far as they could be experienced by
men and reported by them as events like other historical events),
while denying, in each case, that the occurrence or the report
imposes any obligation concerning faith. The acceptance treats the
reports as historical 'truths of one and the same class' whose
verification is by the standard historical methods for the
examination and evaluation of evidence about the past. The denial
rests upon the view that past events and the historical
determination of them are one thing, faith is another. The two are
independent. Truths of the one neither imply nor are implied by
the other. Lessing, after accepting as historical truths that Christ
'declared himself to be the Son of God' and was believed by his
disciples to be such, puts his point thus:

> But to jump with that historical truth to a quite different class of truths, and to
> demand of me that I should form all my metaphysical and moral ideas
> accordingly; to expect me to alter all my fundamental ideas of the nature of the
> Godhead because I cannot set any credible testimony against the resurrection of
> Christ: if that is not a *metabasis eis allo genos*, then I do not know what Aristotle meant
> by this phrase.

The logical type-jump he refers to is that between claims about
what was the case – that is, about what can be included among the
'facts' describing the content of the empirical world historically
considered – and claims about how reality is to be 'understood' and
life to be lived in terms of what is rationally, valuatively and
ontologically ultimate. What Lessing is here setting forward is a

distinction between past events and faith which is not unlike the logical distinction between fact and value which is the basis of the identification of the supposed 'naturalistic fallacy' in moral understanding. It is this distinction which poses for us as well as for Lessing the fundamental problem of the possible relationship between history and faith. The distinction between the two constitutes 'the ugly, broad ditch' which a faith that is actually and not merely professedly grounded on the happenedness of past events must bridge. Lessing asked for help to bridge it: 'If anyone can help me over it, let him do it, I beg him, I adjure him. He will deserve a divine reward from me.' Can anything be done to help him?

The problem that Lessing here raises is expressed in a different way by Kierkegaard in his *Philosophical Fragments* and *Concluding Unscientific Postscript* when he considers the case of the contemporary disciple and maintains that being a contemporary of Jesus would be of no advantage for becoming a Christian believer because 'in all eternity' there can be 'no direct transition from the historical to the eternal'.[18] If he has sufficient zeal, the contemporary may secure eyewitness reports of the activities and instruction of the 'Teacher' which have 'the highest possible reliability', but these alone will not make him a believer.[19] They will only provide him with a mass of data about a particular person of the same kind as could be provided for any other person. The crucial step of faith is the claim, in one sense or another, that 'this man is also God'.[20] But this recognition is not a matter of 'immediate sensation or cognition' so far as 'the direct and ordinary form of the historical is concerned'.[21] Indeed historical data about the individual – the size of his feet, the accent of his speech, the state of his clothes as well as the content of his teaching and the nature of his activities – may well impede this recognition since it presents him only too clearly as a man. The recognition of faith may well be easiest when the historical data about the individual are obscured by the mists of devotion!

Kierkegaard, having posed the problem in his own way, maintains that the gulf between history and faith to which Lessing has pointed can only be bridged by a leap of faith which is not a product of historical investigation or rational consideration but an act of God himself. Historical knowledge is essentially a knowledge of the temporal and so must necessarily exclude knowledge of the eternal, while knowledge of the eternal cannot include temporal and contingent matters.[22] The faith that finds God in the temporal is 'a miracle':

Let no innkeeper or professor of philosophy imagine that he is a shrewd enough fellow to detect anything [*sc.* of God in a human person], unless God gives the condition ... God gave to the disciple the condition that enables him to see, opening for him the eyes of faith.[23]

This is the case with each individual believer in turn. There is no way of receiving the insight from another unless that 'other' is God.[24] Bultmann, as I have already indicated, similarly holds that faith is not a product of historical knowledge of 'Christ after the flesh'. Richard Kroner is another who finds the gulf bridged only by an act of faith which cannot be the product of historical investigations nor justified by them. He puts it:

Every merely empirical explanation of Biblical revelation is out of the question because in that revelation it is the superhistorical which is revealed in the garment of history ... What boldness, what audacity, what foolishness would it be to explore historically the essentially superhistorical![25]

Such a solution may seem attractive because it puts the onus for faith onto God: either he performs the miracles and we believe or he does not. Either way there are no intellectual problems that we are to overcome by our rational understanding. The believer burkes the problem by holding it to be humanly insoluble. He retreats into a fortress whose motto is

Where reason fails, with all her powers,
There faith prevails and love adores.[26]

This fortress is impregnable to rational assault because it refuses to recognize that reason has any powers in the matter. Such a 'solution' to Lessing's problem, however, implies man's irresponsibility for a faith that is grounded upon historical events and the irrelevance of his rationality for part at least of the fundamental structure of the Christian way of life and understanding. It is, therefore, a solution which is perhaps to be avoided unless it is clear that no other rationally satisfactory solution is available, for it follows from this 'solution' that there are no reasonable ways of deciding between truth and error, sense and fanaticism in such matters. Must rational investigation of faith and of the significance of past events for faith show this impotence of reason? Are there any other ways to bridge Lessing's ditch besides that of a divinely occasioned leap?

Lessing's major problem rests on a logical distinction between historical judgments and faith-claims. The distinction is at its sharpest where historical judgments are regarded as something like the straight narration of what are supposed to be the empirically observable facts of the situation under consideration. According to this view a historical account of a resurrection would express what any person enjoying normal sense-experience could have observed of what happened. So far, therefore, as such an account is to be purely historical, it might be better to describe it by a neutral term like 'resuscitation' rather than by a more religiously orientated word like 'resurrection'. Faith-judgments, in contrast, are logically distinct. They may be held to be factual in part since they describe the nature of reality, but the 'facts' included in their understanding are not empirically observable and also involve value-commitments and attitudes as part of their essence. One way, therefore, of trying to solve Lessing's problem may be by challenging the validity of its presupposed understanding of historical judgments, thereby denying either that the gulf exists or, at least, that it is crucial. This response to Lessing's problem can be developed from Richardson's attack on 'historical positivism'.

We have already quoted Richardson's statement that 'the affirmations of the Christian creeds are historical . . . and Christian theology itself is a matter of the interpretation of history'.[27] It is important here not to overlook the term 'interpretation'. While, then, the Christian faith is historical, it is not, for Richardson, simply a telling of a story about past events. It is an 'interpretation' of certain events which finds in them insight into ultimate reality. As such it involves 'personal decision', and its truth cannot be established by reference to the 'facts' of history as if they provide material for objective decisions.[28] Indeed, in spite of his comments about I. T. Ramsey's metaphysical approach, Richardson is prepared to speak of the relation of faith to past events in terms of Ramsey's 'disclosure situations', situations in which the believer finds in certain events 'interpretative clues' to the meaning of historical reality as a whole.[29] In his *Christian Apologetics* he describes 'the Christian understanding of historical revelation' as 'given through certain historical events as interpreted by the faith and insight of the prophets and apostles of the Bible'.[30] What is important for our purposes, though, is that Richardson holds that this interpretative activity is basically the same as that which is involved in all genuine historiography. Rejecting the positivist view of history as 'the scientific establishing and cataloguing of facts' on the grounds that we cannot even establish 'facts' as such without presupposing value-judgments, let alone select and order them into an understandable and understanding account of past happenings,[31] he maintains that 'a true history' depends upon 'the soundness of its principle of interpretation'.[32] It thus reflects the 'personal . . . interpretative imagination' of the historian as well as the public evidence he is assessing.[33] For Richardson

> The historian *is* the interpreter, because the 'facts' themselves are his interpretations . . . In the last resort, as in all historical interpretation, the interpreter's own personal experience of involvement in history will be the deciding factor in his judging, because all historical judgment is unavoidably personal and existential.[34]

On the basis of this view of history, Richardson not only rejects the dichotomy between event and interpretation, holding that ' "what happened" can be rightly assessed only "in the perspective of history" ';[35] he also affirms the methodological unity of our 'knowledge of historical and theological truth'.[36]

We have here, then, a possible way of replying to Lessing, namely through maintaining that there is no ditch between historical judgments and the understanding of faith, since both have the same kind of logical structure as the interpretation of events. Unfortunately this reply appears on examination to be unconvincing. It merely shifts the identification of the locus of the problem from the relationship between historical judgments and faith's understanding to the problem of the relationship between events as they happened and their interpretation by historians and then believers. The effect of Richardson's attack on historical positivism is thus to replace the history-faith dichotomy by a trichotomy of event, history and faith. There are several points at issue here and we will discuss them in turn.

This analysis of the implications of Richardson's work runs counter to his view that there is no possibility of distinguishing between 'the event and its interpretation',[37] since judgments about 'what happened' are always affected by the perspective of the historian.[38] In so far as Richardson is here describing the limits of 'our knowledge'[39] of past events, his view expresses a common but important epistemological point. All our knowledge, be it of objects or of events, is to some extent controlled by the mode of our understanding both as human beings in general and as persons belonging to a particular culture with its conceptual and valuative structures and by the specific questions which determine our perspective in seeking this knowledge. Consequently what we eventually arrive at as 'knowledge' or 'understanding' is a product of the interaction of the character of the object with our human, cultural and personal characteristics. While, though, this means that we cannot ever pretend to be able to know just what happened in a past event in a totally objective and non-selective fashion – even our awareness of our present states is selective according to what we are interested in at the moment – it does not mean that it is neither possible nor useful to distinguish between the object/event and the interpreted knowledge/understanding which we have of it. In fact it is the possibility of this distinction that allows us to question any given understanding of 'an event' and to seek a fresh understanding of 'it'. The 'event' that is referred to will never be grasped 'in itself', and yet as 'what happened' it is a regulative absolute which provides one theoretical absolute for checking our historical understanding of it. To put it in simpler terms, an interpretation is an interpretation *of* something. If, then, as Richardson puts it, the 'facts' of history are interpretations,[40] there must be something of which they are interpretations. Richardson's restriction of the word 'history' to the understanding or interpretation of past events thus requires a theoretical distinction between what happened (the events themselves) and history as the interpretative understanding of what happened. This distinction, though, leaves untouched the problem of how to justify a historical account as a 'correct' interpretation of what happened. If, then, we accept that history and faith are both interpretations of history, we have not overcome Lessing's challenge but converted it into the challenge of how to bridge the gulf between the events as they happened and faith's interpretations of them as historically grasped.

It may be held, following Richardson, that this problem should not be a very troublesome one on the grounds that as the 'historical' understanding of events is a generally accepted mode of knowledge, so the similar kind of interpretation of events found in faith's understanding should be equally acceptable. This response, however, is crucially unsatisfactory because it fails to appreciate that while history and faith may both be regarded as 'interpretations of events', the kinds of 'interpretation' involved (and their respective acceptability) are importantly different. The historian's interpretation is a selection and arrangement of evidence about what happened in the past whose purpose is primarily to show how various factors interacted to produce a particular result, and secondarily to cast light on current situations by analogy with that understanding of past events. The factors considered – such as political, economic, social and personal – are what are held to have been involved in this past situation. The eventual historical understanding is judged satisfactory or not according to the degree to which it relates these factors in a coherent fashion to produce a story which seems to illuminate for us from some perspective what happened in the past and why, and then perhaps to suggest by analogy what might in similar circumstances occur on other occasions. In all this, however, the factors considered and the story produced are primarily seeking an understanding of a specific series of events in their own particular context. Furthermore, even if that 'philosophy of history'[41] which attempts to identify general 'laws' at work in events is accepted as a legitimate development of historical study, the interpretation of events which constitutes history is still not the same as that which is found in faith's understanding. Where the understanding of faith is an interpretation of past events, it is not an interpretation which seeks to provide a way of appreciating the interaction of forces that led to what happened actually happening as it did, or an illustration of general 'laws' governing all relevant events. It is an interpretation which seeks to provide an insight into cosmic, fundamental truth about the nature of God and his relationships to man and the world. Take, for example, the event of the death of Jesus. A historian's concern would be to answer questions like 'Why was he crucified?' and his answer, if ascertainable, would be by reference to factors such as the character of Jesus' teaching in the socio-political context of his day, his refusal to compromise, the response to him by the religious establishment, the delicate situation of the Roman governor and so on. An answer, that is, would be sought which logically would be of the same order as answers to questions like 'Why was Socrates executed?' or Joan of Arc? or Admiral Byng? Those working in the philosophy of history might draw out from the historian's answer to the question about the death of Jesus (probably in conjunction with other cases) claims about men's resistance to change or about their hostility to threats to their convenience. The traditional Christian believer, in contrast, affirms a quite different understanding of the event of Jesus' death. He sees it as an event which in one way or another (depending on the degrees of 'objectivity' and 'subjectivity' in his atonement theology) establishes the reconciliation of man and God through the gracious self-giving of God. In seeing the theological significance of the event in this way he cannot ignore how the historian understands it. It would be difficult, for example, to find the reconciling grace of God revealed in Jesus' death if it appeared historically that he died as a cursing, deluded, politically-motivated fanatic or that he was never actually crucified but that someone else was substituted for him on the way. In this respect what the believer finds in events is not immune to historical investigations. On the other hand, what the believer reaches as faith's understanding of the event is not a product of the kind of investigations that a historian would make into the whats and whys of what occurred. It belongs to a distinct mode of understanding which is concerned with the character, purposes and actions of God and with the consequent possibilities for man. While, then, it may be held that understanding of this kind is a way of interpreting the significance of the death of Jesus, such interpretation is never reached by any degree of historical understanding. The difference is most obvious if we compare examples of the different kinds of understanding that a historian, a philosopher of history and a theologian will come to in the case of the crucifixion of Jesus. Having established that he was crucified, the historian might interpret it as brought about by a combination of Jewish religious conservatism and Roman fear of revolt in the case of an individual who challenged current ways. The philosopher of history, on the basis of how the historian suggests that the event is to be understood, might then compare it with other cases and interpret it as an example of the generally evil character of men and institutions which leads them to oppose, even violently, criticisms of their ways. The theologian, while taking into account the historical ways of understanding the event, interprets it as a saving act for all mankind in which God's character and man's destiny is made known. The first two kinds of interpretation are based on and to be verified by reference to the available evidence of what happened in Palestine seen in the light of our present understanding of men and nature. The third, theological, kind of interpretation, as it employs notions of God and of man's eternal status, finds in the event a significance which no amount of investigation of the historical evidence can confirm. Many men were crucified, some of them may even have been innocent of any crime. Why, then, should Jesus' crucifixion, either as the event that happened or as the historical understanding of that event, be interpreted as having such theological significance? This is the question of Lessing's ditch. We are back to it!

Wolfhart Pannenberg seeks to solve this problem by holding that the resurrection of Jesus establishes the theological significance of his life and death as the proleptic revelation of God's future reign. This occurrence, that is, justifies us in reaching a cosmic, divine interpretation of the events and history of Jesus. He states, for example, that by his resurrection Jesus was 'confirmed in his claim that the final destiny of men is decided by their stand in relation to his message'[42] and, again, that 'it is only in the light of the raising of Jesus that we have reason to speak of a divine incarnation in his person'.[43] What we have here in effect is a version of the traditional proof from miracles of the authenticity of the Christian revelation, a form of argument which was very familiar, if decreasingly attractive, to the eighteenth-century apologetic theologians with whom Lessing was in debate. Unfortunately Pannenberg's 'resurrection' of the argument does not make it any the less problematic. Although we may not consider it necessary to endorse Woolston's comment that the 'evangelical Story' of the resurrection of Jesus is 'a Complication of Absurdities, Incoherences, and Contradictions',[44] we cannot escape recognizing that reference to the resurrection of Jesus as proof of divine significance in Jesus' life and death raises as great problems as it purports to solve.

In the first place there is the problem of establishing the nature and the significance of what was experienced by the people who provide the evidence for the resurrection of Jesus. Pannenberg's own discussion of the issue in *The Apostles' Creed in the Light of Today's Questions* highlights the elusiveness of this problem. On the one hand he affirms that this is an inescapable historical question which must be answered by weighing up 'in detail the exact reality of the evidence' according to 'the methods of historical research'. This he holds to be crucial since 'the conviction that Jesus lives, even today, as the one who is risen, depends on the reliability of this information'.[45] On the other hand, as soon as we try to engage in such historical evaluation of the evidence, Pannenberg claims that we are dealing with reports of 'a transformation into an entirely new life' which must be distinguished from all other accounts of 'the raisings of the dead'.[46] Jesus' resurrection is not to be regarded as 'the revival of a corpse' but as the appearance of a reality which 'is otherwise totally inaccessible to human experience and which can consequently only be expressed metaphorically'.[47] The uniqueness of the reality here confronted by the witnesses of Jesus' resurrection may explain the difficulties which Woolston finds in the reports but it also makes the evaluation of their evidence extremely difficult, if not impossible. How can we judge, in the first place, what must have happened and, secondly, what its significance is for faith when we cannot know what was the reality that was supposed to have been experienced and so cannot tell how far the evidence warrants the claim that it was experienced? Something happened which the witnesses apprehended, sooner or later, by the metaphor of resurrection and which they held to justify their faith about Jesus – 'if Christ was not raised, then our gospel is null and void, and so is your faith'.[48] The very metaphor which they used to describe the event – resurrection – shows that they understood whatever it was that they experienced as an act of God. The agent of resurrection is never doubted to be God, not natural forces nor the accidental reversal of the life-death-decay process. This indicates that those who report the resurrection have, as the consequence of their experiences of something outside our range of experience, leaped Lessing's ditch and apprehended those experiences in terms of God. It does not show us that they were justified in making this leap and reaching a theological interpretation of the events they experienced. Although, therefore, it seems unreasonable to doubt that something strange happened which convinced those who witnessed it as being the result of God's activity, their evidence begs Lessing's question. It does not solve it. Consequently we must either hold that the leap from historical to theological interpretation of events is justified for us by those who made it in the past (and so resting the possibility of our faith's understanding on the actuality of theirs) or we return to Lessing's problem.[49] Since Lessing in part poses his problem about the justification of making the leap from event to faith in terms of the theological interpretation of the resurrection of Jesus, it is not really satisfactory to attempt to answer him by affirming that people have so interpreted the events. A question about the validity of what is done is not to be answered by showing that it is done, otherwise most forms of intellectual and moral skullduggery will be validatable!

Before we see if there are any other ways to meet Lessing's problem, there is a further question to be noted. How is the correct theological significance of certain events to be determined if and when it be established that those events have theological significance? This is a problem which besets. all the attempted solutions which we have so far considered. Take, for instance, the death of Jesus. Traditionally theologians have interpreted it as a saving act. Why should it be given that interpretation? Could it not be interpreted as the sign of man's abandonment by God: their destruction of the perfectly good man or the supreme messenger from God, Jesus, as finally leading God to abandon mankind to self-destruction?[50] The cry of dereliction could thus be seen as reciprocating God's final despair about man. Pannenberg claims that the resurrection of Jesus alone allows us 'to ascribe any saving meaning to his death' and not just 'the failure of his mission'.[51] But how are we to defend the claim that this is the significance of the resurrection event, whatever it was? Although elsewhere Pannenberg speaks of 'God's having been revealed in the fate of Jesus', it is difficult to grasp what he sees as actually having been made known in this revelation beyond the inexhaustibility and infinity of the God whose reign is finally to be realized.[52] If this is what he holds to be revealed, then the 'revelation' seems to be unnecessary in practice and improbable in principle. It seems to be unnecessary in practice because it 'makes known' characteristics of God which can be argued to be implicit in a theistic conceptuality as such; process theologies, for example, reach these claims about God without needing to appeal to revelation, as do other natural theologies which accept the reality of the temporal order in reaching their theistic conclusions. It seems improbable in principle because it is not at all clear how the limitlessness of inexhaustibility and infinity could ever be manifested in specific events. On the other hand, when we consider the theological interpretations of the significance of Jesus which go beyond these formal characteristics into material ones which could only be known by revelation, it is notorious how many divergent meanings are derived from the records about Jesus.[53] The records then appear to be too much like a nose of wax, to be pulled into whatever shape pleases, for the interpretations to carry more weight than that of being more or less possible 'interpretations' of the material. I shall not go further into this hermeneutical question at this point. It is important, though, to recognize that the problem of Lessing's leap is not just the problem of whether and how a theological interpretation of certain events is justifiable. It also involves the problem of how the correct theological interpretation of the events is to be determined.

A different response to the problem of Lessing's leap is to hold that the problem of the relationship between events and faith is misconstrued when it is seen as a question about the possibility of basing religious understanding on this or that specific series of events, taken to a large extent in isolation from the process of history as a whole. According to this answer to Lessing, the value of any particular individual events or series of events is not in the light that they are held to cast on the nature and purpose of God but in the way they can be held to provide an illustration of the process of history as a whole. It is the process as a whole that is to be seen as the revelation – or even as the reality – of God. Lessing's problem is thus dissolved by maintaining that faith is not to be based on events within history as he presupposes in formulating his problem. Hegel, for instance, speaks of 'Universal History' as the stage on which 'Spirit displays itself' in the process of working out the knowledge of that which it is potentially'. For Hegel, 'God governs the world; the actual working of his government – the carrying out of his plan – is the History of the World'.[54] From this it might be expected that religious faith, as the understanding of the material nature and purposes of God, is to be found only by the attainment of an understanding of the whole historical process of events.

Any attempt to provide a *historical* solution to Lessing's problem along these lines is doomed to failure. In the first place the process of history is not complete. We are not at the end of time and cannot envisage when or what it will be. It is, secondly, a story whose twists and turns prevent us from claiming with any confidence that its movement up to now has a pattern leading towards a goal which can be discerned by examining what is known to have happened. Both the incompleteness and the irregularity of the series of past events as seen from the present thus mean that the historian as historian cannot safely claim to ascertain the character of universal history. Such claims are the products of the interpretation of the past from a perspective which is constituted by an independent determination of the ultimate meaningfulness and unity of historical reality. If there is any satisfactory argument on these matters, it will not be from the evidence of the clear unity of history to the conclusion that there must be a God governing it (a historical version of the argument from 'the rule of one', the principle that unity must be the product of a single unifier), but in the reverse direction – namely, that because there is a God, therefore the pattern of historical reality must be a meaningful unity.[55] Hegel sees this:

> That history, and above all universal history, is founded on an essential and actual aim, which actually is and will be realised in it – the plan of Providence; that, in short, there is Reason in history, must be decided on strictly philosophical ground, and thus shown to be essentially and in fact necessary.[56]

In his *Lectures on the Philosophy of History* Hegel describes this 'conviction and intuition' as a 'hypothesis' for the study of history, but one that is proved in philosophy by 'speculative cognition'.[57] Furthermore, so far as most historians are concerned, references to 'universal history' or to 'the process of history as a whole' are not only to what they suspect to be beyond the competence of historians, for who can reasonably claim to appreciate matters on such a scale? They are also regarded as references to what is not the proper object of their concern as historians. Their interest being with establishing the whats, wheres, hows and why of past events and of their significance on a much more restricted scale, they share Isaiah Berlin's view of 'the systems of historiosophers' as 'either too general, vague, and occasionally tautological to cast new light on anything in particular', or providing results which are not confirmed by 'exact scholars in the relevant fields'.[58] Finally, then, the appeal to 'universal history' as a way of meeting Lessing's problem fails because it begs the question, since the essence of the problem could be posed non-theologically as the problem of the relationship between specific events in the past and their historical understanding on the one hand and the claims about universal history on the other. We are back again with the problem of the justifiability of moving from specific events to their theological or universal significance. Lessing's problem has not been solved but rediscovered in another form! Similarly, when Pannenberg maintains that 'because every individual entity has meaning only in relation to a greater whole, universal history in the sense of the total meaning of all history is an inescapable theme of historical work,'[59] he shows that his view of historical activity depends upon presuppositions which cannot be derived from that activity. If events are finally to be understood only in terms of 'universal history', the character of universal history cannot be discovered from a study of past events but must be known independently of such understanding of the events in order for the events to be understood in terms of it.[60] In other words, we cannot derive the correct perspective for appreciating the significance of events from a study of events since it is the perspective by which we view the events which determines how their significance will appear to us.

Here we arrive back at issues with which this essay began, at questions about the value of epistemology, philosophy, abstract concepts referring to God and metaphysics in understanding the grounds, nature and truth of the Christian faith. In spite of the evident role of past events in determining that faith, the conclusion which is indicated both by this investigation and by a systematic consideration of the relationships between past events and the interpretation of them (for which there is no space here) is that while such references may point to where, for psychological reasons or because of traditional ways of seeing, the truth of that faith is generally perceived, the final justification of that faith rests upon epistemological-metaphysical reasoning which either supports the understanding of faith directly (if the relationship to events is held to be of the story and moral type), or supports the understanding of events as partly due to the agency of God (if the relationship is of the event and agency of God type). In both cases the fundamental court of appeal is not to history but to metaphysics. If Lessing's 'ugly, broad ditch' is to be bridged, it will only be by a metaphysical argument that can justify the claim that God can be seen at work in a specifiable way in specifiable events for a specifiable reason. If such an argument is not acceptable, then there is no way of justifying religious faith by reference to events. The relationship between the two is the accidental one that certain events happen, as observed or as related from a particular perspective, to evoke or to illustrate religious insights which must be confirmed in their own right. Surprising, then, as it may seem to those who emphasize the historical character of the Christian faith, the material as well as the formal content of that faith is thus to be decided by the metaphysical reasoning of natural theology. The justification of that faith depends on the work of those who seek, among other metaphysical questions, to find satisfactory models for divine activity[61] and to show why Jesus is 'the key image'[62] who 'focuses for us the recognition and the realization'[63] of the theistic nature of ultimate reality.

NOTES

1. A. Richardson, 'Ian Ramsey of Durham, An Appreciation and Review', in *The Ampleforth Journal* LXXIX, Summer 1974, p. 68. The comment in brackets is by Richardson.
2. A. Richardson, *Christian Apologetics*, SCM Press 1947, p. 108.
3. A. Richardson, *History Sacred and Profane*, SCM Press 1964, p. 13.
4. Cf. John 1. 14; I Cor. 15.3; I John 1. 1f. For this view of the significance of Jesus Christ, cf. my article 'The Incarnation as a Continuing Reality', *Religious Studies* 6. 4, December 1970, pp. 303ff.
5. M.F. Wiles, *The Remaking of Christian Doctrine*, SCM Press 1974, p. 118.
6. V.A. Harvey, *The Historian and the Believer*, SCM Press 1967, pp. 280-283.
7. This paper is concerned with the logical problem of the derivability of religious faith from past events. It does not attempt to consider other problems concerning the relationship between faith and history such as the theological problem of the compatibility of God's perfection with the view that he made knowledge of himself dependent upon historical events accessible, by the nature of

things, only to a few. Nor does it deal with the problem of the possible confirmability/disconfirmability of religious beliefs (such as about the status of the papacy or the role of episcopacy) by reference to what has actually occurred in the past.

8. The references to Lessing are to his 'On the Proof of the Spirit and of Power' as translated in *Lessing's Theological Writings*, ed. H. Chadwick, A. and C. Black 1956, pp. 51-6.

9. They were, however, replaced by so-called 'internal' proofs which were equally dependent on historical evidence and so vulnerable to Lessing's criticism. But this is not to say that the proofs of miracle and prophecy were abandoned; cf., for example, their use by Liddon and Mozley a century ago and by Richardson and Pannenberg today (nn. 42ff. below).

10. It is interesting – and somewhat puzzling – to note in this connection that Richardson seems regularly to misquote Lessing's conclusion by speaking not of the 'accidental' but of the 'incidental truths of history', although his references are to Chadwick's translation: cf. A. Richardson, *The Bible in the Age of Science*, SCM Press 1961, p. 39; *History Sacred and Profane*, pp. 28, 95, 120f., 125, 148.

11. J. Macquarrie, *Principles of Christian Theology*, SCM Press 1966, p. 79.

12. S. Kierkegaard, *Concluding Unscientific Postscript*, translated and edited by D.F. Swenson and W. Lowrie, Princeton University Press 1941, p. 188.

13. R. Bultmann, *Faith and Understanding*, Eng. trs., SCM Press 1969, p. 132.

14. Ibid., pp. 137f; cf. Richardson, *Christian Apologetics*, p. 151.

15. For further discussion of this subject cf. my two articles, 'Theistic Verification' in *The Living God*, ed. D. Kirkpatrick, Abingdon Press 1971, pp. 48-75; and 'Can the Theologian Legitimately try to Answer the Question: Is the Christian Faith True?', *The Expository Times* LXXXIV, August 1973, pp. 325 ff.

16. Voltaire, *A Philosophical Dictionary*, London 1843, vol. 2, p. 10.

17. W. Pannenberg, 'Response to the Discussion', *Theology as History*, ed. J.M. Robinson and J.B. Cobb, Harper and Row 1967, p. 274.

18. Kierkegaard, *Concluding Unscientific Postscript*, p. 89.

19. S. Kierkegaard, *Philosophical Fragments*, translated and edited by D.F. Swenson, Princeton University Press 1936, p. 48.

20. Ibid., p. 36.

21. Ibid., p. 71; cf. pp. 46f., 51.

22. Cf. ibid., pp. 50, 62f.

23. Ibid., p. 52; cf. p. 46.

24. Cf. ibid., p. 56.

25. R. Kroner, *Between Faith and Thought*, Oxford University Press, New York 1966, p. 22.

26. Isaac Watts, *Hymns and Spiritual Songs*, Book III, No. 38.

27. Richardson, *History Sacred and Profane*, p. 13.

28. Ibid., pp. 293f.; cf. pp. 197ff.

29. Ibid., p. 224.

30. Richardson, *Christian Apologetics*, p. 92; cf. *The Bible in the Age of Science*, p. 146.

31. Cf. Richardson, *Christian Apologetics*, pp. 96f.

32. Ibid., p. 147.

33. Richardson, *History Sacred and Profane*, p. 156; cf. pp. 235, 294.⁻

34. Ibid., p. 294.

35. Ibid., p. 235; cf. *Christian Apologetics*, p. 147. This view of history as

essentially uniting the event and its interpretation still leaves us with the problem of determining the appropriate structure of interpretation by which to understand what happened in particular cases. Mr John A. Harrod has pointed out to me that Richardson himself seems to adopt different structures for different series of events. Richardson claims, for instance, that 'the historical evidence for the resurrection, regarded simply as historical evidence, is strong'. Consequently he criticizes those who use 'the canon of positivist historiography' to deny 'the historicity of the resurrection', on the grounds that they use an inappropriate canon of historical understanding (*The Bible in the Age of Science*, p. 128). On the other hand, when he mentions the events of the Exodus in *History Sacred and Profane*, p. 224, Richardson seems to be regarding such a structure of understanding (or something like it) as appropriate for understanding the reports of the Exodus, for he writes that 'it is probably beyond the power of historians, using all the resources of modern scientific historical method upon the materials at their disposal, to reconstruct in detail the story of "what happened" at the coming out of Egypt. Perhaps nothing externally happened in Egypt or at the Red Sea or in the Wilderness which we today would not account for by natural means . . .' The 'we' here, however, might well be rejected by a person of Jewish faith on the grounds that a structure of understanding involving divine intervention is needed to understand the Exodus and that to find historical understanding of the Exodus which does not involve such intervention is to adopt a false historical positivism. Such a view might be defended by the same kind of argument that Richardson uses to defend the resurrection of Jesus, namely, that only the presence of some events which cannot be explained 'naturally' can account for the rise of the believing community. This response to Richardson is not 'frivolous', I think, but points to the way in which non-historically determinable factors decide how we understand history; cf. *Christian Apologetics*, pp. 175f.

36. Richardson, *Christian Apologetics*, p. 11; cf. the similar view in Pannenberg, 'Response to the Discussion', *Theology as History* (see n. 17 above), pp. 234, 256ff., 275.

37. Richardson, *Christian Apologetics*, p. 147.

38. Cf. Richardson, *History Sacred and Profane*, p. 235.

39. Richardson, *Christian Apologetics*, p. 147.

40. Cf. Richardson, *History Sacred and Profane*, pp. 293f.

41. This is only one use of the notion of 'philosophy of history'. While it is clear in itself and refers to the metaphysical and moral understanding of history as a whole, such as is found in Hegel or Augustine, it should be carefully distinguished from the philosophical activity which deals with the logical nature and status and content of historical judgments. In this latter sense of the notion, this paper may be described as an essay in the philosophy of history. To save confusion, however, the notion will be restricted in this paper to the former – and to me questionable – usage.

42. W. Pannenberg, *Basic Questions in Theology*, Eng. trs., SCM Press Vol. I, 1970; Vol. II, 1971; Vol. III, 1973: Vol. II, p. 24; cf. Vol. I, p. 8.

43. W. Pannenberg, *The Apostles' Creed in the Light of Today's Questions*, SCM Press 1972, p. 96; cf. 'The Revelation of God in Jesus of Nazareth', *Theology as History*, pp. 114ff. Richardson makes a similar point in *Christian Apologetics*, pp. 167f., 172f., but cf. *History Sacred and Profane*, pp. 205ff.

44. T. Woolston, *A Discourse on the Miracles of our Saviour*, London 1727, Vol. I, p. 57.

45. Pannenberg, *The Apostles' Creed*, pp. 104, 108; cf. p. 107.

46. Ibid., pp. 97, 100.

47. Ibid., p. 111; cf. pp. 97f.; cf. also 'The Revelation of God in Jesus of Nazareth', *Theology as History*, p. 115, and the criticism of this view by K. Grobel in an essay entitled 'Revelation and Resurrection' in the same volume, pp. 168 f.; *Basic Questions in Theology* II, pp. 24f.

48. I Cor. 15. 14.

49. It is on these grounds that Richardson's strongest argument for the resurrection fails to show that the resurrection reports provide a way of meeting Lessing's problem. According to Richardson, the most convincing proof of the resurrection is that only the apostles' belief that such an event had occurred can explain their faith, commitment and preaching. He says, for instance: 'Whether the original disciples were right or wrong about the fact, it cannot be gainsaid that their conviction that Jesus had risen from the dead was the starting-point of the Christian faith' (*Christian Apologetics*, p. 167; cf. *The Bible in the Age of Science*, pp. 127f., 173). What such an argument may reasonably be held to show is that belief that the resurrection of Jesus had occurred is alone able to explain the rise of the apostles' faith after the crucifixion of Jesus and especially of their belief about the significance of Jesus as the revealer of God (cf. *Christian Apologetics*, p. 168). What it does not show, however, is the nature of the events that evoked that faith nor the justifiability of seeing those events as verifying that faith both for them and for us. There is no need to be so sceptical as to deny that something happened to turn the presumably disturbed disciples into committed believers, and that that 'something' is what they described as the resurrection of Jesus. Unfortunately the converting power of that 'something' for the disciples does not allow us to determine its significance for us.

50. Cf. Matt. 21. 33ff.

51. Pannenberg, *The Apostles' Creed*, p. 96.

52. W. Pannenberg, 'Dogmatic Theses on the Doctrine of Revelation', in *Revelation as History*, ed. W. Pannenberg, Eng. trs., Sheed and Ward 1969, p. 138; cf. Pannenberg, *Basic Questions in Theology* II, pp. 24f., 110, 114.

53. Cf. the delightful story quoted by L. Hodgson in *For Faith and Freedom*, SCM Press 1968, Vol. 2, p. 7, of the 'girl of deep Christian piety' who, as demanded, compared the stories of the raising of Jairus' daughter and that of Lazarus. She stated that Jesus went immediately to Jairus' daughter whose father was 'wealthy and influential' but 'delayed three days and went at his ease' in the case of Lazarus 'who belonged to a poor family'. Hodgson points out that as the details were correct, she earned full marks. On the other hand the class awareness that is revealed in the presentation of the story might not be so obviously a 'correct' understanding of Jesus for some of his current followers!

54. G.W.F. Hegel, *The Philosophy of History*, translated by J. Sibree, new introduction by C.J. Friedrich, Dover Books 1956, pp. 16, 17f., 36.

55. Cf. Pannenberg, 'Response to the Discussion', *Theology as History*, pp. 254ff., and 254 n. 61.

56. G.W.F. Hegel, *Philosophy of Mind*, translated by W. Wallace, Clarendon Press 1894, p. 148.

57. Hegel, *Philosophy of History*, p. 9; cf. p. 36.

58. Isaiah Berlin, 'The Concept of Scientific History', reprinted in *Philosophical Analysis and History*, ed. W.H. Dray, Harper and Row 1966, p. 23.

59. Pannenberg, 'Response to the Discussion', *Theology as History*, pp. 242f; cf. *Basic Questions in Theology* I, pp. 12f., 98.

60. Pannenberg holds that such a view of the totality of history is possible in terms of the significance of Jesus as the manifestation of the end of history. This revelatory significance of Jesus, however, is only to be established for Pannenberg by reference to the resurrection, an argument which we have already suggested to be unsatisfactory. Pannenberg also seems to consider that the authenticity of our grasp of the revelation in Jesus can be checked by comparing it with the known pattern of history, but this is to beg the question. We cannot have Jesus as the clue to the pattern of history and that pattern as the clue to the correct understanding of Jesus without either finding ourselves in an unsatisfactorily circular argument or having to hold that the pattern of history is ascertainable independently of the revelation in Jesus, which is what I suggest to be impossible.

61. This is the title of a series of lectures by I.T. Ramsey, published posthumously by SCM Press, 1973.

62. Harvey, *The Historian and the Believer*, p. 283.

63. Wiles, *The Remaking of Christian Doctrine*, p. 118.

~ 7 ~

The Authority of the Christian Faith[1]

RICHARD HANSON

I

The Authority of the Word

Ultimately all authority in the Christian religion must go back to the Word of God. The authority of the church can only be valid if it is the Word of God that gives the church its authority. The authority of the Bible can only be of any weight if the Bible is accepted as the record of the Word of God. The authority of religious experience can only be impressive to those who believe that such experience is in communication with the Word of God. Theoretically the Word of God is preached every Sunday in pulpits all over this country. It is supposed to be a large part of the duty of every priest and minister of religion to be very zealous to discover and to disseminate this Word. Theoretically all Christian people should have a working idea of what the Word of God is.

In fact, however, the concept of the Word of God is a complex one, of which very different accounts have been given during the course of Christian history. Catholics, in as far as they have tended to take any notice of this particular mode of stating the authority of the Christian faith, have been inclined to encapsulate or confine the Word in dogmatic formulae. For them the Word has often meant in effect the authoritative teaching of the church, especially as laid down in historic and classical statements of councils and theologians, prelates and popes, through the ages, in such forms as the Nicene Creed, the Chalcedonian formula, encyclicals and catechisms. This way of conceiving of the Word of God has at least meant that the Word is accessible and comprehensible; you know where you are with it. It also means that the Word can be worked up into a consistent scheme of theological thought, like the scholasticism of the thirteenth century. Above all it means that the Word can be controlled, that the church is firmly in charge of it, and can develop, apply, modify and even suppress the Word as it chooses. This advantage does not only appeal to an authoritarian church governed by a sacerdotal caste. Anglican churches and Anglican theologians have at times regarded the Word of God very much in this way. One has only to look at a book such as *The Christian Faith* written by the late Dr C.B. Moss, in many ways an admirable man and an intensely Anglican theologian.[2]

But there are grave objections to this interpretation of the Word of God. It comes perilously near to controlling God. Men have always wanted to control God. It is always tempting to think that we can manipulate God, shut him up in a box like a genie, gain a monopoly of him like a capitalist, or confine him in a reservoir whose taps we can turn on or off. But the Word of God is not bound, either by Catholics or by Protestants.

Again, it is impossible to exhaust the content and fully express the meaning of the Word of God in formulae. No language is ageless; there is no *philosophia perennis*. Even the most sacrosanct language eventually needs explanation, re-statement, re-definition, bringing up to date. The example of the doctrine of transubstantiation is an obvious one. But there are others: 'he descended into hell', 'consubstantial with the Father' are far from self-explanatory terms today. The Word of God, therefore, cannot be finally, unalterably expressed in dogmatic or doctrinal propositions. This does not, of course, mean that such statements are useless or improper or unsuitable, but that the Word of God cannot be permanently captured or fossilized by them.

It must next be pointed out that there are quite as many dangers in the conventional Protestant treatment of the Word of God as in the Catholic. The chief Protestant danger is the one which Paul Tillich pointed out – that of imagining that the Word means words. In Protestant churches in countries where Protestants are very conscious of being Protestants (such as Ireland) you will find few pictures or icons and almost no statues; these are considered to be dangerously like Roman Catholic practice. But you will find words written up all over the place, the Ten Commandments, the Lord's Prayer, quotations from Scripture, verbose memorials of bygone worthies and so on. And Protestant services consist almost wholly of words, exhortations and sermons and petitions as well as (sometimes wordy) psalms and hymns. The impression must often be created that serving God consists in talking continuously: in the beginning was the Talk.

Again, if the Word is identified with doctrinal formulae, at least it is defined and comprehensible; but the Protestant conception of

the Word of God can lead to the identification of the Word with
some very queer phenomena. Richard Hooker once complained of
some Puritans that when they and their Bibles were alone together
they immediately took whatever strange thought came into their
heads to be the teaching of the Holy Spirit. In our own day the
followers of Moral Re-Armament have made not dissimilar claims.
The thought that he is speaking, or is authorized to speak, the
Word of God can intoxicate a man and render him irresponsible
and fanatical. 'Whenever sermon-making and temple-building are
thought of as an ultimate human occupation,' says Karl Barth,
'whenever men are aware of divine appointment, of being entrusted
with a divine mission, sin veritably abounds – unless the miracle of
forgiveness accompanies such activity.'[3] Attempting to speak the
Word of God can lead to doctrinaire arrogance, as in all
sectarianism, whether that of the Covenanters in Scott's *Old
Mortality* or that of contemporary Paisleyites. It can also lead to an
irresponsible subjectivity and indulgence in whimsy.

If we go to the Bible to discover the meaning of the term 'the
Word of God', we receive, as we might expect, a very diverse
answer. But it would be quite inadequate to say that in the Bible
the Word of God simply means people preaching. There is one
element in the concept which is present in almost all the
occurrences and which goes beyond just preaching: the Word of
God usually means the act of God. When the prophetic books tell
us that the Word of God came to Isaiah or Jeremiah or Amos or
Hosea, it does not simply mean that the prophet had a good idea or
a bright thought or an inspiring message; it means that God acted
through the prophet. When in the creation narrative in Genesis
God speaks, his speaking is also a creative act. Deutero-Isaiah, the
prophet of the exile, declares that God's word does not return to
him empty (Isa. 55. 10f.; 45.18; 46.10). The book of Wisdom
describes God's Word as leaping down from heaven to do his will, a
drawn sword in its hand (Wisd. 18.15f.). This is true of the New
Testament also. Jesus appears in Galilee preaching a Word, a
gospel. But it does not just consist of moral exhortations, and it is
not very obviously 'inspirational'. It is eschatological, it tells of the
arrival of the kingdom of God, the kingly rule of God, at the last
time, of something *done* by God. And in the rest of the New
Testament, the Word of God is much more like the activity of God
than like preaching about God. Of course apostles and disciples do
preach the Word, spread the Word and serve the Word. Paul
describes himself as 'conducting a sacrificial cult of (*hierourgounta*)

the gospel' (Rom. 15.16), spending his energy and life in its service. The author of Hebrews says in a well-known phrase that 'the Word of God is living and active and sharper than any two-edged sword' (Heb. 4.12). These references to the Word suggest neither that the Word is simply sermons, or doctrine, nor that it can be satisfactorily presented just by talking about it. The Word, in short, is not just words. The Fourth Gospel, one of the latest books of the New Testament, goes so far as to say that Jesus Christ was the Word made flesh (John 1.14), the active being of God himself appearing uniquely and finally in human form. This is the last and furthest development of the thought about the Word of God in the Bible. Clearly there can be no greater authority in the Christian faith than this: this must be the ultimate court of appeal in all its diverse manifestations.

This concept of the Word of God is not, however, a simple one, open though it may be to simple people. Even in the comparatively short time-span covered by the writing of the New Testament, one can see that the Word, or the gospel about the Word, has a history. Our earliest witnesses to it are not the gospels but the letters of Paul; our latest witness is not the book of Revelation, but the second epistle of Peter. The concept of the Word is profound and complex. In the Fourth Gospel it has connections with rabbinic teaching and Greek philosophy. The history of Christian doctrine during the first four centuries is the history of a tangled and far from straightforward exploration of the possibilities latent in this concept of the Word, the *Logos*. It is neither a story of simple biblical exegesis nor a tale of steady and disastrous corruption of scriptural truth by Greek philosophy or Oriental gnosis. And the history of Christianity ever since the fourth century presents us with a varied and many-sided tapestry of the possibilities, for good and bad, which this concept of the Word of God contains. In this tapestry is woven superstition and sanctity, the wildest hopes and the profoundest thoughts, misunderstanding and the insights of genius, exploitation and heroism, darkness and light, folly and wisdom, brutality and tenderness. There figure on it such contrasts as St Augustine and St Jerome, the Children's Crusade and the Franciscan movement, John Hus and Pope Alexander VI, Luther and Titus Oates, John Wesley and Bishop Hoadley, Karl Barth and Ian Paisley.

This Word of God must in the final analysis represent for both Catholics and Protestants God himself, his own activity, his self-communication, his character, however we conceive of it or apprehend it. The rest of this essay will attempt to explore, even though briefly and sketchily, what is the evidence for the Word of God, what are its signs and proofs, that is the authority of the Bible. Next it will consider by whom the Word is to be taught, perpetuated, disseminated and developed, that is the authority of the church. Finally, it will try to discover how the Word can be apprehended as truth, that is the authority of the Christian faith.

II

The Authority of the Bible

Ever since the revolutionary intellectual movement which we call the rise of historical criticism began about two centuries ago, it has been peculiarly difficult to determine the nature of the authority of the Bible. It may well be that the immediate reaction of the reader of the last sentence will be 'Why bother?' Why should we go in for all this analysis, examination, assessment of historical authenticity, search after literary and oral sources, this investigation of provenance, milieu and background, all this reconstruction, hypothesis, re-interpretation, all this arousing of uncertainty, disturbance, alarm and despondency? Why should we not be content with the simple, age-old, traditional acceptance of the Bible as true and trustworthy? Why not just believe the Bible as our grandfathers and great-grandfathers did?

Many replies could be made to this very understandable plea. It could be said that our ancestors did not accept the Bible in a simple, straightforward way. They found it necessary to allegorize the Bible, or to ignore large parts of it, or to read into it ideas of a much later day. Origen in the third century believed that in many instances where the gospels appear to contradict each other, one account is meant to be taken literally and the other allegorically, symbolically only. All through the ages Christians have found it impossible to take large parts of the law-codes of the Pentateuch at their face value. The framers of the confessional statements of the Reformation period, for example the Augsburg Confession, the Thirty-nine Articles and the Westminster Confession, unreflectingly accepted very much later formulae, such as the Nicene Creed, the Chalcedonian Formula and the Athanasian Creed, as simple, transparent interpretations of scripture, which they certainly are not.

We cannot, anyway, ignore those discoveries of the human intellect which affect our interpretation of the Bible: the doctrine of evolution, the vast extension of knowledge of ancient history opened to us by archaeology, the great advance that has been made in the understanding of ancient religion. We cannot put the clock back and pretend that in regard to the Bible we stand innocently where our forefathers stood two centuries ago.

Finally, it is impossible to escape uncertainty and conjecture by simply canonizing our own point of view. The opinions of the simple believer, or of the simple clergyman, gain no authority just by the fact that they are strongly held. They have no more authority nor certitude than the opinions of the biblical expert; indeed they have less, for he at least is an expert. We cannot render ourselves invulnerable to biblical criticism by just ignoring it, any more than the ostrich can render himself immune from the hunter by burying his head in the sand.

But it is certainly true that the present period is a particularly difficult time in which to estimate the authority of the Bible. Biblical study has recently manifested an alarming centrifugal tendency, a tendency to analyse without synthesis, to see divergence, fragmentation, diversity, heterogeneity and inconsistency everywhere in all parts and sources of the Bible. The Old Testament prophets become, not recognizable characters, but a school of anonymous atomistic figures operating in a haze of oral tradition. Israel's history is found no longer to be unique, nor its tradition of prophecy; these things can – indeed they must – be parallelled elsewhere. Narratives which appear to be historical, such as the 'we-passages' in Acts, are not historical but legendary or purely fictitious. Primitive Christians have been found to be people with appallingly defective memories but very vigorous and fertile imaginations, blind to history but infinitely credulous about legend. This new method of looking at the past is not confined to biblical study. Its impoverished, reductionist spirit can be seen in the study of the classics and of modern history too. It represents a form of loss of nerve among the intellectuals of the Western world.

Most serious of all is the state of study concerning the authenticity of the career and teaching of Jesus. We may well have become accustomed, accepting honestly the verdict of scholarship, to regard the Fourth Gospel as an interpretation of the significance of Jesus rather than as an authentic record of his deeds and words. Such a view has far-reaching consequences for christology and trinitarian doctrine, and these consequences must be accepted and worked out. But the synoptic gospels, which are rightly reckoned to be documents of a different sort from St John's gospel, are today placed in a gravely uncertain position. Study of them appears to be afflicted by an incurable subjectivity. Most scholars agree that Jesus existed and that he taught, but what did he do and what teach? *Quot homines tot sententiae.* If the basic assumption of form criticism is accepted, that the material about Jesus was altered and modified according to need during the period of oral transmission, then a reason can always be found why any given incident or saying in the gospels might have been invented. Study of the motives of the evangelists' arrangement of their material seems to have reached a point where the more we study the motives, the further we are from being able to judge the authenticity of the material. Even the most bizarre reconstructions, provided that they are presented with erudition, are now given some credit: the bold fancies of Brandon, the imaginative selection of facts given by Morton Smith, the gastronomic fantasies of Allegro.[4] The hounds of criticism will have to cast again and pick up another scent.

The old assumptions about the Bible have crumbled, and to a superficial glance only chaos has come to fill their place. The doctrine of original sin seems to be left hanging in the air now that the opening chapters of Genesis can no longer be regarded as a scientific account of the origin of the human race, of culture and of civilization. The proof from the predictions of Christ in the Old Testament has now been removed from the case for the divinity of Jesus Christ – a loss that cuts deep, for this type of proof is deeply embedded in the New Testament itself. Moses, David, Solomon and Ezra have been deprived of their numinous reputation as authors of the Old Testament. Joshua did not stop the sun, nor Daniel encounter the lions nor Jonah the whale. The oracular view of the Bible is dead. The doctrine of the Bible's inspiration has become the shadow of a shade, useless for theological purposes.

Would it not be better, then, to dispense with the Bible, to do without its authority altogether? We could perhaps rely instead on tradition. When Newman in 1860 saw the devastating effect which the volume *Essays and Reviews* had on the Protestant reliance on the Bible, he rejoiced in a private letter that Catholics were bound to no such reliance but could fall back on tradition. Or we might rely solely on the authority of the church. Or we might, going to the other extreme as some sixteenth-century Anabaptists did, rely on our charismatic insights; our second baptism in the Holy Spirit might supersede Scripture. We could, in short, fall back on the authority of religious experience. We might even produce as an alternative some attractive synthesis of all sacred literatures or of all the higher religions of the world.

It certainly is true that in the past Protestants have tended to use the Bible too much. They have read into it doctrines which are not there. They have attached themselves, for instance, to the eccentric idea, justified neither in scripture nor tradition nor reason, that Christians are bound to treat their Sunday as Jews were, or are, bound to treat their Saturday. They have baselessly appealed to the Bible to give authority to their forms of ministry. They have – or at least Anglicans have – imagined without good ground that they could find the rite of confirmation laid down in the New Testament. Perhaps this over-use of scripture by Protestants has been punished by their now being deprived of the possibility of using it effectively for any purpose.

But when all has been said and done, it is utterly impossible to do without the authority of the Bible. To despair of the Bible is neither necessary nor desirable. There is no conceivable substitute for it. The church can only establish its authority by pointing to the Bible. Tradition is either a repetition of the Bible's substance, or an interpretation of it; any other form of tradition is false. Religious experience alone cannot take the place of the Bible: to try to follow this guide would be to follow a will-of-the-wisp likely to land its follower in a bog of contradiction. Newman in his *Development of Christian Doctrine* suggested that in the end what determines true doctrine is not so much its consonance with scripture as the authenticity of the church that teaches it. But the only way any church can establish its authenticity is by appealing to the Bible.

Without the Bible Christianity is rudderless or, in another nautical metaphor, it has lost its anchor. The Bible was deliberately canonized by the church to be its norm, and that church originally put itself irreversibly under the authority of the Bible. The Bible moors the church to a history which cannot be undone. Without the Bible the church would inevitably embark upon an exciting but utterly misguided doctrinal space-flight. At one time, between 1854 and 1950, it looked as if the Roman Catholic Church was going to take off thus. But the Second Vatican Council is no doubt a sign that it has drawn back.

If we are to discover the authority of the Bible, we must first note two facts. The first is that the Bible is testimony, witness, not oracle. The Bible is the record or documentation of the Word of God; it is not the Word itself. 'The written Word of God' is a most misleading expression. Any explanation of the Bible which maintains that God wrote the Bible or that the Holy Spirit is author of it, even though it fall short of a theory of verbal inspiration or dictation, must be discarded. It has been reduced by historical scholarship either to meaninglessness or to falsity. It rests upon the traditional doctrine of the inspiration of the Bible, and that is now an impossible one. The Bible is the written witness to the activity and character of God, the testimony to the Word of God. It is, of course, enormously diverse testimony; it consists of dozens of books, written in three different languages by hundreds of writers, many (perhaps most) anonymous, and its documents span a period from 2000 BC to AD 120. The literary forms which it embraces are almost endless: saga, legend, myth, history, law, prophecy, gnomic utterances, drama, philosophy, diaries, gospels, letters, novels, diatribe, apocalypse and many others. But as a whole it constitutes a variegated witness or testimony or documentation to God's activity and character. This is the Bible's nature and function. It is not an oracle, nor an encyclopaedia, nor a theological treatise.

The second point to be remembered is that the Bible must be understood within a worshipping community; otherwise it ceases to function properly or ceases to function altogether. All the documents of the Bible have always been read, and almost all were written, from faith to faith, for a worshipping community by a worshipping community. The Bible is not exegetically autonomous. It demands, indeed it creates, a tradition in which it is used. The Bible is, in fact, deliberately canonized tradition; authorized interpretation of the original revelation as well as an account of that revelation itself. And there is a certain arbitrariness about the canon of the New Testament. At its edges the New Testament lapses into early Christian literature, with no hard and fast line between. In such a collection of documents providing testimony, the fact that the edges are blurred is not significant.

We can now see what the authority of the Bible must be. It is the authority of canonized witness or testimony to the Word, that is to the activity and character of God, witness deliberately chosen by the church when it was in a position to know what was good evidence and what was not – a state of affairs long since past. The Bible is indispensable testimony – basic, original, irremovable testimony – by which all Christian teaching must of necessity be tested. But as far as doctrine goes, it only provides the raw material, not the finished product. It is the duty and business of the church to make the raw material into the finished product. This is in today's circumstances a daunting, difficult, demanding but stimulating task, which involves nothing less than a re-assessment of the Christian faith. But the task must be faced and affords us some reasons for hope, if the following conditions are fulfilled.

First, clergy and teachers must accept the results of historical criticism of the Bible more openly, honestly and whole-heartedly. The church at large can hardly be said to have done this yet. Such an attitude must include the acceptance of the Fourth Gospel as interpretation of the significance of Jesus Christ rather than as a record of his *ipsissima verba*; the final relegation of Abraham, Isaac and Jacob to legend, where they can join Adam and Noah; the realization that Paul's letters, and not the gospels, are the earliest documents of the New Testament; the understanding of the eschatological nature of the New Testament. Historical scholarship is, of course, an uncertain discipline, but we must cease to look for an old-fashioned demonstrable certainty and learn to live with uncertainty in the sense of recognizing those areas where we have no right to ask for certainty.

Secondly, the problem of the relation of the Jesus of history to the Jesus of the church's faith must at least be recognized as a problem, as something which each of us most face honestly. Most clergy seem to be quite unaware of it as a problem at all. It was always undesirable, and is today impossible, to make the words of Jesus our final authority. We must start off with the risen Lord, the Lord of the church's *kerygma*. Bultmann is right here. But we must not, we cannot stop short here. We must look back through the preaching of the primitive church to see the Jesus who walked the lanes of Galilee and the streets of Jerusalem. The two, far from opening the possibility of playing off one against the other, are closely interdependent. What we can see and reconstruct is not indeed a life or biography of Jesus, but his character. It is impossible to deny that Paul knew the salient facts about the character of Jesus; he preached no empty apocalyptic Messiah, a mere lightning-flash from heaven, but a Christ of gentleness, humbleness, compassion and resolution who deliberately accepts the way of the cross. It may be that we shall end by agreeing with the interesting argument of Professor R.S. Barbour of Aberdeen University, put forward in a recent book,[5] that the interpretation of Jesus by the men of the primitive church is a reflection of the impression which the Jesus of history made on them.

Thirdly, we must admit a graduation of authority within the Bible. Some parts are clearly more important than others. Both Jews and Christians have always tacitly admitted this in their use of the Bible in lectionaries and in teaching. But we should now honestly allow, not only that Amos is more important than Ehud and the anonymous writer of Isaiah 40-55 than the author of Esther, but that the genuine epistles of Paul are more important than the Pastoral Epistles, that the epistle of Jude and II Peter must have very little authority because of the late date when they were written and canonized. We must see Paul, John and the author of the Epistle to the Hebrews as so many profound interpreters of the significance of Jesus Christ. And in expounding them we must allow for the fact that the gospel has a history: Paul is by far the earliest, then comes Hebrews, and then the Johannine literature. The New Testament is not like a manual of instructions. It is more like a series of lenses through which we look at the same object, or like the light of a great lighthouse, brilliantly bright in the middle, but becoming dimmer the nearer you come to the edge.

Lastly, we must recognize the sort of language in which the Bible is written. It is not wholly historical, matter-of-fact, everyday language. The reader will remember that the Rev. Theophilus Pontifex in Samuel Butler's *The Way of All Flesh* thought of Eve being taken from Adam's side as a straightforward operation which might have happened at the bottom of his garden. But that is not the sort of language which the Bible normally uses when it speaks of God. Nor is its language usually scientific nor philosophical. It uses imagery to convey truth which often can only be conveyed by. imagery: equivocal, analogous, symbolic language. This use of language lands us in all sorts of difficulties. Where is Abraham's bosom? Can it be examined by a stethoscope? What is the blood of the Lamb? Can we assign it a blood-group? But some biblical imagery at least is perhaps more lasting and effective than any other mode of communication, because it appeals, not merely to the intellect, but to something deeper within us.

We need not, therefore, disparage the Bible, nor despair of its influence nor reject its authority. Through history it has found its own way of asserting itself. Were space to allow, one could expatiate upon several examples: the influence of the Fourth Gospel upon the Arian controversy, the rejection of Apollinarianism in the fourth century, the effect of the book of Psalms upon the thought of Augustine, the constant tendency of eschatology to return to Christian theology even when it has been decisively banished, the return to a biblical doctrine of grace in the sixteenth century, the new interest shown in our own day by the Roman Catholic Church in the Bible. After all, story and drama are the basic forms of literature which will always appeal to all people; they are ageless. The Bible gives us both a great story and a great drama. It will exercise its regulative power upon the Christian faith in its own way.

III

The Authority of the Church

It seems beyond dispute that the church is intended to have authority. There can be no doubt that the church from the earliest moment of its existence has behaved as if it had authority. The primitive church demonstrates this fact as clearly as the church at any other period. The primitive church was in many ways quite unlike any Christian group known today. It was anarchic, fragmented, living in an eschatological and charismatic atmosphere; it had no New Testament, no creed, no permanent ministry; its eucharist, if we are to judge by the tenth and eleventh chapters of Paul's first epistle to the Corinthians, must have been like a noisy picnic; the relationships of baptism, faith and Holy Spirit were still undecided. But the church's confidence in its own authority was remarkable. The choice of Matthias, the decision to admit Gentiles, the sending of Paul and Barnabas on a missionary journey, the appointment of the Seven, all show the church unself-consciously exercising its authority. But a much stronger proof of its possessing authority lies in the fact that the church undertook to forgive or retain the sins of its members. The New Testament is full of examples of the exerting of this authority, and the conviction that it is the privilege of the local church as a whole to forgive sinners, and not merely of the clergy, survived for a much longer period than many other primitive ideas. There were still lingering traces of this conviction visible in the life of the church as late as the fifth century. However the church may have exercised its authority, it certainly behaved from the beginning as if it possessed authority, the authority of Christ.

Again, the church is part of the gospel. It is utterly impossible to dissect the Christian revelation and remove the church from it. St Paul's doctrine of the church as the body of Christ shows that this fact held true in the primitive period. But it is no less true today. It is impossible to imagine any circumstances in which anyone should hear the message of Christianity at any period without the interposition of the church at some point in the line of transmission, either by preserving or circulating the Bible or by communicating doctrine or preaching the gospel. It is unwise for any Christian group to ignore even the subject of the continuity of the church, because the continuity of the gospel, or of the Word, is bound up with it. If any person celebrates a sacrament or preaches a gospel, neither is necessarily self-authenticating. Sooner or later the question must be asked, What authority has this celebrant or this preacher? How do we know that God hears their ritual petitions or that he is authentically proclaimed in their words? Catholics are all too conscious of this question, but Protestants tend to dismiss it airily as unimportant. It cannot be dismissed, if Christianity of today claims to be the authentic successor of primitive Christianity.

Further, the church is necessary, not merely to preserve, circulate and interpret the Bible. It is necessary to complete it, to round it off. Immediately after the first century, when the church began to move into a Gentile milieu away from its Jewish matrix, it was faced with the necessity of answering three questions:

1. What is the relation of the being of Jesus Christ to the being of God?
2. What is the relation of God to history in view of the career of Jesus Christ?
3. What does God do to man in Jesus Christ?

The Bible does not answer any of these questions directly. It was the inescapable task of the church to give an answer to these questions. It attempted to do this by a process of trial and error which resulted in the fourth and fifth centuries in the classical doctrines of the Trinity and of the Incarnation to answer questions 1 and 2, and in the gradual formation later of a body of doctrine about grace and about atonement to deal with question 3. In a word, the process of creating tradition is inescapable. Tradition is the result of the church interpreting, worrying over, brooding upon scripture. There is no prefabricated theology in the Bible; the Bible is not a textbook of doctrine or ethics or ecclesiology or liturgy. The thought of the Bible has to be related to the thought of each age. The church has this vast and complex task, and this means that the church is as necessary to the Bible as the Bible is to the church.

Lastly, institutions are as inescapable as tradition. Though each separate institution has to justify itself on its own merits, there is nothing wrong with institutions as such. Institutions are the carapace against the destructive forces of change and history set up by every society which exists in time. What contemporary Christians should seek for is not the abolition of institutions, but the right institutions. If we try to found a Christianity without institutions we shall end with an institution devoted to abolishing institutions, just as if we try to dispense with tradition we shall end with a tradition of having no tradition.

The authority of the church can only be based on the authority of the Word of God. It will not do to base it on its foundation by Christ in the days of his flesh, on such passages as Matt. 18.16ff. The origin of the church lies not at Caesarea Philippi, but in Easter and Pentecost. The church springs out of the resurrection. St Paul, our earliest authority, gives us an ecclesiology of the church as the body of Christ living in the Spirit. To base its authority on its institution as a society, like the Society of Jesus and the Salvation Army, is to look at it 'after the flesh'. Even less satisfactory is it to base the church's authority on a succession of bishops or the hierarchical status of its officers. What gives the church its authority is the Word of God. This does not mean the loquaciousness of God; it means God disclosing himself in Christ active in the Spirit. The church is where the Word of God acts: it is the locus of the Word of God.

Such authority is in its essence not legal or judicial but moral and spiritual, and it is not inconsistent with its being expressed in institutions, in such things as a permanent ministry and a definite discipline and agreed formulae of doctrine. Indeed, it is inevitable and to be desired that it should be so expressed. Had it not been so, it is doubtful whether Christianity could have survived the threat of Gnosticism in the second and third centuries, and even more doubtful whether it could have encountered in the fifth century the collapse of the Western Roman empire without succumbing. Men are not pure spirits, they are not just incarnate moral principles, though Protestantism is always liable to fall into the Ritschlian fallacy of thinking that they are. If the Word of God is to gather together a church, that church will be composed of men and women of flesh and blood, with unconsciouses and appetites, subject to the laws that govern tangible sublunary things. Therefore the Word of God must be expressed in institutions, in concrete, particular, observable ways. Further, this society that is the church must be involved to some extent in law, both ecclesiastical and secular law. There is no virtue in either anarchy or injustice. Ecclesiastical law grew up very simply, innocently and naturally out of the church's claim to forgive sins, and it always was from the beginning well mixed with other sorts of law, with Jewish law and Roman law and Stoic ethics.

Still, the authority of the church is basically only moral, and the church must always be prepared to recognize this. Ever since the emperor Constantine between the years 313 and 337 recognized

and patronized the church, it has had a public image of an
authoritarian, authority-bearing institution which relies on law.
Sixteen centuries of history have stamped this image deep. But in
the nineteenth century the image began to break up. All over
Europe the church began to be divorced by the state or to take
measures to divorce itself. At the same time in most denominations
coercion to conform backed by the law of the land or by public
opinion began to collapse. Though it is only in our lifetime that this
process has reached the Church of Rome, still it is visible now even
there. The church has learnt by the hard way that its authority is
only moral. In Scotland the courts of the Kirk could no longer
trouble a Robert Burns, were he to appear. In England the bishop
knows that his authority rests on the moral influence of his office or
his character, not on ecclesiastical law. The Pope has been forced to
abandon his secular rule and has in consequence gained greatly in
moral authority.

At the same time it must be admitted that it is difficult to see how
the authority of the church as a whole can be expressed today. The
church today is deeply divided by an internal schism. I will not here
enter upon the reasons which appear to me compelling for
concluding that the situation is not such that one body alone
claiming to be the church can be regarded as authentic and the rest
as in schism. Anyway, all the major divided bodies agree that the
others are in some sense part of the church; unchurching them
raises more problems than allowing this point. But there can be no
doubt that the condition of dividedness impairs the authority of
every body which claims to be the church.

The conventional, traditional ways by which the church has
expressed its mind and made its decisions in the past do not look
effective today. Pronouncements by hierarchs or conclaves,
followed by coercion; general councils or local councils; confessional statements – all seem inadequate and ineffective in the light
of today. Democracy in church government is by no means a
necessary or invariable part of the church's life, but it has in our
time come to stay for the foreseeable future; it will probably in the
end even reach the Church of Rome in some form. It is much more
difficult to achieve decisions and agreements in a democratic
church and to persuade the rank and file to agree to formulae and
concordats. The failure of the recent Anglican-Methodist Scheme
of Union shows this. We are, in short, living in a period when
inevitably, as far as the authority of the church goes, weakness and
uncertainty are more in evidence than at any time since the
sixteenth century.

But there are certain forces making unobtrusively for the unity and authority of the church. One clearly is the ecumenical movement. This can, of course, be dismissed as a racket, a bandwagon run by successful careerists for their own profit, or as an attempt by bankrupt companies to survive by pooling their resources. But it seems to me much too serious an enterprise to be written off like this. In the first place, consider who are the opponents of the ecumenical movement: disciples of Cardinal Ottaviani; anti-intellectual pietists; the followers of Ian Paisley. God preserve any cause from friends such as these, and God bless any cause that has such enemies! Secondly, in recent years new and genuine interest in the ecumenical movement has been shown by two powerful but very different groups, the government of the Union of Socialist Soviet Republics and the Roman Catholic Church. This does not suggest ineffectiveness. Thirdly, the ecumenical movement is beginning now after over sixty years of existence to show some solid results. It can sincerely claim a large share of the credit for the formation of the Church of South India, the Church of North India, the series of remarkable agreements on such controversial subjects as the eucharist achieved in recent years between theologians of the Roman Catholic and of other communions, and the impressive agreement on christological doctrine reached in two meetings in Bristol and in Rhodes by theologians of the Orthodox and the Oriental Churches.[6]

Another force which appears to be working towards unity in the church is one that has been already mentioned, the movement of all traditional denominations away from domination by or association with the state. This movement could be traced, did time permit, taking place among established or major churches in many of the countries of Europe from about 1800 onwards, and in ecclesiastical bodies as far different as the Church of Scotland, the Lutheran Church in Denmark and the Roman Catholic Church, and perhaps most strikingly in the Anglican Churches of England, Ireland and Wales. It looks as if while society everywhere becomes more secularized, Christians everywhere have been realizing that their convictions and beliefs have more in common with each other than they have with those of the societies within which they live. This, almost inevitably, makes logically for church union.

Finally we must note the emergence in the period since the end of the last war of a kind of Scholars' International which unites trained theologians of all ecclesiastical traditions not only in a common discipline but in a common search for Christian truth across and beyond the denominational barriers. The long-term effects of this free-masonry of trained theologians are incalculable. They cannot but make for Christian unity.

One can therefore see the possibility, perhaps even the probability, of greater unity and therefore of greater authority accruing to the Christian church in the future. But if it is to come, it will come only in the form of authority that is moral and not legal, spiritual and not jurisdictional. It will have to be authority that is seen to be the authority of the whole church, not only of a section at the top, and it must be achieved by painful heart-searching, patient ecumenical endeavour and dialogue, which renounces party spirit as the work of the devil. Only ecumenical thinking can create an ecumenical church, and only an ecumenical church can have full authority, can properly represent the authority of Christ.

Before we finish considering the authority of the church, something must be said about the limits of the church's authority. The church's authority is subject to the same condition as are all authority and all phenomena in the New Testament except one. It is not absolute; it exists in a dispensation of faith, not sight; it is still authority whose nature is inaugurated but not consummated eschatology. The church is a church *in via*, a pilgrim church which has not yet arrived. Its authority is exercised between the cross and the end, between the resurrection and the parousia. It is subject to the 'relativism' of the New Testament. This means that the church never has the right to say 'Now, when so-and-so speaks, or now, when this group pronounces, this is Christ himself speaking; here are no qualifications and no human, creaturely imperfection.' Neither pope, nor council nor assembly nor – worst pretension of all – inspired individual can carry the absolute and final authority of God. The church has no more right than the individual to claim that it enjoys or imparts direct unmediated knowledge of God; this is for the next life, not this one. Wherever the church exercises its authority it must do so with the humility that recognizes that its judgment may be corrected or reversed at the last judgment.

But we must revert to the exception to the rule which I have just enunciated, the exception to be found in I Corinthians 13. Love is the only phenomenon that is not liable to revision at the last judgment; it alone is exempt from the 'relativism' of the New Testament. This can remind us that if the authority of the church is the authority of Christ – and we claim no less than this – then we have a clear picture of the pattern of the church's authority. Christ's authority expressed itself as the authority of self-giving love. He 'did not please himself' (Rom. 15.3); he did not exercise authority as the rulers of the Gentiles do (Mark 10.41-45); he came to minister and not to receive the ministration of others, to be the servant of all; he washed the feet of his disciples; he utterly eschewed the way of violence and self-assertiveness. The church undoubtedly has authority, but its pattern of exerting that authority must be Christ's pattern and not Pilate's. The church must be a servant church and if necessary a suffering church. We need not be Donatist about this, courting persecution and regarding it as the norm; but we must not be triumphalist either. Dostoievsky's story of Christ before the Grand Inquisitor is nearer to the heart of Christianity than Pope Boniface VIII's Bull *Unam Sanctam*. In order to preserve Christ's authority, the church must be prepared, like Christ, to forgo worldly authority.

IV

The Authority of Faith

It is one thing to define what we mean by 'the Word of God', to clear our minds about the authority of the Bible, to delimit the authority of the church. It is another to answer the final question, 'Does the Word so witnessed and so commended come to us with the authority of truth?' The whole affair could be a vast delusion or a vast fraud, in which case it has no authority at all.

Experience suggests that those who are officially commissioned to preach and to teach the Word consider this question very seldom. They are ready to explain how Christianity is good, useful, comforting, helpful and improving, that it will make you moral or happy or both. But they do not often consider whether it is true, or how it is true. They might perhaps plead, with some justice, that the average Christian in this country does not want to be perplexed with such a deep question as this. But even if the believer is not concerned with this question (and some certainly are), the unbeliever often is concerned, and often the case for Christianity goes by default. It is often assumed without challenge in the press, on television and in contemporary literature and drama that Christianity is a myth, a delusion, an obsolete creed, to which no intelligent man can any longer give credence.

We cannot any longer rely on the scientists and philosophers to help us in this situation. From the first we shall find at the best neutrality, and we are more likely than not to encounter positive hostility from the second. A century ago things were different; the church has scarcely become accustomed to the cruel change. A century ago, indeed up to forty years ago, idealist philosophy everywhere held the stage and made the running. Idealist philosophy was a type of thought which largely originated with and was certainly given its finest and deepest expression by the German philosopher Hegel. It was based on the axiom that we cannot separate the reality of any object from our thinking about it, and that therefore the supreme and ultimately sole reality in the universe is mind. It went on to build on this foundation a dazzling series of speculative philosophies which undertook to explain the whole of reality, including the Christian religion. The idealist philosophers offered the theologian the alluring prospect of proving philosophically (and therefore scientifically) that the Christian religion was true. The theologians fell in large numbers for this attractive offer. Most Protestant theologians between 1850 and 1930 were idealists of one sort or another. Only a few brave souls, such as the Dane, Søren Kierkegaard, protested against this movement; he said, among other things, that to be a professor of theology was to crucify Christ! The rest, however, preferred to believe that they had never had it so good, and hastened to accept the slightly patronizing support of idealist philosophy. William Temple was perhaps the last eminent representative of this school.

But today theologians are living in a different climate of opinion, and a much colder one. Today philosophy offers almost no help at all to theology. The philosophers of today have abandoned widespread and lofty claims to know the nature of existence, and of almost everything else as well. Instead of ranging widely over the universe, they concentrate upon one square inch of territory, on the meaning of meaning, or on perception, and try to understand that. In consequence they find it possible to offer almost no help to theology. Truth, the philosophers seem to say, is to be found by logic or by science or not at all. And neither logic nor science can tell us anything about God. The situation is not in fact one of despair. Some philosophers of religion are making serious and impressive attempts to build a natural theology in modern terms, and some philosophers are rather less confident than they were of the omnicompetence of logic and science. But it is a struggle. We must not pretend that the path of finding truth in Christianity by way of philosophy or science is an easy or obvious one.

Besides, Kierkegaard was right about one thing; it ought not to be possible to prove the existence of God or the truth of Christianity simply by philosophy or science. Christianity demands self-commitment. God can only be known in the Christian tradition by faith. We cannot exhaustively know, familiarly handle, God. We cannot grasp him as we grasp a theorem, prove him as we prove the existence of a comet, understand him as we understand some grand general explanation of the universe. Knowing God involves a movement of our whole persons, an act of faith. God cannot therefore be decisively, demonstrably known and proved to be by a careful consideration of nature or history or of 'this sorry scheme of things entire'. We must not, of course, entirely rule out the aid of science or philosophy or, for that matter, of history in the enterprise of examining whether the Christian faith is true. But we cannot prove its truth simply by demonstrating that it is true from these disciplines, not only because it is by no means easy to do so, but because we ought not to want to do so, because if God could be proved true in this way he would not be God. And if someone suspects that this is a theological version of the story of the fox who had lost his tail, it can be pointed out that Kierkegaard proclaimed this doctrine, not when it seemed very difficult to prove the truth of Christianity from philosophy and so on, but when it seemed the easiest thing in the world, the obvious common-sense solution, with all the prestige of the highest intellects behind it.

Can we perhaps, in our search for the truth of Christianity, call in the witness and authority of religious experience? People do experience God, or they think and say that they do. Why cannot we take them at their word? There have been sensational conversions, those of St Paul and Blaise Pascal and John Wesley. There have been, and there still are, people who have profound mystical experiences. The argument from religious experience has been popular ever since it was first distinctly propounded by Friedrich Schleiermacher early in the nineteenth century. It may even be said to form part of the theology of Rudolf Bultmann. At least his 'Christ-event' must be presumed to take place wholly or largely in the religious experience of the individual.

But the difficulty of appealing to religious experience, if we support our appeal with no other arguments, lies in our inability to recognize the experience as authentic unless we call in other criteria as well. Bernadette Soubirous in 1858 thought that she saw the Blessed Virgin Mary appearing to her at Lourdes and heard her say, 'I am the Immaculate Conception'. Joseph Smith in 1830 put on a pair of sacred spectacles that he had made for himself and saw a series of visions which led to the founding of the Church of the Latter-day Saints, popularly known as the Mormons. These were certainly religious experiences. Which was authentic? They could hardly have both been authentic. Why should not Bultmann's Christ-event take the form in some cases of a Mary-event? A former editor of a British communist paper, Douglas Hyde, was some years ago converted to the Roman Catholic faith as he knelt before an image of the Virgin in a church. Was this a genuine form of religious experience? Moslems and Hindus have religious experiences. Buddhists who do not believe in any God have religious experience. We seem to have reached the point of proving too much.

In short, to appeal to the authority of religious experience alone is to appeal to an intensely subjective or individualistic authority or norm. The argument can be improved by appealing, not to the religious experience of the individual, but to the corporate experience of the church. This was the great argument of the Roman Catholic Modernist, George Tyrrell, and handled as ably as he handled it the argument sounds impressive. But it still suffers from a fatal diversity. The church has had different religious experiences at different periods of its existence. Protestants have different experience from Catholics, and even if we were – ungenerously and unjustly – to dismiss the spiritual life of Protestants as inauthentic, by this Modernist argument we open the gates wide to what the French usefully describe as 'folklorisme', the kind of thing that goes on at Lourdes and Fatima. Most theologians, even Roman Catholic theologians, would regard such a development as highly undesirable.

We have reached the point then, if the argument of this essay has been followed, of estimating accurately the authority of the Bible and of the church, but of realizing that this is not enough. We do not make an act of faith in God as disclosed in Christ simply by believing the Bible as taught by the church. But when we believe in Christ we believe in Christ and not in the Bible nor the church instead. We could not believe in Christ without the Bible or the church, but when we believe, we believe on the authority of the truth which we find in Christ. We still have to answer the question, 'Why should we believe the Word witnessed to by the Bible and taught by the church to be true?'

I suggest that the Christian faith has the authority of the highest good that we know. What more attractive and satisfying account can be found of our destiny, purpose and status in the world? I believe that if we start from this point we shall find the other kinds of authority falling into place. St Augustine saw God not only as the supreme Intellect, as Aristotle did; not only as the supreme Good as well, as Plato did; but as the highest Good which attracts by love. Augustine became convinced by his observation of the human mind – largely by observing his own mind – that our will is only free when it chooses that which is good. We do not for purposes of moral choice stand on a neutral island between good and bad; we are not in this sense morally autonomous. We must be either enslaved by choosing the bad or free by choosing the good. We believe in God when the power of love which he exercises attracts us to choose him and to choose that which is good. It is not simply a matter of correct rational analysis, it is a matter of the will being filled with impulses from the highest good. Belief indeed involves the intellect, it is not whimsy or bigotry or wishful thinking or self-deception. But it is still true that we can only believe if we want to believe. What makes believers believe is the attractiveness of the proposition which the Christian faith presents to us.

The church commends to us the proposition that God loves us and seeks us in Christ, and produces the Bible as documentation for this proposition. We do not, of course, come across this proposition in a vacuum. We meet it in a worshipping community of believers, we meet it in action; we meet it, so to speak, being practised. We may find this proposition an attractive, satisfying account of things. We may, perhaps we must, note that the church has had in the past and still has in the present a way of getting between us and the proposition, obscuring and even distorting it. And we may observe that the Bible has often been in the past and still in the present sometimes is interpreted narrowly, unrealistically and stupidly. But if we find this proposition an attractive and satisfying account of things, then we test it by our knowledge and by our experience. We ask if it is positively contradicted by philosophy and science in such a way that we can be quite sure that philosophy or science is right and this proposition wrong. We ask if we know any better account of things, if this account of things appeals to what in ourselves we take to be good, to be the best. Does it engage our minds at the deepest level? Is our predilection for it more than fancy, more than a liking for intellectual fireworks? Do we even perhaps faintly begin to feel that we *ought* to believe it? If we can answer questions such as these satisfactorily, then we make the move of faith and decide to believe.

We can only grasp or respond to this proposition in faith, by an act of faith, indeed by a life of faith. If this proposition could be shown to be true demonstrably or mathematically or scientifically, there would be no room for faith, nor would God be the God whom Christianity knows and worships. To know that God is true we must make an act of personal commitment; that is the only way to this knowledge. But in order to do this, we must first be convinced that the act of faith is worth making; our mind must be persuaded that this is the sort of thing that we ought to do. We must be sure that we are not following a mere whimsical fancy, that we are not making a plunge into the irrational out of a love of the irrational. In today's climate of opinion a plunge into the irrational would be fashionable and admired, but it would be wrong. Faith is a safeguard against irrational belief. We must, in short, be deeply convinced that truth is likely to be found, not just in commitment, but in *this* form of commitment, and then we must commit ourselves to the best and highest that we know.

When we do commit ourselves, we find that this belief is true. This is the only way to find truth, but truth it does find. The sign that we have found truth is that we discover finally that we are under a compulsion, an obligation, to believe. We find our minds and wills engaged by an obligation which we cannot disavow, cannot dispense with. Christianity is not in the end a purely voluntary occupation, like bird-watching or photography, and faith is not an arbitrarily given capacity like an ear for music. We find ourselves being called by God. It is his Word that calls us.

It must be added that this process of belief, though it ends in a sense of obligation to believe, does not necessarily carry with it a sense of pleasure, nor a release from the ordinary ills and disturbances that affect our wills, our passions, our sentiments or our psyche. Nor does it necessarily solve all our moral problems. Some apologists for Christianity speak as if it has this panacea-like result, as if it were a cure for all stress and strain. It *can* be a comfort and resource, of course, but it is not necessarily so. Many believers have found their psychological problems exasperated by their faith: one could instance St Paul, St John of the Cross, the poet William Cowper and Søren Kierkegaard. But they still were convinced that they must believe. This is because they were not merely operating a psychological gimmick, taking a trip, undergoing an experience for the sake of the experience, but encountering truth, meeting someone outside themselves. Why did Regulus go back to Carthage? Why did Socrates refuse to escape from prison? Why did the Buddha leave his palace? Why did Jesus go up to Jerusalem for the last time? Why did Fr Damien have himself put on the leper island of Molokai? Why did Dietrich Bonhoeffer return to

Germany from the USA just before the last war? All these people knew in their heart of hearts that they must do what they did because they were attracted by the highest good. This was their discovery of truth.

When, lastly, we accept the authority of the Christian faith and accept it as the Word of God which speaks to us, we are not indulging in self-deception nor yielding to mere whimsy. Our act of belief is subjective; all commitment-in-truth must be subjective. But it is not individualistic, for it is a commitment into a society, the church, and it has the weight of Christian tradition and experience behind it. Christian belief is indeed open to competition. Other people can reach quite different beliefs by apparently much the same process. Christianity can only compete on its own merits, but it should not be afraid of this. Christian belief can, of course, be corrupted into bigotry, greed, aggressiveness and self-assertion. But so can the best of creeds. Men have always tried to manipulate God as well as to worship him. God has in the deepest sense made himself vulnerable to men, but he has seen to it that in the end he turns the tables on them. This is the message of the crucifixion and resurrection of Jesus Christ. In judging God men judge themselves. If we meet the truth we are either attracted by it or shown up by it.

NOTES

1. This essay represents the substance of the Stephenson Lectures delivered to the University of Sheffield during four days in March 1974.

2. C.B. Moss, *The Christian Faith*, SPCK 1943.

3. Karl Barth, *Commentary on the Epistle to the Romans*, Eng. trs., Oxford University Press 1933, p. 136.

4. S.G.F. Brandon, *Jesus and the Zealots*, Manchester University Press 1967; *The Fall of Jerusalem and the Christian Church*, SPCK 1951; J.M. Allegro, *The Sacred Mushroom and the Cross*, Hodder and Stoughton 1970; Morton Smith, *Clement of Alexandria and a Secret Gospel of Mark*, Harvard University Press 1973.

5. R.S. Barbour, *Traditio-historical Criticism of the Gospels*, SPCK 1972.

6. See the reports: 'Unofficial Consultation between Theologians of the Eastern Orthodox and Oriental Orthodox Churches, ed. J.S. Romanides, P. Verghese and N.A. Nissiotis', *Greek Orthodox Theological Review* X.2, Brookline, Mass., 1964/5; and 'Papers and Discussions between Eastern Orthodox and Oriental Orthodox Theologians, The Bristol Consultation', ibid., XIII.2, Fall 1968.

~ 8 ~

Love and Justice

JOHN BENNETT

The discussion of the relation between love and justice is central in any Christian approach to political ethics. Differences of conviction or of emphasis as between individual thinkers or traditions about the proper stance of the church in relation to politics or about Christian guidance for particular political decisions often follow from contrasting ways of relating love to justice. I shall first explain how I am using those familiar words.

We inherit both a radical conception of the justice of God that reaches down to the people most oppressed or deprived from the Bible, and endless analyses of the concept of human justice in philosophical ethics from Plato and Aristotle to John Rawls.[1] There is much to be gained in clarity and precision from these analyses, but without the pressure on consciences of the biblical radicalism, Christian approaches to political ethics often lead to little more than minor re-arrangements of institutions and policies.

It is helpful to start with what Aristotle calls 'particular justice' with emphasis on the distribution of goods in the community. The formal meaning of justice in this sense, the assumption that goods should be distributed according to what is due to all the parties involved (*suum cuique*) is only a beginning, for it tells us nothing about what is due to anyone. Rights and claims, even conceptions about what is fitting in terms of punishment, have been in a continuous historical process of transformation. The question as to what constitutes justice today must take account of the result of many changes in the status of various categories of persons. When Aristotle spoke of these matters, he took slavery for granted.

Today what I believe and what most readers of these words believe about justice is the result of social revolutions which have enabled neglected or exploited portions of the human race to gain enough power to call attention to their rights and claims as human beings. Industrial workers, non-white races, peoples under colonial rule, and women have all been heard from.

Now the idea of justice is under the pull of the idea of equality. There is room for prudence in weighing the actual effects of measures that may be taken to secure greater equality on the well-being of all concerned. Yet all structures of justice that are unequal and that have stereotyped defences in terms of prudence need to be reviewed in the light of the social effects of the inequalities of condition and of opportunity which they create and also in view of the unlimited capacity of people in power to rationalize their advantages in terms of the common good. The only justice that can have any standing in Christian ethics is justice that is continually being transformed and that is continually transforming, as the effects of institutions and policies upon people, near or far, come to be imaginatively understood.[2] Concepts of justice must make room for the pressure of neglected interests or neglected people on the minds of those who discuss them. It is a historical question which will never be settled how much Christians have moved to an acceptance of this radically transforming justice because they have become more responsive to biblical teaching and inspiration and how much they have been driven by events, in spite of themselves, to respond to the many human groups that have become articulate and have gained power to press their claims. I think that both factors have been important, but that most often the second has prepared the way for the first.

Roman Catholic ethics has come to use 'social justice' as almost a technical term which covers the meaning of justice that I have in mind. Father Bernard Häring in *The Law of Christ* makes clear that social justice transforms traditional views of the distributive justice. He says that social justice 'looks beyond in the interest of the community, above all, to those who are economically and politically weak, who, though they have nothing to give, still have natural rights to be respected both by the community and by men of property and possession'.[3]

The familiar words of the Magnificat point to the dynamic justice of God that creates new situations in which the meaning of human justice comes to be more fully understood: 'He has put down the mighty from their thrones, and exalted those of low degree: he has filled the hungry with good things and the rich he has sent empty away' (Luke 1.52.) The process continues as new mighty and new rich rise to the top, and there is always the question how far these can be made to share their power and their wealth.

Contemporary students of ethics, who may acknowledge only their debt to the philosophical tradition, often give support in principle to the position that I defend here on biblical grounds and as a response to our experience of the capacity of neglected portions of humanity to make their claims convincing. John Rawls continually emphasizes the following two principles as central to his idea of justice:

The first requires equality in the assignment of basic rights and duties, while the second holds that social and economic inequalities, for example inequalities of wealth and authority, are just only if they result in compensating benefits for everyone, and in particular for the least advantaged members of society.[4]

Those principles as stated provide an open door for the ideological rationalizing of inequalities by those who benefit most from them, but the emphasis on 'the least advantaged members of society' Rawls takes seriously. His hundreds of pages of philosophical analysis probably do not of themselves lead to this emphasis or to the intensity with which Rawls presses it, apart from the direct or indirect influence of the Bible, or the perceptions of what is important in human terms that have come from many social revolutions.

The analysis of justice in philosophical ethics has been paralleled by great attention to the analysis of love in theological ethics. Anders Nygren's *Agape and Eros* has been a landmark in all recent discussion of the subject even though I know very few who fully accept his position.[5] He has scoured those two concepts so that they are so clean and so separate that neither is very close to concrete human experience. However, Nygren's analysis has helped a generation of theologians to see what some of the issues are. *Agape* for him is pure self-giving love that is unmotivated by the desirability of the object loved. It exists in pure form only in God's love for the sinner as revealed in the cross of Christ. *Eros* for him is love for that which has value to the lover and its highest expression is love for God. There is a debate as to whether *eros* is basically egocentric because it is directed to what has value for the self. But the very act of valuing, ultimately of worshipping, directs attention away from the self. This is one of the criticisms of Nygren by Father D'Arcy in his book *The Mind and Heart of Love*.[6]

If one asks in a preliminary way about the degree to which there is kinship between the *agape* motif or the *eros* motif and justice, I think that we may find some such pattern as this. *Eros* with its

movement upward to that which has most value can easily divert
attention away from the worldly struggles for justice. Even when
eros becomes an expression of love for God this may be so. In the
way in which the great Augustinian synthesis relates love for God
to love for neighbour we see that there is a problem. Paul Ramsey,
for example, says that 'in the total thought of St Augustine the true
meaning of love for neighbour is blurred by its combination with
love for God, interpreted not as "obedient love" but as the soul's
desire for beatific union with God'.[7] I realize that there are so many
varied nuances in Augustine's thought about love that it is easy to
be unfair, and any spelling out of the love for God can very well
make full place for the concern for justice for all neighbours since
God loves them. In Matthew 25 the service to the hungry and
thirsty, the stranger and the naked and the imprisoned, was
revealed to be service to Christ, and in our time it is clearer than in
most periods that such service must take the form of political
activity on behalf of a transforming justice. Yet the *eros* motif may
become a diversion from such concerns unless one stands well
corrected by the gospel.

Agape may seem equally remote from the claims and counter-
claims of the struggle for justice, for it has no place for such claims
for the self or for one's own group. I shall have much to say about
this issue later. Yet the downward motion of *agape* is consistent with
the caring about the victims of society who are furthest down the
ladder or who may be on the other side of conflicts. It includes love
for enemies. The *agape* motif, as Nygren presents it, only indirectly
gives value to these least or to other persons as human beings. God,
according to this view, always keeps conferring value on human
beings, but does not the fact that persons by their nature are the
appropriate receivers of such value set them apart from all other
beings? The abstract analysis of *agape* that leaves persons as empty
vessels in themselves except as the divine *agape* confers value upon
them is such artificial and bloodless thinking that I appeal from it
to direct respect for the human as human which for most people
must be part of their concern for justice.

Reinhold Niebuhr's concept of mutual love, which is more akin
to *philia* than to pure *agape* or pure *eros*, is seen by him as related to
the problems of justice in society. Mutual love is a blend of *agape*
and *eros*. Love for another which is a part of a mutual relationship is
not completely dependent upon reciprocity though it is supported
by reciprocity. It has enough of *agape* in it so that it intends to
continue regardless of rebuffs and frustrations and sacrifices. I

doubt if Niebuhr's concept of mutual love quite meets the need for an idea of love that is immediately relevant to justice. In one sense it does, for it is a human possibility. It is not as perfectionist in relation to the problems of society as is perfect *agape*. Yet it seems to me that it does not really cover love for distant communities of neighbours who cannot reciprocate, a form of love that does not involve any felt mutuality at all. I suggest that there are two aspects of love which need emphasis in this context. One is mutual love on a very broad scale that includes shared concern and loyalty in relation to various communities. The other is the caring for neighbours at a distance when shared concerns and loyalties do not bind us to them. They may be too far away to be involved in such consciously shared interactions, or they may be on the other side of national or cultural or ideological boundaries which tend to create hostilities, or they may be future generations for which we have responsibility. The extension of love for the neighbour in these ways is essential if it is to be relevant to the problems of justice.

There are two ways of relating love to justice which I believe to be mistaken. I shall deal briefly with each.

The first is the tendency to separate love and justice so that they are not expected to influence each other. Among recent writers this is most noticeable in Emil Brunner, especially in his book *Justice and the Social Order*.[8] He defines love in such a way as to limit it to face-to-face relations. However, I remember a conversation with him in 1946 in which I asked him about this matter and he surprised me by saying that justice is 'institutionalized love'. This may be too static a way of overcoming the separation of love and justice, but it differs from the impression of dualism that much of Brunner's work conveys.

There is a better-known dualism in Luther's thinking that distinguishes between two aspects of the activity of God: God's *opus proprium* which expresses his aggressive *agape* and his *opus alienum* which involves judgment and wrath. This contrast within the nature of God is reflected in the contrast between law and gospel and between the 'two realms', both of which are in line with the separation of love and justice. I have learned that it is not safe to make generalizations about Luther because his defenders are always ready to do battle. Also any writer whose works are often polemical and who uses vivid and provocative language is easily misinterpreted in a one-sided way. The renaissance of Luther studies has helped to deliver Lutheranism from one-sided stereotypes, especially from the way in which the doctrine of the two realms came to dominate German Lutheranism with fateful political consequences. Yet I do not see how it can be denied that there is this dualistic tendency in Luther, according to which the love of the realm of redemption does not sufficiently interact with the order-preserving activities of princes, soldiers and hangmen. There is not enough emphasis on the love that should transform the legal structures and the justice imposed by princes, which because there is so little influence of love upon it actually has more to do with order than with justice. There are great problems in relating love to the policies of government, but to allow Christians to project two standards, one developed around love and the other around justice with the second degenerating into police justice, into the imposition of order to maintain the *status quo*, leads to the grave distortion of both love and justice. Whereas when love and justice interact, we may see the institutions of justice become informed by an aggressive concern for their own victims, by the raising up of the neglected and exploited majority of people to new levels of opportunity and participation, to new levels of welfare and dignity. The protection of them at these new levels becomes the aim of justice, and then its aim is the discovery of more people who must be raised to those same levels. The revolutionary dynamism of justice has love in it, though it does create problems for love that I have yet to discuss.

The interaction between love and justice must really be a two-way movement. The impulses of love need to be related to the structures of justice that enable those who are weaker to resist the paternalistic temptations that often accompany love and distort it. We are living at a time in which this resistance is taking place on all sides, for the people who in weakness have been on the receiving end of paternalism are now telling the world how things look to them and are finding their ways of resisting many well-intended forms of domination as well as those that are expressions of greed and the will to power. This is true, for example, of the relation between churches in Europe and North America and churches established by missions in other continents. The eyes of love need to understand what is happening.

There is an opposite view of the relation between love and justice. It unites them by leaping over the ambiguities and the complexities connected with the implementation of justice in a stable society or in the struggles for justice in the midst of social conflicts. Sometimes this involves chiefly the assimilation of justice to love, and it expresses an idealism of love often present in the liberal social gospel and in much Christian pacifism that refuses to reckon with these ambiguities and complexities. Another tendency is to unite love and justice in such a way that it is difficult to say whether justice is assimilated to love or love to justice. I have in mind the discussion of this subject in Joseph Fletcher's *Situation Ethics*. Fletcher has a great gift for stimulating thought by coining vivid and provocative but simplistic slogans. His basic position is that 'love is the only norm', and he develops it by saying in the title of one of his chapters: 'Love and justice are the same.' He expands this as 'Love and justice are the same, for justice is love distributed, nothing else.'[9] What it means to speak of 'love distributed' is not clear to me. This identification of love and justice is given the technical name of 'pure act agapism' by Professor Frankena in his helpful analysis of the ways in which ethical theorists relate love to rules of any kind, including rules of justice.[10]

One example shows how easily Fletcher can let down his guard and allow love to be assimilated to anything that in his judgment can possibly be defended. He speaks of the decision by President Truman to drop the atom bombs on Hiroshima and Nagasaki as being made on what he calls 'a vast scale of "agapeic calculus"'.[11] To me this is a *reductio ad absurdum* of his position. It assimilates love, not to justice, but to the crudest form of a doctrine of military necessity. President Truman's decision, whatever the motives behind it (and these were probably based on the sincere judgment that it was the surest way of preventing a greater evil), represented a final stage in the deterioration of moral standards in relation to war during the Second World War. The destruction of Dresden and Tokyo and of many other cities prior to the use of the atom bomb was morally similar to the destruction of Hiroshima and Nagasaki, though the latter presented a fateful precedent as humanity entered the nuclear age.

Frankena in the essay just mentioned writes:

> Pure act agapism admits no rules or principles other than the 'law of love' itself, and it also does not allow that there are 'perceptual intuitions' about what is right or wrong in particular situations independently of the dictates of love.[12]

Like the analysis of *agape* and *eros* by Nygren this produces an utterly self-consistent concept that seldom guides anyone's actual conduct. Fletcher does have rules that are ordinarily applicable and that do give guidance, but the difficulty is that under the cover of love he can by fiat set aside these rules so completely that they no longer remain as qualifying factors or sources of restraint. If he is sure that he can say that what he does is done from love, not only is anything permitted but there is a refusal on his part to admit that what is done may still be objectively evil though the lesser evil.

I have rejected the idea that love and justice should be kept in separate compartments and I shall now mention the ways in which love should influence decisions about justice, indeed all decisions in the political sphere.

Love should first of all control motives. Love is not the same as justice but it should seek justice.

Love should be a source of the transforming aspect of justice which I have emphasized. It should increase one's sensitivity and imagination both in regard to the goals of justice to be sought and in regard to the people whose claims and interests and needs are to be considered.

Love should give priority to the changes in structures and policies which will benefit the most disadvantaged people. It should cut through conventional systems of justice that are designed to benefit those with most power in society. One of the most important ethical passages in the writings of Karl Barth with which I am familiar is the following from his remarkable essay on 'The Christian Community and the Civil Community', an essay about which I am led to comment that the wrongheadedness of its methodology is equalled by the soundness of its conclusions. Barth writes:

> The Church is witness of the fact that the Son of man came to seek and to save the lost. And this imples that – casting all false impartiality aside – the Church must concentrate first on the lower and lowest levels of human society. The poor, the socially and economically weak and threatened, will always be the object of its primary and particular concern, and it will always insist on the State's special responsibility for these weaker members of society.[13]

Today the most difficult choices for people living in the wealthier northern nations come from the presence of a billion people in the world who are threatened by famine or who are already the victims of famine. This is a reality that none of our conventional systems of justice have any place for, and only justice transformed by love is likely to discern its meaning.

Love points to structures in communities that encourage both mutuality and participation by those whose lives are affected by them.

Love sometimes has a veto. It sets limits to the methods that are tolerable in the pursuit of any ends. Every reader is likely to have a different list of possible vetoes. I suggest two as illustrations: the use of torture to force persons to do the will of those who control their bodies, and the destruction of centres of populations in war. I realize that there are situations in which in regard to the first it may be said that the information secured by the torture of a few persons may save many persons from becoming victims of a régime that lives by a system of torture. I am not interested in judging others who are driven to desperate decisions in harder situations than I have known, but I think that this brutal use of power over others is a betrayal of the human in those who are tortured and in those who torture. As for the destruction of centres of population I can conceive of no exceptional circumstances in which it would not be vetoed by love. If a state does this in desperation no Christian should justify it. I believe that the least that we can say has been said by the Second Vatican Council: 'Any act of war aimed indiscriminately at the destruction of entire cities or of extensive areas along with their population is a crime against God and man himself.'[14] The missiles of the nuclear powers on both sides are aimed to do this.

There will always be debates between those who stress a 'teleological' and those who stress than a 'deontological' approach to ethical decisions, and the former will be wary of these vetoes. Yet I think that at least they should be willing to admit that if laws do not set specific limits to conduct under all conceivable future circumstances or under circumstances that cannot now be conceived, they should always be felt as strong moral pressures against particular acts of inhumanity, and that if they are driven by some circumstances to make exceptions the pressures remain as sources of restraint.

I shall now deal briefly with the relation between justice and other social values or goals and especially order and freedom. I was fascinated by the words of Archbishop William Temple which Alan Richardson quotes twice with approval to the effect that 'it is desirable that government be just; it is essential that it should be strong'.[15] Richardson says that 'No Christian realist would be so foolish as to transpose the adjectives "just" and "strong" in this pronouncement.' So long as either Temple or Richardson or others of their spirit are the ones to follow up on such a statement I do not quarrel with it, but such a statement coming from the rulers of most nations in the world today would worry me a great deal. A more dialectical conception of the relation between justice and order-maintaining strength seems to me to be essential. Unless the strength of a government is used with some regard to justice it may become so oppressive that there is justification in seeking to overturn it if that is a possibility, or if all efforts to do it are not believed to be counter-productive. Perhaps they usually are counter-productive, but that does not in principle rule them out. Indeed the continued strength of a government depends in part upon its being believed to have some justice in it by those who live under its authority. I shall have more to say about the possibility of justifiable revolutions later.

The relation between justice and freedom involves the interpenetration of one by the other. Freedom itself is a matter of justice: it is the due of people to have basic human rights. One of the remarkable facts about the churches in the world today is that they have become in country after country champions of human rights, not only the rights of Christians or churches but the rights of all persons. Unless there is freedom to expose and protest against many forms of injustice, there is little chance of overcoming them.

One recent episode illustrates the role of the church as a defender of human rights. On 5 June 1974 there was a service in the Cathedral in Santiago, Chile, in honour of Cardinal de Silva Henriques who has been the most powerful defender of the victims of the post-Allende regime in that country. The report of that service said the following: 'The audience today, mostly poor and lower-middle-class people, included relatives of political prisoners and many sympathizers of the Allende government who have come to look on the Cardinal and an important segment of the Catholic Church as their protectors.' The Catholic Church is doing this in several other Latin American countries, in the Philippines and even in South Vietnam, and both Catholics and Protestants share this role in South Korea.

There remains a very great dilemma so far as the basic rights of expression of mind and conscience are concerned. The situation in which I see that dilemma most clearly is China. The people of China have under their Communist régime overcome mass poverty, and I doubt if this has happened to the same extent anywhere else. They have also gained freedom and dignity as a nation. They have come to embody on a large scale concern for neighbours and for the community. They do not have the rights of personal expression of mind and conscience and, though it is recognized that the revolution must continue, those who have the power are likely to manipulate new stages of the revolution. What has been achieved has been so extraordinary and there have been so many gains for aspects of justice that I have no zeal for emphasizing the lack of personal freedom as of now. I am enough of a realist to wonder how long the gains for justice will survive without freedom to criticize those who have the political power. The problems of oppressed humanity are so stubborn and complex that in this case I think that we should celebrate the overcoming of so many cruel forms of oppression. I perhaps feel this all the more as an American because the United States until recently willed the destruction of the Communist régime that has done so much for China. Professor Rawls states as one of his principles of justice that 'the principle of equal liberty' should be ranked prior to 'the principle of regulating economic and social inequalities'.[16] I think that sometimes that may be right but, as Rawls later admits, it depends upon the degree of the social oppression or economic impoverishment. To invoke that principle now in regard to China would be the reading of the meaning of justice too much in terms of an individualistic ideology. I say that without denying the truth in the insistence that justice should include freedom of expression for mind and conscience.

Love should will justice, but justice, as I have said, does often create problems for love. The most difficult tension between love and justice is present when the struggle for justice or the defence of justice involves serious conflict. The political process at its best is coercive as one party displaces the party in power, but when there is general acceptance of the coercive aspect of the process, this takes much of the sting out of the coercion. Far more difficult is the use of raw power in an economic conflict, and more difficult than that is the use of violence. The acceptance of police force in a well-ordered society creates problems for love even though love may be expressed through it, but these problems are minimal compared with those that we have in a situation of disorder, whether it is an international war or a civil war or revolution. Those who are absolute pacifists in their interpretation of the responsibilities of love escape the most perplexing dilemmas in the relation between love and justice. I shall not deal at length with the use of violence in international war except to say that recent experience even for non-pacifists should greatly narrow the possibilities of justifying war. Though there are complexities related to deterrence, the use of nuclear weapons in war seems certainly to be off limits. Also, as an American I am convinced that a war of intervention by a great power to prevent revolutionary change in the third world is also off limits. I cannot deduce from the experience which has led to that statement that there are no conceivable circumstances in which the limited use of military force can be justified, but there must be a heavy burden of proof on governments in this regard, especially in view of their capacity to deceive the people. This shift of the burden of proof from the citizens to the government can be a momentous change in all thinking about justified or unjustified wars.

When we come to revolutionary violence I think that we need to heed the warnings in Alan Richardson's book *The Political Christ* against romantic attitudes toward revolution and in regard to the repressive character of régimes that have often followed revolution. In his brief discussion of revolution he seems to allow for the possibility of its justification in situations where there are no constitutional means of bringing about necessary changes. He is himself the beneficiary of two revolutions since the early seventeenth century, and I think that these were at the deepest level most important for the freedom of the people of the United States than the American revolution!

It is pretentious to speak of a 'theology of revolution', but I believe that it is important to state that there is a theological permission for resistance to political authorities that is recognized within more traditions than has been the case in other periods. I believe that Richardson is right in his emphasis on the importance of governmental authority, but I think that he overstates the case for the beneficent effects of Romans 13. Those verses about obedience to the governing authorities have been a proof text for the support of tyranny throughout Christian history. The efforts to gain freedom from the injunction in Romans 13 as a law, through the exegesis of the text, is a fascinating study. Those words have sometimes been seen to be time-bound and an expression of Paul's somewhat satisfactory experience of the Roman government when he wrote them and, perhaps, as a prudent way of securing toleration for the church. They have been seen as including criteria that should control their application in the words: 'Would you have no fear of him who is in authority? Then do what is good, and you will receive his approval' (v. 4). Are we not free from any duty to obey such authorities when this is clearly not true of them, when we have authorities which in the words of Karl Barth are 'liars, murderers and incendiaries . . . which wished to usurp the place of God, to fetter the conscience, to suppress the church and become itself [as a government] the Church of Anti-Christ'. In such a situation Barth said that 'it could well be that we could obey specific rulers only by being disobedient to God, and by being thus in fact disobedient to the political order ordained of God as well'.[17] Another approach to the exegesis of the first seven verses of Romans 13 is to see them as part of the much longer passage which

includes v. 8, which lifts up the love commandment as supreme. To
do this is to subordinate the specific injuctions of Romans 13 to
love, and this may relativize it as a law, for obedience to it may be
seen to be against the law of love.

Pacifist objection to violence in revolution is not affected by
theological permission for resistance to political authorities, but
those who are not pacifists in regard to international war should
not become pacfists in principle in the context of revolution. The
current discussion of the legitimacy of revolutionary violence
almost always emphasizes the reality of what is called
institutionalized or systemic or covert violence. It is remarkable
that not only radical theologians of liberation but even the Latin
American bishops meeting at Medillin, Colombia, in 1968 used the
phrase 'institutionalized violence' to describe the present situation
in Latin America. They warned against overt violence to counteract
this institutionalized violence on prudential grounds for they feared
that it would result in even greater evils. Alan Richardson in
discussing the arguments for violence based upon the reality of such
institutionalized violence says that this should be seen as 'force'
rather than 'violence', and he implies that it is merely a case of the
legitimate order-preserving force that governments always use. But
in many countries it is a system of unjust coercion that determines
the conditions of life of the great majority, a system that often uses
force directly and this at time takes the form of violence.
'Institutionalized violence' may not be visible and bloody violence,
but it is the destructive and even lethal nature of the whole system
of coercion which, for example, crowds people in large number into
hopeless slums or ghettoes and condemns their children to
malnourishment and most of the population to a life expectancy
that is half that of those who are more privileged. This is as lethal as
the most bloody violence. Where such realities are the dominant
fact I do not see how there can be any moral case, except on pacifist
grounds, against violent revolution in principle, although it may be
imprudent and counter-productive and, if it fails, terrible
repression may be the result.

All discussion of revolution should be situational. It should avoid
the assumption that because a revolution may seem morally
necessary it is possible. There should be realistic estimates of the
troops that are available for revolutionary action and not merely of
the generals or the theorists. Archbishop Helder Camara's warning
against armchair guerrillas is always in order. There should also be
realistic estimates of the extent to which the population is ready to

support a revolution and the extent to which the existing government is in a state of deterioration or decay. I note very little emphasis on such calculations in Christian writings about revolution. Without them .there is the likelihood that if revolutionary initiatives are taken they will lead a people into catastrophes that may be worse than the original injustice.

Justice in the midst of these social conflicts does create problems for love, even though love should control the motives of those who seek justice. Also, love leads us to see that these struggles for justice are always in need of correction. Adversaries should never be written off as non-persons. It often may seem hypocritical to speak of loving enemies who are seen as 'oppressors', but in the Christian context it is essential to see one's own side as sharing with adversaries common human finiteness and sin without annulling the difference that does separate those who profit most from systems of injustice from those who are their victims. Those on the other side are seen to have status as persons loved by God, no matter how right it may be to struggle even by violent means to displace them as holders of power.

Love should also have a veto on methods, as I have already suggested, and this may be a matter of utmost difficulty in the hardest situations. It is not for me to write as an armchair judge of what the limits of action are in situations remote from my experience. Yet I have confidence that there would be important practical differences in action between those who are restrained by love and those who are swept away by vindictive fury and who forget the humanity of enemies who may be in their control. It is significant that the group appointed by the World Council of Churches to discuss the issue of revolutionary violence was able to agree that there are 'some forms of violence in which Christians may not participate and which churches must condemn'. The group was not able to agree on the general question of violence, and it had members who felt compelled to say that 'nonviolence does not present itself as an option unless they would withdraw totally from the struggle for justice', and yet they were able to join with others in saying the following:

> There are violent means of struggle – torture in all forms, the holding of innocent hostages and the deliberate or indiscriminate killing of innocent non-combatants for example – which destroy the soul of the perpetrator as surely as the life and health of the victim.[18]

This statement has great importance, for it is no armchair judgment.

Love and justice come together, in spite of the problems that activities in behalf of justice may create for love, when those who seek justice keep in view reconciliation beyond the conflict. Love and the confession of sin and the recognition of the special temptations that accompany justified revolutionary partisanship belong together. Humility and a response to the mystery of God's love that transcends both sides in any conflict prepare the way for reconciliation.

NOTES

1. John Rawls, *A Theory of Justice*, Oxford University Press 1973.
2. Paul Tillich, 'Transforming or Creative Justice', *Love, Power and Justice*, Oxford University Press 1954, pp. 64f.
3. Bernard Häring, *The Law of Christ* I, Eng. trs., Mercier Press, Cork, 1962, p. 519.
4. Rawls, op. cit., pp. 14f.
5. A. Nygren, *Agape and Eros*, Eng. trs., 3 vols. 1932-39; 2nd ed. in one vol., SPCK 1953.
6. M.C. d'Arcy, *The Mind and Heart of Love*, rev. ed., Faber and Faber 1954.
7. Paul Ramsey, *Basic Christian Ethics*, Scribner, New York, 1950, SCM Press 1953, p. 119.
8. Emil Brunner, *Justice and the Social Order*, Eng. trs., Lutterworth 1945.
9. Joseph Fletcher, *Situation Ethics*, Westminster Press, Philadelphia, and SCM Press 1966, p. 87.
10. William K. Frankena, 'Love and Principle in Christian Ethics', in *Faith and Philosophy*, ed. A. Plantinga, Eerdmans, Grand Rapids, Michigan 1964.
11. Fletcher, op. cit., p. 98.
12. Frankena, op. cit., p. 221.
13. Karl Barth, 'The Christian Community and the Civil Community', *Against the Stream: Shorter Post-War Writings, 1946-52*, SCM Press 1954, p. 36.
14. 'The Constitution on the Church in the Modern World', par. 80 (in *The Documents of Vatican II*, ed. W.M. Abbott, Geoffrey Chapman 1966, p. 294).
15. Alan Richardson, *The Political Christ*, SCM Press 1973, p. 98.
16. Rawls, op. cit., p. 43; for qualification of this principle see pp. 542f.
17. Karl Barth, *The Knowledge of God and the Service of God*, Hodder and Stoughton 1938, p. 230.
18. 'Violence, Nonviolence and the Struggle for Social Justice', *The Ecumenical Review* XXV, October 1973, p. 443.

~ 9 ~

Reflections on Theologies of
Social Change[1]

RONALD PRESTON

I

The ecumenical movement has been of immense importance for
Christian social ethics. Indeed it would not be too much to say that
the churches have made more progress in social ethics in the last
half century than since the break-up of mediaeval society. It is
because the search for the *renewal* as well as the unity of the church
has been at the heart of the ecumenical movement that this
progress has been made. One aspect of the quest for renewal has
been a determined effort to investigate what exactly is going on in
the world, so that the churches understand the situation of their
own day, and do not go on preaching and teaching and formulating
their priorities either oblivious of what is happening or
misunderstanding it. The churches were caught out in this way
when what is commonly called the industrial revolution began to
accelerate social change in Britain, with effects that have become
cumulative and world-wide. They had little or nothing relevant to
say at the time and have been slow to catch up since. Pioneers in
the ecumenical movement wanted to avert the same mistake at a
time of new social changes and pressures in this century. This has
meant that traditional theologies, confessional or not, all of which
took shape in ages when social change was so slow as to be almost
imperceptible from one generation to the next, have had to be re-
fashioned to cope with rapid social change. For, as we all know,
social change is now so rapid that it is extremely hard for the next
generation to take over from the previous one. Fathers and sons, for
instance, find it hard to understand one another, because their
formative experiences in their teenage years have been in such
different circumstances.

The Oxford Conference on 'Church, Community and State' in
1937 was an attempt to cope with twentieth-century social change.

In a sense it did so defensively against the challenge to the Christian faith of political totalitarianism; with concern for mass unemployment in the economic sphere not far behind. It produced theological insights of very high quality which are by no means exhausted. The Geneva Conference of 1966 on 'Christians in the Social and Technological Revolutions of our Time' which was deliberately planned to be a successor to Oxford in the new circumstances of the mid-sixties, was more on the offensive in its desire for Christian initiatives to influence the processes of social change, which were now taken for granted. It was no longer necessary to urge that theology take social change seriously, to point out that all previous theologians of any influence in all the main confessions, whether emanating from monasteries, seminaries or universities, had taken the *status quo* too seriously, and had thanked God for 'creation, *preservation* and all the blessings of this life' but not for change, whether evolutionary or revolutionary. At Geneva the mood was very different. It was there that a major ecumenical Christian conference outside Latin America first heard of a theology of revolution. It was there that the rapid social changes being brought about everywhere by the ongoing technological changes in the 'Western' world were faced. At the same time the protest against them by many of the affluent youth in that world began to be heard. It was at Geneva, too, that the break-up of the monolithic Marxist world was registered, and with it the rising expectations of the politically decolonialized third world, and their sharp criticisms of the wealthy world.

Since the Geneva Conference we have seen a very marked growth of theologies of social change. The term 'political theology' has been coined. Within it there have been theologies of development, of revolution and of liberation; and there has been Black theology, which is also essentially one of social change. They are all related to theologies of hope; and in all the emphasis is much more on terrestrial than on celestial hopes. They are clearly vigorous and important. Indeed I do not think that nearly enough attention has been paid to them in Britian. Nevertheless I also think that some cautions need to be expressed about them. This essay is an attempt to reflect on Christian social responsibility in the last quarter of the twentieth century in the light of these recent developments. Working on the assumption that it is the continued advances in pure science and technology that bring in their train economic, social and political changes, it begins by giving a rough sketch of what is going on in the world, with particular stress on the first world, of which Britain is a part, and the problems it raises for us. These problems are seen to be essentially political ones; and as Christian insights need to be brought alongside empirical situations if they are to guide, fortify and inspire us, an examination of the contribution of these political theologies naturally follows after the sketch of the empirical situation. But as they all give a decisive place to New Testament data the essay, before examining them, looks at the New Testament teaching on Christian hope, and then asks how far these political theologies have used that teaching in an illuminating way in spelling out Christian social and political responsibilities and choices in our time.

II

A mood of pessimism has overtaken the first world after an unprecedented twenty-five years of economic growth and the comparative optimism of the mid-sixties. This is partly due to the shock caused by the power exercised by the oil producers of OPEC over oil prices and supplies (the first time the affluent world has been treated in a way it has been accustomed to treat others). But it is also due to our inability to control inflation, which had been occasioned, well before the dramatic rise in the price of oil, by the rise in food prices as a result of bad harvests in Russia and India. It showed how dependent the whole world is on each part and on the weather; even the affluent, though much less vulnerable, cannot insulate themselves. A third reason for pessimism is that the affluent have become more aware of the social ills in their own countries, which with all their wealth they have failed to solve.

Nevertheless we must not be too impressed by what is probably a temporary mood. There may be economic and social disaster ahead; and of course should a major war break out the disaster is scarcely calculable. However, international relations is not the theme of this essay, and it will assume that a major war will not break out. In that case the material resources and scientific skills of the affluent world are so great that it is likely that the immediate economic problems will reach a tolerable solution in three or four years' time, and that the underlying factors which have been in operation in the last few decades (and some of them far longer) will still operate. In particular, through the continued development of pure science and technology the processes of economic growth and rapid social change will continue.

From this angle human history was one of relative stagnation until about the year 1760. Since then we have seen an ever increasing control of matter and energy, and a steady long-term growth of the economy at an over-all rate of not less than 3% p.a. GNP. The affluent world is more and more deliberately organizing knowledge by creating the intellectual tools for grasping and deliberately changing the world. We are often told that 50% of all the natural scientists who ever lived are alive now. We are also told that organized innovation is 99% sweat and 1% genius. We shall, therefore, expect to see an increased speed in the application of technical discoveries. Recently there has been a breakthrough in processing information by computers, and we are on the edge of a breakthrough in distributing it by computerized learning processes and telecommunications by satellites. Our powers of calculations have increased by a factor of 10,000 in the last fifteen years, and at a rapidly falling cost. In many sciences knowledge doubles in ten years. In some, four-fifths of what will be relevant knowledge at the turn of the century is not yet known. Man's age-old economic problem of the scarcity of basic food, clothing and shelter for the bulk of the world's population may be in sight of solution in perhaps fifty years; the equivalent of the sound barrier in this matter can be broken. This is vital to about 2,300 millions of the 3,600 million people now alive. But whether they *will* benefit from the growing affluence of the technologically advanced world is a fundamental question addressed first to us who live in it.

None of this will happen without difficulties. I mention three.

1. First of all there is difficulty in forecasting developments in any one science, let alone its interaction with other sciences. Kahn and Weiner in their study of *The Year 2,000* mention a survey of the future made in 1937 which missed atomic energy, the computer, antibiotics, radar and jet propulsion.[2] The problem is that established knowledge is itself a conservative force, and that the absorption and even retrieval of it becomes a daunting task. Also, few of us have new ideas after the age of 25. In short, it is extremely hard to look ahead more than fifteen years with any confidence; and if in economic terms the future is discounted by 10% p.a., that too means that little weight is given to more than fifteen years ahead. Certainly we need to think ahead as efficiently as we can, but it is unlikely that we can project with much certainty beyond fifteen years, a length of time when a great deal can in fact change. If I am told, for example, that the world's iron reserves as at present known will be exhausted at present trends of consumption in 93 years I am unimpressed;

there are too many imponderable factors in that time scale. We cannot be responsible for a future we cannot foresee.

2. Next there is the difficulty of forecasting the use which will be made of discoveries. The German chemist who a hundred years ago compounded polystyrene had no thought that it could be used to make a superior napalm, enabling it to stick more effectively to its victims. This difficulty is a fact of life with which we have to live, endeavouring to be responsible in our own generation and leaving it to succeeding ones to face their responsibilities. In our time we have to face the fact that the explosion of knowledge since 1940 has been such that our monitoring devices and safeguards have proved inadequate, so that we can no longer take clean air, earth and water for granted. This is the truth in the ecological controversy of the last few years; and the problems to which it has drawn attention are beginning to be tackled. Although much depends on inter-national co-operation, and progress is patchy and hazardous, there is no reason to suppose they will not be tackled, at least to a reasonable extent. Beyond this the demand for a 'stable state', that is to say the end of economic growth, is a mistake. In a nutshell it depends upon an argument that we are using up irreplaceable natural resources because population is increasing exponentially (that is to say at a constant rate over time), and therefore so is the rate of consumption and pollution. It ignores the fact that technological innovation is also increasing, and this is affecting all the other variables. The need is rather to use economic growth to cope with the necessities of the people already born (whilst doing what we can to reduce birth rates). We must not be deflected from removing crippling poverty from over half the world's population.

3. A political difficulty emerges from these other ones. The complexities and uncertainties of decision-making require the continual feedback of information and re-ordering of priorities. This in turn requires a very sophisticated decision-making process just at the time when more and more people are rightly wanting to participate in it. A high degree of political wisdom will be needed to cope with this. Indeed what speed of change can political institutions themselves cope with? Western-type political democracies do not find it easy to cope with rapid change. If governments demand it they are likely to be voted out of office. And how much change can people stand? How

malleable and mobile can they be? What institutions are needed to help them to face change? The answer to these questions is not clear, and they suggest caution; but if ordered change is not secured a dangerous backlog builds up which leads to social explosion.

At this point we note the rejection of the technologically affluent future by many of the younger generation. The cry of the Paris students in 1968 was 'death to the technical reason' and 'all power to the imagination'. To many of the student generation the rich of our age appear poor and detestable. They reject what appears to be the likely future of a mass consumption society. They have a sense of alienation in the midst of abundance. They seek a non-competitive communal life. In one sense it is ironical that they are bored by the affluence which their parents have created and which they have enjoyed, since it is the basis of a welfare state which enables them to opt out whilst being able to presuppose a level of basic securities below which they will not be allowed to fall. Yet it is a healthy sign that concern for the quality of life comes to the fore once a certain standard of living has been reached, provided it does not turn aside from the task of seeing that the majority of the world's population can experience what the students can take for granted as underpinning them. The control of technological power and the use of the resources it provides remain the key issue. It is a *political* one, not a technological one. There must be no turning back on the political task.

III

In many respects the second world is similar to the first in basic economic and technological background. Starting a long way back in economic development, governments which cannot be removed from office by the electorate have been able to impose a rate of forced saving on their populations which the electorates of the first world would not tolerate. So they have had a very rapid economic growth. The same difficulties have to be faced as in the first world and, all in all, the second world is neither more nor less successful in solving them than is the first world. Again some of the younger generation are disenchanted with the quality of life they find and are expected to look forward to; and a significant number of the older generation also question whether the material transformation of which Marx spoke is enough to satisfy human aspirations. There has been something of a break-up in monolithic Marxism, and a cautious improvement in the conditions for the flourishing of the human spirit. Under the utopian theory that once the advance guard of the workers has seized power all *fundamental* political problems are solved, the tactical struggles which inevitably accompany bids for power in the political processes are interpreted as counter-revolutionary moves, and repressions and purges have been the result. Now these are somewhat abated, but there is no clear alternative explanation of political processes. Marxism in China is clearly making an effort to avoid Russian fossilization, and it is a source of inspiration for many in the third world who have no time for the Russian version of Marxism. China is also a country with a pronounced this-worldly orientation, and without the secularized biblical undertones which are unmistakable in Soviet Marxism. For these reasons the theological significance of Maoist China is a question of the first importance, but not one which can be pursued further here.

When we turn to the third world it has now become necessary to separate the newly rich oil states from the rest. For our present purposes we need say no more about them, but turn to what now is being called the fourth world. Asia, Africa and Latin America differ in important respects from one another, but these differences will be ignored in my brief comment. Here the speed of change is even more traumatic, as traditional societies are hit by the effects of the technology of the first world without the infrastructure of social and political institutions which developed in the latter in the last century. Tribalism and the caste system are instances of additional complications. Half of the population is under 29, and it is set against authoritarian and bureaucratic structures and restlessly in search of a new future, broadly interpreted as a socialism of self-management. Awareness of the growing economic disparities between their world and the rest has led to a growing demand for a greater share of affluence, and a more fundamental demand for liberation from oppressive power structures, both neo-colonial and domestic, and by force if necessary. In Latin America the search for a new society is related to the process of 'conscientization' by which those on the margin of society become self-conscious of themselves and their state of life in the act of grasping that change is possible and of moving themselves towards changing it. Meanwhile the influx into the cities of the fourth world is becoming a cascade. Driven from the villages where there is no work, people settle in the shanty towns on the edge of the cities where there is also no work, and where the social restraints of village life no longer hold. This is perhaps the most potentially explosive social factor of all.

How can the fourth world exert enough pressure on the other worlds to secure that the vast resources of those worlds are used towards a more just international economic and social order? It seems clear that the comfortable do not take seriously the burden of rectifying injustices until the under-privileged both become articulate and have enough strength to make a dint on them. The fourth world has become articulate, but it is in a weak position against the other worlds whose economic and technological power gets relatively greater against theirs. In the long term a humane and just world is a gain for all, but in the short term the wealthy are only too likely not to see beyond their immediate interests. Will they learn in time?

At any rate in the first world, governments are influenced by their electorates and respond to pressures. It is also in the first world that Christians are strongest and still represent in most countries a significant element in the electorate. Is it possible that they could become more alert and informed and thus politically more effective? What theological resources have they for coping with social change? And what are their hopes for the future? We are now offered the various political theologies of hope and change, all relating themselves to the New Testament. Therefore it is to my own understanding of New Testament hopes and their significance that I refer before reflecting on the various political theologies.

IV

New Testament thinking is both eschatological and apocalyptic. Eschatology is concerned with the 'last' events in time in the sense of those which are of lasting and ultimate significance for the whole; apocalyptic is concerned with the end of ongoing or routine time. Both carry on categories of thought which are of central significance in the Old Testament. The key to the ministry of Jesus (in word and deed) is its eschatological character. He presented his hearers with a challenge to moral and religious discernment; those who had eyes to see were to realize that the hoped-for 'last days' in the Jewish religious tradition, when Yahweh would vindicate his purposes, had already dawned in his own ministry, paradoxical as it was, since, while in some respects it fulfilled Old Testament hopes, in others it negated them. The powers of the 'last days' were thus already at work in the world. At the same time it is very likely that Jesus had a foreshortened expectation of the future of routine time, that is to say that he had a lively apocalyptic expectation that it would soon come to an end with a *parousia*, when the eschatological powers now already at work in the ongoing world would achieve an evident triumph, of which his own ministry was a proleptic indication. The earliest Christian community certainly had this double eschatological and apocalyptic outlook. It had no doubt that 'the light of the knowledge of the glory of God' had been seen 'in the face of Jesus Christ' (II Cor. 4.6); that in a decisive sense it was living in a new age; that the powers of the age to come were already at work. Yet the present age still continued, though not (it was believed) for long. Soon would come the *parousia*, the return of Christ, and the end of the present time series. The early Christians lived with the sense of membership in a new community of the Spirit, based on faith in Christ, love to God and to one another through him, and hope for the imminent final triumph of what Jesus had begun. They lived in the two ages at once; they lived between the kingdom of God drawing near in Jesus and its soon-to-be-accomplished consummation.

The Christian's hope in the New Testament is of the final triumph of good over evil, that is to say the abolition of sin; the final triumph of the new life in Christ over human finitude, that is to say the abolition of death; and the fullness of love, joy and peace, that is to say the end of that boring aspect of routine time which is so pungently expressed in the book Ecclesiastes. This hope is epitomized in the thought of being 'with Christ' and of having a new resurrection 'body'; and thus it transcends what is within history and continuous with our space and time, and apocalyptically looks to what is discontinuous with it and with our bodies with their present space and time equipment. There is an inescapable 'other-worldly' stress in the New Testament. But this is in no way to be confused with the Platonic idea that this world is only a shadow of the real world. In both Testaments *olam* and *aion* are used both for this age and the coming one.

Christian hope lies between ignorance and knowledge. It neither indulges in unnecessary curiosity, for example about the date of 'the end', nor does it wait passively on events. It eagerly grasps adumbrations of the new age already experienced and is active and eager in its outlook. In hoping for what we do not yet see we show our endurance (Rom. 8.25), but it is much more than a passive endurance. What we already know of the eschatologically ultimate in Christ is the basis of our future expectations; we are betrothed and we look to the marriage; we are eschatologically renewed and we look for the *parousia*.

In almost all the New Testament these hopes are foreshortened, so that there is no hope for the terrestrial future. The existing institutions of society, notably slavery, are accepted and humanized within the Christian community with no thought of change. In St John's gospel, however, a drastic theological reconsideration has taken place. The imminent apocalyptic expectation has gone, but the radical eschatological Christian outlook is no whit diminished – if anything the radical contrast between its light and the surrounding darkness is intensified – and is left as the permanent possession of the church through indefinite ongoing chronological time. It was of immense importance that this theological shift took place when it became clear that no imminent *parousia* was likely. But its effect on immediate decision-making is negligible. The Christians are to continue with the same active eager attitude to chronological time, and they are to continue to grasp adumbrations of the new age as before. Whether there is only a little routine time or a lot – scores or hundreds or thousands of years – makes no difference. Each day is an occasion of joyful response to the eschatological nearness brought about by Christ.

Apocalyptic is a dispensable thought-form. This means that Christians should have a positive and forward-looking attitude to the future, that they should have criteria for judging in which direction they wish to influence it, and that they should be on the look-out for all signs of renewal as judged by these criteria. But it does not mean that they have any clear picture of what is to happen in the course of chronological time. They have no grounds for *a priori* theological pessimism which thinks that little or nothing can be done, or that things will get worse. No limits have been set by God to human achievement if humanity responds to his call and is sensitive to human need. Neither are there grounds for *a priori* theological optimism. There is no assurance that humanity will become more obedient, or that there is any built-in process leading to a better world. There may be catastrophes; or perhaps a series of renewals and catastrophes. This is because each generation has to make its own the moral advances made by its predecessor, and if possible extend them. If it fails at least to do the former, the disasters caused by the collapse of something superior is more than that of something less so. Moreover the subtler temptations arise out of genuine moral achievements. A society which presupposes co-operation and fails to get it is worse off than one that appeals overwhelmingly to self-interest, as *laisser-faire* did. That was what was so shocking about the regress to synthetic technological barbarism in Nazi Germany. Social change (unlike biological evolution) can be rapid but it is also precarious. Good and evil may well grow together until the end of time. What we know of the recalcitrance of human beings makes us cautious just as what we know of their potentialities of goodness makes us hopeful. But the basic ground of our hope, and in the Christian outlook hope vastly outweighs gloom, is in what we already know and have experienced through Jesus. It leads to the affirmation that history will not ultimately defeat God's purpose (but not that that purpose will be achieved in the continuities of our present historical order), and that no human effort to work for the good of humanity is wasted.

To repeat, our hope in Christ does not give any detailed content to our hope for our terrestrial future, though it gives us ground for taking that future seriously and positively. It is true that there has been much spurious other-worldliness in the Christian tradition, and this has given plausibility to the Marxist criticism of it; but finally the Christian hope is 'other-worldly' in the sense that its fulfilment transcends this world. This is important in a future-orientated society which may easily be tempted, as Marxism is, to inflict cruelties on the present generation in the interests of future ones. Aldous Huxley once said that a future-orientated society without a hope of heaven would be a tyranny. It is just because we have no abiding city that we can laugh rather than sigh, and that we must take the needs of our present fellow-members of the earthly city so seriously.

The Christian emphasis is on the call to be obedient today within the perspective of the future that can be reasonably foreseen. Man 'come of age' has great powers and great responsibilities under God. He is not bound by the past but free for the future; he is liberated to commit himself to the world in hope and to look for the common grace and the hidden grace at work in it. Fear of the unknown future is a major obstacle to making a creative response to a time of rapid change. This is particularly acute in affluent societies who are conscious of what they have to lose; their heart is where their treasure is. It is all the more serious if Christians are timid and fearful. Instead they should discern hope in the midst of the struggle for human conditions without giving way to zealotry or escapism. Of course it is possible to have courage without hope, and we must honour many humanists who possess it. It is possible to have fanatical hopes, and these need mitigating by a dose of Christian realism. It is also possible to be quietist and 'other-worldly', and this needs correcting by a lively Christian hope as a source of vision and strength in facing the human future.

IV

What I have just written has some affinities with the political theologies of the last ten years, but it would by no means be accepted by them in its entirety. But first of all we need to understand what is meant by the term 'political theology', which I take to be in itself a witness to an important truth. Negatively it is a protest against the 'privatization' of theology; positively it is not so much a 'theology of politics' as we might have one of industry, or art, or education or sport, but rather an assertion that politics is not a *part* of theology which one may or may not engage in according to one's choice. To think theologically is willy-nilly a political activity, whether one is conscious of it or not. This is because *all* thinking takes place in a social context; and the social and the political realm overlap to a considerable extent. It is true that in some aspects of theological study, textual criticism for example, the influence of the social context is negligible. In descriptive studies, historical and contemporary, it has more place. To understand the Chalcedonian formula one has to understand its vocabulary, and that arose in a social context; St Anselm on the doctrine of the atonement is unintelligible without a knowledge of feudalism. As each generation re-writes history with questions, insights and perspectives occasioned by its own situation, so the church continually reflects on her own past and sees it in new ways. 'The faith once delivered to the saints' (Jude 3)is seen very differently at different times. When we come to think theologically in our own time, the political context of that thought is inescapable. To think we can be neutral is a delusion; it is impossible to escape out of our milieu and to avoid conditioning factors, as if we could be 'pure' reasoners, with reasoning in pure mathematics as the model in our minds. Of course we can be partially aware of conditioning factors and partially overcome them, but not completely so. Moreover the political realm is one of conflicts of groups and institutions, from which churches are not exempt and which Christians cannot escape. The importance of the ecumenical movement is that it makes us relate our thinking to that of Christians and churches from different contexts (often adding also the vividness which comes from personal encounter) within the fellowship of the whole church, so that we may learn from one another and make a more adequate response to the issues that face us, holding inevitable conflicts within a deeper commitment to the crucified and risen Christ.

There can be no dichotomy in the Christian task between changing persons and changing structures. This is a false antithesis which never quite dies down. Even the most 'personal' preaching of the gospel requires an interpretation which itself is in a social-political context; and structures of life (family, work, citizenship) mould persons from their infancy onwards, so that the way they work cannot be left unexamined. In an important sense theology is inescapably political. Those who have stressed this have also stressed how often it has conformed to the *status quo*, or imagined it was neutral and a-political (even in the case of a man like Charles de Foucauld), and how little it has challenged current structures. They ask whether this is true to the stance of the biblical data, once the time-bound situation of the early church is allowed for.

The theology of hope has been a pervasive political theology in the last decade or so. It does not stress faith in God's past actions so much as hope for his eschatological action in history in the future. It professes to empower the lives of Christians from the end or fulfilment of history with an eschatological vision of a fulfilled kingdom of God, as the basis for breaking up existing social and political structures and establishing new ones; and also for keeping perseverence and hope alive in defeats (for it is not blindly optimistic). It criticizes a stress on present eschatology as leading to a bourgeois and spurious other-worldly individualism. In doing so it undoubtedly has the kind of personal pietism associated with Bultmann in mind, with its stress on an inward relation to God and the realization of an authentic but a-historical self. This, however, is an over-simplification. Ethics has never been a main interest of Bultmann; he has little to say about it, and that of limited use. There is no necessity for a stress on present eschatology to have that effect. The Berrigan brothers, for instance, or Bishop Colin Winter, find the roots of their hopes in the presence of Christ in the eucharist, and from this derive their challenge to established structures. Moreover, those who have in fact most stressed future eschatology in Christian history have generally thought of it in very individualistic terms: 'salvation for my soul after death'. In fact both present and future eschatological emphases can be subject to individualistic distortions and the neglect of social change and social justice.

On the other hand the theology of hope is in danger of its own characteristic distortion, a utopian strain, to which I shall turn shortly. But it need not be. Indeed on occasions it does warn against canonizing *any* order, even as it stresses the infinite possibilities of the open future. But on whether its projected transformation of the world is to be part of, and continuous with, our human history or not, it appears to be ambiguous. More important still is that with its stress on looking for the radically new from God as 'the power of the future', quite unlike what we know of the present or of human potentialities so far, it fails to make clear how what is radically new in the future can guide ethical action now. Rather, we can only base ourselves on our *present* understanding of the *past*. This is not to say that we are in bondage to either the past or the present, but we are compelled to go back for our criteria today to what we know now of the revelation in Christ. In fact when we come to what the theologies of hope say about the present we find they are wrestling with the same problems as others, with no clearer or agreed answers (for example to the problem of violence). They express a change of mood, and one which when not utopian is positive and valuable, but otherwise a great deal of the theology of hope seems to involve the moving of biblical material in a different pattern without much greater theological illumination. It seems an involved way of urging Christians to take the future seriously and work to make it more just and human. It is still too much a theology of the Word, in the aftermath of Karl Barth, attempting to move too directly from scripture to the modern world. Scriptural revelation does not tell us of our terrestrial future; from it we can derive an attitude to and criteria for dealing with the different foreseeable futures that different generations and societies have to face. The call is for joyful obedience today; the material for decision comes from the empirical data of the day.

Some theologians of hope stress the importance of apocalyptic for expressing confidence in the completion of the disclosures of God's triumph at the end of history. This may be only a question of the terms in which convictions are expressed rather than of their content, but in view of the importance of the distinction between eschatology and apocalyptic in the New Testament, and the fact that the distinction between present (or realized) and future eschatology is a good way of expressing the Christian hope, it seems better to abandon apocalyptic as a category no longer useful in Christian theology, especially since as inherited in the Christian tradition it has had some serious drawbacks. (1) It has laid too much claim to precise knowledge of the future in God's intentions, continually forecasting the date of the *parousia*, and not being willing enough to live by faith. (2) It has had a pessimistic view of history, assuming that things would get worse before Yahweh intervened to sort out the mess and vindicate his faithful. (3) It has not attached much importance in any case to the ongoing events in human history in view of the expected cataclysmic future. (4) Its hopes for an absolutely new future have been too discontinuous with the ongoing events in human history. (5) Believers have been too certain of their place in the new post-apocalyptic order, and too certain that it is an exclusive place. There is a hope for the 'nations' in the New Testament; and the more conscious we become of the plural nature of the world, and the greater the insight we attain into other religions and philosophies, the more we are coming to see a relation to Christ in them, even though they are unaware of or would deny it.

V

From the theology of hope has come the theology of liberation, whose provenance has been Latin America, even though its ingredients are all European. It has many merits. It takes seriously the injustice and oppression in the world about which traditional theologies have been far too complacent. It stresses the violence embedded in existing structures in which theology has been too ready to acquiesce. It sees that technological development can easily reinforce these injustices. It wants to rouse those on the margin of society to realize their own potentiality in envisaging social change and taking steps to bring it about; in doing so they will express love to their oppressors by liberating them from the alienating effects of their own oppression. It stresses that neutrality is impossible when considering social injustices; and that it is necessary to find the sufferings of others intolerable and be willing to forgo a clinging to personal innocence, and to bear the toils and conflicts needed to remove them. It calls for a quickening of imagination to envisage social goals which are more precise than an utopia and less so than a technically developed model (which it thinks will be too conservatively influenced by the present).

However, some cautions need to be expressed. (1) In practice it adopts without arguing for it a Marxist or neo-Marxist social, economic and political analysis. This seems to be considered self-evidently correct, but the assumption needs defence. It can hardly be a *theological* judgment that Marxism is the 'scientific' political and social analysis. Therefore it must be argued out in political and social terms. In the trivial sense that 'we are all Marxists now', in much the same way as we are all Darwinians or Freudians now, the assumption is justified. But in a more rigorous sense it is not. The Marxist theories all embody useful insights, but each one taken separately, and the whole lot taken together, are sufficiently defective as a basis for prediction (which is the point of claiming to be a scientific theory) to provide a very unsafe ground for action. This is not least because Marxism is clearly related to the nineteenth-century state of British and West European thought and society out of which it grew (aware of conditioning factors in all other thought except its own). To justify this verdict is not possible within this essay; all that can be done here is to draw attention to the assumption about Marxism so widely found in theologians of liberation. Gutierrez, for instance, writes of the need for a 'scientific' approach in order to discover laws proper to the political world which will give revolutionary activity effectiveness, and assumes he has found that approach in Marxism. To him it provides a science of the facts but lacks mobilizing force; whilst Christianity is a faith which nerves to action by providing an imaginative utopia of a society without class and liberated from all oppressors.

The Movement of Christians for Socialism, which met in Santiago in 1972 at the time of the UNCTAD Conference and not long before the overthrow of the Allende Government, said, 'Today an awareness is growing of a strategic alliance between Christian revolutionaries and Marxist revolutionaries in the liberation process' and refers to 'walking in common' towards 'a common global historical liberation process'. In the Philippines, Fr Luis Jalandoni, the son of a wealthy landed family, was captured in September 1972 after being on the run for a year with the New People's Army, the military wing of the Communist Party, in the struggle against President Marcos. He had been working for basic trade union rights for poor sugar workers against sugar planters with their own private armies, and had got nowhere. He became convinced that only armed struggle could avail and so he threw in his lot with the Marxists. I quote him rather than the better known Fr Camilo Torres. But there are many others. From these examples one can see why the Marxist analysis appeals, but that does not of itself mean that it is correct. We can also see why one might ally with Marxists for tactical reasons, not 'scientific' ones. However, it is these latter that theologies of liberation advance.

(2) There are strong messianic and utopian strains in these

theologies which need calling into question. The projecting of the pervasive New Testament language of the 'new' on to the political future leads in many of these theologies to an explicit emphasis on a messianic hope, held in what is described as the revolutionary present, for a qualitatively new future which will transfigure politics and involve a fundamental transformation of history. Rubem Alves, for instance, makes much of a distinction between humanist messianism (by which he means Marxism) and a Christian messianic humanism.[3] There is a frequent appeal to the saga of the exodus. Gutierrez says it points to a unity between the social-political and the redemptive dimensions of life which was fulfilled and deepened in Christ. There are not two histories, one sacred and one profane, but one history in which God acts in a way of which the exodus saga is the model.[4] This ignores the fact that there is a vital difference between the two Testaments at this point. In the Old Testament there is one kingdom which is both church and state. The theme of the Old Testament is the formation of a people of God which in some sense or other has an universal mission, but which is centred in the Jewish state in the various forms it took in the Old Testament period; that is why no attention is given to those who were driven out of their lands in order that the people of God might occupy it. In the New Testament there are two kingdoms. The people of God has been reconstituted; it has broken the bounds of the Jewish state and has become in principle universal. Christians now live in two kingdoms, two cities (Augustine), two realms (Luther), not one. In the kingdom of God the messianic role has been accomplished in the ministry of Jesus. It is quite illegitimate to transfer it to various movements in the kingdom(s) of the world. God's action in history (to use in passing a term which needs careful explication) is providential, not messianic; his rule in history is more hidden and history more ambiguous than biblical messianism would suggest. In spite of the exodus saga the people of God found themselves in exile; and revolutions can be counter-revolutionary! A strain in Zionism which holds still to the one kingdom view adds dangerous religious dimensions to an already strong nationalist fervour in Israel.

This messianism is one aspect of a tendency to move directly from biblical categories to the modern world in a way which is dangerously *simpliste*. It obscures the need to come to terms with empirical evidence *en route*, and leads to the absolutizing of current positions in political ethics. It moves too easily to and fro between biblical symbols and motives on the one hand and interpretations of current history and commitments to political programmes on the other. It is a legacy to some current political theology of biblical theology out of the Calvinist tradition of using scripture. An examination of Puritan preaching in the twelve months after the execution of Charles I shows innumerable sermons being preached on Psalm 149.8, which refers to 'binding their kings in chains and their nobles with links of iron', transferring the text to the current situation in a way which seems foolish now, but is being paralleled in much of the recent theologies of change. Much Black theology, for instance, thinks of Blacks as a 'chosen people' because they are oppressed, transferring the category from the Bible to where it does not apply, and adding a dangerously uncritical messianic overtone to a proper concern for social justice, a concern which would be even better if it showed more awareness of other oppressed groups of other colours and situations.

(3) Utopian strains are found in the theology of liberation which are closely related to messianic ones. The classical discussion of utopias in the last forty years has been that of Karl Mannheim. There is an interesting ambiguity in his book *Ideology and Utopia* at this point, arising from the fact that the different sections of the book were originally written in German at different times. The main thrust is a cool dissection of ideologies as the rationalizations of privileged social groups and classes, and of utopias as those of unprivileged classes. In effect to set them in a social context by the techniques of the sociology of knowledge is to remove some of their absolute character, when their purpose is in fact to evoke precisely that character for those who hold to them. Yet Mannheim also holds that utopias are necessary or men will not have the vision and drive to produce a more humane society, so that 'man would lose his ability to shape history and therewith his ability to understand it'.[5] So utopias are both in a sense deceitful and yet necessary. Reinhold Niebuhr came to a similar conclusion in his earlier writings which were more influenced by a Marxist analysis; at the end of his *Moral Man and Immoral Society*, he hoped that the workers would retain their illusionary dream of perfect justice long enough to overthrow the worst oppressions of the present. 'The illusion is dangerous because it encourages terrible fanaticisms. It must therefore be brought under the control of reason. One can only hope that reason will not destroy it before its work is done.'[6] The remark needs some qualification in any case as a political generalization, but the question for the Christian is, are Christian hopes of a kind already mentioned not enough, or do we need

misleading utopias as well to move us to forward-looking action?

Using the term in a different sense from Mannheim, Christians are often urged by theologians of liberation to develop ideologies for action; to grasp our environment with active systems of hope-filled meaning and to commit ourselves to the action they call for. The influence of the Marxist Ernst Bloch has been great at this point. His *Das Prinzip Hoffnung* (1959) has regrettably not been translated into English, for it lies behind a good deal of liberation theology. His challenge is to 'dream forward' as a cognitive act; to push beyond the 'objective possibilities' – that is, everything which can reasonably be expected or cannot be excluded by present evidence – to the 'real possibilities' yet to mature, since they will grow out of a new reality. Moltmann urges us not to be hamstrung in our hopes for a desirable future by the constriction of a calculable future based on extrapolations from the present.[7] The danger of utopianism in such exhortations needs guarding against. It leads to the despising of precise goals and the presentation of impossibilities as possibilities; it leads to the atmosphere of holy wars. If utopian movements are successful they are likely to lead to tyranny because of their claim to embody a greater perfection than the facts warrant, and if unsuccessful to ever greater repression by the powers that be. The refusal to pay attention to the evidence of the present quickly leads to anti-intellectualism and to stereotyped judgments. There is enough of both in the world without Christians adding to them. Yet in saying this I am conscious that Christians too often will not sustain the slog of continued political effort unless a crusading utopian mood can be worked up. It is one of their biggest failures. For politics, to quote an anonymous reviewer, is a realm 'in which men of muddled motives and mixed ambitions have to make choices that threaten their principles, strain their affections and wear out their nerves'.

In order to sustain the ongoing political task deep commitment and reserves of patience, perseverance, courage, wisdom, hope – not to speak of faith and love – are needed. Men and women know something of these in their own lives by virtue of their sheer humanity, and on the basis of these qualities numbers of them have served their fellows in the political sphere. Those who are Christians should be even more alert in this realm, for their faith can be a source of further strength to them. All the virtues just referred to have a deep light shed on them by Christ; indeed it is what we know of them already which enables us to see how much they are deepened by him. Christians have greater resources to draw on through the 'new creation' brought about by Christ, and in particular they are given a commitment to the basic equality and fellowship of all men in Christ, which in itself continually calls in question accepted institutions, and issues in a particular concern for the poor and disadvantaged. Furthermore, vision and imagination is needed in order to understand both other people and social and political situations; it is not just a matter of a technical mastery of the 'facts', indispensable as that is. A wisdom beyond that is needed to assess their significance and context, in short to understand a situation in depth. Also, it is necessary to create models to simplify the task of grasping with the mind a series of complex and varying phenomena. All this is true. But it is a long way from the call to ideologize or create utopias. It is vital to see things as they are to the best of our ability, making all allowances for conditioning factors, as the basis for seeing what is a realizable as well as a desirable future, in the direction of which we should try to move by the next steps which have to be taken. There are indeterminate possibilities for the future, but no utopia is on the way; moral ambiguities and precarious balances of power are a permanent human condition.

The utopian element in these theologies of social change is closely related to their preoccupation with the Marxist analysis. In Marxism two elements are curiously related. One is the claim to be a 'scientific' theory of social change, to which I have already referred; the other is its utopian horizon in its picture of the coming classless society. Related to these is the curious tension in it between the 'scientific' theories which purport to uncover the dialectical power struggles through which social change will inevitably proceed until the classless society is reached, and the view that men should create for themselves and seize revolutionary opportunities to push the process on. Many liberation theologies exhibit the same dual attitude. They accept too easily the Marxist claim to be scientific, and at the same time say that Christianity and Marxism are congenial because both drive us to take hold of our future and heighten our powers to do so. (They also add very truly that Christianity also includes the dead in its hope, whereas Marxism cannot.) However, Marxism is of great importance for Christians, who need to see it as an 'unwitting servant of Yahweh', like the Assyrians and Cyrus in the Old Testament.[8] There is every reason to take the Marxist-Christian dialogue seriously and to be ready for it whenever the chance occurs. The period between the publication of Pope John XXIII's encyclical *Pacem in Terris*, when it got seriously under way, and the Russian invasion of Czechoslovakia was brief. But sooner or later dialogue will be resumed. Christianity is seen already by some Marxists to be very different in principle from the spuriously other-worldly and individualistic forms of it which Marx and Engels encountered and presumed; and the break-up of monolithic Marxism is producing a community of questioning in many Marxist circles akin to that in Christian ones. When it comes, the Christians will have to try, with Pannenberg, to show the Marxists that human alienation requires a deeper cure than social change can provide. To put it in another way, Jesus liberated in his lifetime, liberates now, and will liberate in the future. The Christians must also show the Marxists that belief in the transcendent God does not cramp and restrain human possibilities but sustains and liberates them. They will be tempted in doing this tacitly to accept the Marxist claim to be a 'scientific' analysis of the facts of the present, and will therefore be in danger of continually mistaken tactics based on a defective over-all analysis. But to criticize Marxism as 'scientific' can only be done in the political, social and economic context in which the analysis is expressed. There is no direct route from the Bible to it. This is a position no different from that in which the Christian is placed in respect to secular disciplines in general, for instance both the natural and social sciences. He needs to pay attention to them, and it is good that theologians are now taking them seriously, but they must beware of being swept along by intellectual fashions (which occur in every intellectual discipline), without examining more carefully how well they are founded. The inadequacies of the Club of Rome report on 'The Limits to Growth' or *The Ecologist's* 'Blueprint for Survival', to take two examples, can only be realized by participation in the debate they have provoked; there is no direct route from the Bible to the matter.

VI

Little needs to be added on the theologies of revolution. The word does not necessarily imply physical force, but rapid, radical and discontinuous change. Nevertheless force often accompanies political revolutions. The theologies of revolution join in pointing out that established theologies have far too readily sanctified the *status quo*. The preservative action of God has been overstressed. Now, however, consideration of criteria for just wars in modern conditions has been extended to those for just revolutions. But in changing the emphasis to God's concern for the poor and oppressed, and his activity in overthrowing the mighty out of their seats and exalting the poor and weak, greatly inflated claims for revolutions have been made. It is said that they are parabolic signs of the transfiguration of politics, bearers of a righteousness not their own, God's instruments for exposing the falsehoods in established structures, always more likely to have truth on their side than established patterns. Lehmann holds that the emphasis on law and order is a vast distortion, and that freedom always has priority over order under God as justice has over law. Here one distortion has produced its opposite, and theology, instead of illuminating the tensions and ambiguities within which human life has to be lived, has given an uncritical sanction to one side of the human situation.

The truth in this is that to be radically concerned with persons and for the humanization of the structures in which persons live in is an important sense a revolutionary stance. It means that Christians cannot be content with existing structures (unless they have strong reasons to believe that no better is possible at the moment). It means that they need to work at theologies which have a built-in ability to cope with change, and which fortify them in the arduous task of making constructive use of the changes which in our world will be going on anyway. To think one can be a-political is in fact to be covertly *pro* the *status quo*. They need to bring love, joy and creativity to a world which is either too fearful of change or too cocksure about it, but not at the cost of falling a prey to a political innocence compounded of messianic and utopian illusions.

VII

Although all the elements of these various political theologies are European in origin, none of them has yet made much impact on the British scene, though to some extent they find a hearing among Christians of student age. Yet in a world where our policies affect others all over the globe, and where in the ecumenical movement great progress has been made in mutual understanding in the last half century, it is disturbing to find British theology and church life so insular. It is not that the British churches and British Christians give the impression of being particularly alert and active with respect to their own political responsibilities in the light of rapid social change. Quite the contrary. Yet to ask that they pay more attention to these theologies, not least out of a concern for what has seemed to so many Christians in the fourth world to speak to their condition, is not to ask that they be accepted without criticism.

Queries must be put against their easy acceptance of the Marxist analysis as 'scientific', and their tendency to dismiss all queries of it as reactionary; the danger of their biblicism and utopianism need pointing out. But in doing this we are in no way impugning particular actions and stances taken by Christians in situations quite different from ours, which we cannot fully appreciate from outside. Rather we deal with our own situation. We must show why the Marxist 'scientific' analysis does not fit it, but only as a step in wrestling with an economic and political analysis which does fit, and which throws light on goals for the next fifteen years or so which need to be worked for. This is a theme for another essay.

These political theologies have had a powerful effect in opening the eyes of every part of the ecumenical movement, not least the 'Faith and Order' aspect of it, to political tasks which cannot be shirked. British Christians need this stimulus and should be grateful for it. For the rest the New Testament present (or inaugurated) and future eschatological perspective, liberated from the 'time-bound' apocalyptic elements which are there associated with it, is the best basis for political theology. Reinhold Niebuhr expressed this in his own characteristic way in 1952 in *The Irony of American History:*

Nothing that is worth doing can be achieved in our lifetime, therefore we must be saved by hope. Nothing which is true or beautiful or good makes complete sense in any immediate context of history; therefore we must be saved by faith. Nothing we do, however virtuous, can be accomplished alone; therefore we must be saved by love. No virtuous act is quite as virtuous from the standpoint of our friend and foe as it is from our standpoint. Therefore we must be saved by the final form of love which is forgiveness.[9]

There is a slight overstatement here in the first sentence, where if 'ultimately' were inserted before 'worth doing' it would be less open to misunderstanding. Nevertheless this is a better theological horizon within which to work at a positive and forward-looking theology of social change, than that advanced in most of the political theologies of the last decade.

NOTES

1. Some of this essay was originally part of a public lecture given for the Board of the Faculty of Divinity in the University of Cambridge in November 1972, but it has been considerably rewritten and extended. The most convenient survey of the theologies discussed is to be found in *A Reader in Political Theology*, ed. Alistair Kee, SCM Press 1974. See also Paul Lehmann, *The Transfiguration of Politics*, SCM Press 1975.

Roman Empire was destroyed in the early years of the fifth century. Ancient history then ended and mediaeval history began. The second was reached at the turn of the fifteenth century when mediaeval history came to a close and modern history was born. The feudal culture was no more. Manor and serf gave way to the entrepreneur and the wage-labourer. Christendom as a theocratic political unity collapsed before the forces of nationalism to give the system of sovereign nation-states. Scholasticism as the pattern of correct thinking gave place to scientific method and historical study of origins as the correct methods for discovering truth.

All these victories were successes of a new social class who demanded, fought for and won a substantial control in the affairs of state. In achieving power they tore down all the fences based on the identification of privilege with the ownership of land as they successfully inserted contract in the place of status as the juridical foundation of society. When they had finished, no longer were the land-owner, the ecclesiastic and the knight-errant symbols of social prestige. The banker and the merchant, later to be joined by the manufacturer, took their places. The members of this new class soon worked out its equivalent to the code of chivalry and system of canon law that had provided mediaeval society with its standards of value and its social *mores*. Whereas the feudal system of mutual dependence based upon personal loyalty harmonized with the mediaeval system of salvation by sacraments controlled by the ecclesiastical hierarchy, the merchants relied on written documents which, like the Bible, could be understood by all men. Like their mediaeval ancestors they, too, believed that 'Where your treasure is, there shall your heart be also.' But their treasures lay in a different place, and so they evolved a code of conduct to govern economic affairs which sharply reversed long-established Christian teaching about the danger of money-making. Indeed, their entire ethical system was based upon the conviction that the life of business enterprise was not as spiritually hazardous as the mediaevalists had taught. Instead, they regarded it as the most appropriate field of operation for the saved soul, and the idea of credit in the bank available for the merchant of sound commercial standing replaced the mediaeval notion of stored merit in heaven under the control of the ecclesiastical hierarchy on earth. In short, the leaders of the commercial middle classes were Protestants.

However, just as ancient history and mediaeval history came to an end, so too, we argued, 'modern' history has reached its finale. All the differing realms of human thoughts and activity, politics, economics, and education were being basically transformed. We pointed out that the recent war had simply hastened a process already begun and had thereby thrown into a clearer relief what was already to be seen by those who, following Niebuhr, Tillich and Berdyaev, could recognize the signs of the times. In industry and commerce, free enterprise was giving way to an ever-increasing measure of economic planning. Even in the USA, where no one any longer believed in the just price of the mediaeval canonists, a secularized equivalent to it had been achieved in the idea of a 'floor' for prices in time of depression and a 'ceiling' for them in time of war. In domestic politics, whether Republican or Democrat, all had come to believe in the 'welfare state'.

All this we saw, but in seeing it as the end of Protestantism we did not go far enough. What we perceived as having come to an *end* was what had *begun* at the end of the Middle Ages. What we should have gone on to do was to give attention to the whole Christian period itself, when by 'Christian period' I am referring to what began with Constantine.

When the Christian church expanded beyond Asia Minor and carried its message to the furthest corners of the Roman empire, it soon had to face a simple but inescapable issue that was a matter of life or death. Its parent, Judaism, had been able to arrive at a concordat with the authorities of the empire whereby the Jews were unmolested since their religious code allowed them to pray *for* the emperor even if it did not allow them to pray *to* him. The imperial authorities accepted this compromise with supercilious tolerance: the Jews were not politically a threat to the Roman régime, whereas the Christian church was rapidly becoming dangerous since the Christian church was universal in a sense in which the Jewish fellowship did not claim to be. To the Roman magistrate there was no problem so long as the Christian would regard his saviour as one god among others. The deities of Persia had been acclimatized to the atmosphere of Roman temples. Why not this Jesus whom Christians, if not Jews, called the Christ? But the early church from the first was willing to seal its rejection of this simple solution with the blood of its martyrs. *If they were to continue to be Christians* as distinct from devotees of some man-made faith, this was no solution. In terms of our modern English vocabulary, the struggle was not simply 'religious'. It was political in the sense in which the modern Communist or the ancient Greeks would use the word 'political'. For the imperial authorities salvation lay in membership of the community whose geographical bounds were fixed by the lines of the furthest Roman legions. But the Christian believed not in *pax Romana*, limited in space and time, but in the kingdom of God which had *no* frontiers. The issue between church and empire was not that, while they both believed that the latter was eternal and the former was of the earth, they could not agree on the relation between them. In other words, it was not a question of what should be rendered to God and what rendered to Caesar; although that was how the Christians as distinct from the civil authorities sometimes tried to construe the matter. *Pax romana* was eternal according to the imperial voice. It was precisely this conviction that the Christian church refuted.

The quarrel therefore was about the question: Where had the eternal irrupted into time? The Christian reply was clear and unequivocal: in the risen Lord. He was the true *kyrios* and the real Caesar just as the true community was the Christian *ekklesia* and not the Roman empire. By AD 300 the Christians had virtually conquered. As T.R. Glover long ago used to say: 'They had out-lived, out-thought, and out-died the pagans.' It was then that Diocletian, seeing the issue 'Caesar or Christ' with overwhelming clarity, began the terrible persecutions of the years 303 and 304. But it was too late. The Christian church was too well established, particularly in the cities and among army officers and leading citizens. As Professor E.R. Hardy of the Episcopal Seminary in New Haven used to say: 'What was the effect on gods or men when half the soldiers in the guard of honour at a state sacrifice protectively crossed themselves at the most solemn moment?'

Emperor-worship had never been to the sophisticated Roman citizen what we naive and literal-minded Westerners conceive it to be, *viz.*, the worship of a man. It was much more like the Nazis' worship of Hitler or the Soviet adulation of Stalin as in each case embodying a whole way of life and thought. Although it was not so much the emperor as a man but rather his 'genius' that was adored, yet the path of adoration was not an easy one when twenty-five emperors ruled in eighty years and only four died in their beds! Diocletian soon decided that discretion was the better part of valour and he voluntarily retired in 305. It took eighteen years before the resulting dynastic struggle was finally resolved for Constantine the Great to become the sole ruler of the Roman world.

The Christian church under Constantine[2] had now to face a real issue and one for which its bishops and thinkers were hardly prepared: 'Was the Christian church to witness to the work of God in the world by staying aloof from the world, or was its task to try to redeem the world by entering it?' They took the latter decision. Subsequent history has been what it is just because they did so.

The whole of the subsequent history of Europe and its cultural offshoots in North and South America and Australasia has been based on this decision of Constantine and those who followed him. St Augustine of Hippo grappled with its tremendous theological and political implications in his *The City of God*. The monastic movement tried to purify the life of a church grown worldly, by withdrawing from the world. Luther and Calvin tried to do the same by staying in it. So, too, did the Baptists, Congregationalists and other rebels against classical Protestantism. And this was true all through the succeeding centuries when liberal Protestantism conquered the more traditional modes of theological thought. In short, throughout all the tattered pages of church history from Constantine on to and beyond the Pilgrim Fathers, the Christian faith was conceived of as the true *religion* of society in the original sense of the term: that which binds a community together.

But this is no longer true. To the sociologist the most revealing index is what has happened to the celebration of Christmas, for the declining significance of a holiday in its original sense is a crucial sign that a culture has lost its coherence. As the *New York Times* literary critic, Anatole Broyard, recently pointed out, 'the celebration of holidays is an index of conviviality, from the Latin *convivium*, "a living together". While Christmas literally drives us into one another's arms at department store counters, this could hardly be called convivial.'[3]

That is why the word 'theology' has such an odd ring on the campus of a contemporary university, for an intellectual system like 'theology' or 'science' is not just a set of ideas but a way of looking at life which either is or is not operative in the minds and souls of men and women in a particular society. Let me illustrate my thesis by considering any discussion about students, curriculum and the like at a Senate meeting in a British (or so far as that goes, French, Swedish or American) university.

If the professor of political science gets up to speak and points out that the issue in question is one which should be considered 'democratically', his colleagues, by and large, will listen with both interest and a sense of relevance. If the professor of philosophy then gets up to make his contribution and suggests that the issue is one which should be seen in terms of the 'philosophical' issues involved, his colleagues will still listen with a sense of relevance, even if their

interest tends to wane. The same would be true if the professor of
mathematical statistics suggests that the 'statistical' evidence for
certain conclusions presented by the students should be more
rigorously examined. Interest might be restored and a sense of the
relevant still maintained if the professor of psychiatry speaks from
the standpoint of the 'emotional' tangles which might emerge in the
lives of the affected students. Yet we can be sure that if the professor
of theology were unwise enough to rise and suggest that the
problem should be considered in its theological perspective, his
enemies would be annoyed and his friends would be perplexed.
They would all agree that he was introducing that which, even if it
is intelligible, is irrelevant to the ongoing life and thought of a
faculty meeting. Perspectives of the kind which he is urging might
be relevant, it would be thought, in discussions in the Faculty of
Divinity, but certainly they are hardly relevant, so it would be
taken for granted, in the discussion of any question elsewhere in the
university.

There was an equally significant illustration, a few years ago, at
one of America's leading institutions of higher learning, Princeton
University, of the thesis which I am now making. The academic
authorities in question initiated a new approach to the problems of
human relations whereby there would be created that which would
be the expression of an integrated study rather than the specialized
studies of the particularized social sciences. This desirable end was
to be achieved by a 'Council on Human Relations' which would
seek 'the fundamental principles in this field'. The President of
Princeton described this new venture in the following terms:

... the new council would bring together faculty members in history, politics,
economics, sociology, anthropology and social psychology. All will be concerned
with the study of human resources, human relations and human organization.
Moreover, synthesis will be the dominating theme of these studies since the
tensions in human relations in the world today no longer permit the slow
accumulation of bits and pieces of research in the various specialized branches of
social science. The findings of social psychology must be put to work immediately
in political science, and sociology must help enlighten economic analysis.

What is quite clear from such a statement is that there is no point
at which 'theology' is construed to have any relevance in the
intellectual consideration, *even when synoptically undertaken*, of the
relations between human beings and their behaviour.

As the distinguished English educator and historian, M.V.C.
Jeffreys, pointed out twenty years ago,[4] 'it is impossible to
introduce any specifically religious conceptions such as sin or
salvation into a modern discussion about education without

producing the sort of impression that one would create by going out to dinner clad in a bear skin instead of a dinner jacket.' Similarly, in our departments of classical languages the study of Hebrew has no status. I have in mind here the reply by one of America's most distinguished classical scholars to one of his students who had suggested that he should study Hebrew: 'You have no need to study Hebrew: that's in religion.' The odd fact is that the student in question wanted to study seriously the emergence of the Latin alphabet from the Greek alphabet. In conversation I had pointed out that he should look into the origin and evolution of the Greek alphabet, too, from the Arabic mainland where the Phoenicians had changed in the late second millennium BC from syllabic writing to a primitive alphabet. I had shown to him the appropriate diagrams in W.F. Albright's and Frank Cross's work, and that is why he had seen the importance of a knowledge of a Semitic language. Hence his perfectly logical suggestion to his professor only to be met by the ignorant reply, 'Hebrew is in religion.'

The professor could equally have had in his mind the word theology, for the words were interchangeable. In his circle of intellectual acquaintances the words meant the same, either at worst words of abuse or at best interchangeable terms. Yet no less a figure than Erasmus could regret to the end of his days that, as he pointed out in one of his letters to Colet, he was too old after his years in Oxford to learn Hebrew when he got to Paris. Here I can only explain what has happened by saying that even in the minds of our professors of classics, the Renaissance has been conquered by the Enlightenment, so aptly described by the Austrian epigrapher and linguist, Ernst Dobhofer, as the 'tireless search for knowledge and truth, allied to an uncritical contempt for everything which had for so long been considered the sole refuge of this truth'.

Thus we arrive at a tragic conclusion. Theology, which, whatever else it may be, certainly involves a consideration of man, his place in the universe and his relation with his fellows, in terms of his ultimate loyalties and ultimate principles of interpretation, is construed as being irrelevant to the intellectual purposes of the modern mind.

Yet 'theological' issues are not irrelevant in the perplexity which is our modern situation in art, the stage, politics and education alike. These issues are simply not recognized as such.

In my own experience over the last ten years this fact has vividly been brought home to me by four assignments with agencies of the American government. In each case I had been asked to help in the solution of a burning social problem and each was of such a character that for its solution the use of scientific knowledge by itself was not enough, but the application of this knowledge to the social situation involved humanistic insights before a solution could even be dimly seen.

I have used the word 'humanistic' just now for want of a better word, because with rare exceptions the scientists and civil servants with whom I worked would have been scandalized if I or anyone else had used the word 'theological'. Yet the issues which had been raised could only be adequately described by such a term as is clear from an examination of what went on in the four ventures.

Financed by the Office of Education of the US Government, the first of these assignments examined how we can *understand* what is happening to our universities. For years research in higher education had been a commonplace activity receiving substantial financial support from the private Foundations and the American government. Yet this research had been assumed to begin and end with the social sciences. I was invited (oddly enough as a sociologist) to act as chairman of a group of scientists and scholars in other fields which would raise deeper issues, since so much research in education had been largely sterile in producing improvements upon the educational scene commensurate with the sums of money which were being spent. We soon found out that our task was nothing less than raising the question of whether a 'humanistic' idea, like a sense of the tragic, might not be as useful in understanding our universities as is a sense of the metrical. The context of my activity was the Regional Education Laboratory for Higher Education of the Carolinas and Virginia, now the National Laboratory for Higher Education.

The second assignment was the result of an invitation to serve for a year as full-time consultant on the humanities as a member of the National Goals Research Staff of the White House. In addition to the contribution of civil servants from the widest reaches of the Washington governmental spectrum, together with a social psychologist from Harvard University and an economist from New York University, it was decided that the 'scientific' efforts should be complemented by the hopeful help of someone who, as the nation looked towards the coming bicentenary of its foundation, would stand for a humanistic dimension of life.

The third assignment was that of helping to deal with the problem of the increasing pressure of population growth in the developing countries of the world. Here again research had been largely the monopoly of the social sciences and the biomedical sciences, yet it was obvious to the simplest mind that the size of a family and therefore the overall size of the population of a country or a continent was the result of the fact that human beings, husbands and wives, made certain decisions, and it was not obvious that an understanding of these decisions was exhausted in what the sciences could say statistically or psychoanalytically about them. The locus of my activity here was the Carolina Population Center of the University of North Carolina at Chapel Hill and my activities, financed by the American State Department, took me to various African and Asian countries.

For the fourth assignment – for which I received the oddest title of all – I was attached as the 'sociologist-moralist' to a team of America's leading authorities on renal disease. There were five surgeons who specialized in kidney transplantation and five physicians who specialized in treatment using the artificial kidney. The Bureau of the Budget of the US Treasury had set up this team, supplemented by a lawyer, a psychiatrist, an economist, a hospital administrator and myself, to produce a report which would help the Treasury to deal with the wide ramifications of what had become the extremely expensive but successful methods of dealing with a malady which up to then so often had fatally afflicted men and women as they became productive citizens and parents of children. The problems were and are complex beyond all words. For example, how are a surgeon and his colleagues to decide which, to quote an actual case we were confronted with, of two women should receive a kidney available for transplantation when it is virtually a complete 'tissue-match' for an ailing prostitute but just less so for an ailing mother of four small children? The verdict of 'science' is of course the prostitute, but what is the verdict of ethics and social responsibility? And if it is the mother, what then does one do or say to the unfortunate one? Whichever decision the surgeons make is the wrong one. The issue has moved beyond 'ethics' as it had moved beyond 'science'. The question is no longer what is the 'right' thing to do but rather an even more perplexing one: How are we to make sense of the mystery of human existence when there is no good way out, only a tragic burden to be borne? That 'ethics' is meaningless without 'theology' is a lesson which echoes – alas only rarely being recognized as such – a million times a day in our sick rooms, our hospitals and our nursing homes.

The common lesson to me from these experiences in such disparate realms, from the plight of higher education to the

treatment of renal disease, is that at no time in the history of
Western civilization has a sense of theological relevance been so
widely even if unconsciously spread, yet at no time has the
relevance of the whole Christian theological scheme been dismissed
in such a cavalier fashion. What is true of 'theology' is just as true of
'religion', however it may be described. Yet the fact is that St Paul
would say of us, as he said of the Athenians in the middle of the
Areopagus, 'I perceive that in every way you are very religious.'

The signs he saw then were of the worship of many gods and he
would see these signs today, for we live in the West where
Christianity, sociologically speaking, has become one religion
among many others. That is why in Britain, in the USA and in
continental Europe the study and research in the sociology of
religion has gone ahead by leaps and bounds. But it is no longer the
traditional sociology of the Christian churches or the sociology of
Protestantism or Roman Catholicism. These studies are still
vigorously pursued, but there is even more activity in the analysis of
the many religious movements *outside* the churches that we now see
on every hand.

What is even more significant is that sociologists are turning
their attention to what are religious movements even when they are
not so recognized. This is true, argues a distinguished American
sociologist, Russell R. Dynes, of sociology itself in his recent
penetrating article, 'Sociology as a Religious Movement'.[5]

Thus we have now moved to 'comparative religion', to use the
term literally since religions are being 'compared'. Professor Dynes
is 'comparing' one movement of religious faith with another such
movement, but it is 'comparative religion' with a difference from
the conventional discipline of that name in a Faculty of Theology.
The 'older' comparative religion is primarily the expression of the
literary and linguistic interests of 'the humanities'. What is most
important in its study of Islam, Hinduism, Buddhism and the other
religions of the world is the historical investigations of their origins
together with textual studies of the systems of thought embodied in
their sacred scriptures. It is this historical aspect which has
provided (as at the University of Leiden in the Netherlands and at
the University of Chicago in America) an alternative to the label of
'comparative religion' in the shape of the phrase 'the history of
religions'. Oddly enough, both phrases seem to exclude, in the
minds of those who normally use them, the study of Judaism and
Christianity. Yet it is also true to say that this humanistic pattern
followed in the study of comparative religion shows much of its

Christian antecedents in its methods of study, from the time of
Renaissance scholars such as Erasmus to the fully orbed critical
studies of the Bible which were well under way by the end of the
eighteenth century. The newer approach, which has been dubbed
the 'new comparative religion', is no less interested in the scriptures
and in the theologies of the religions being studied. But it wishes to
go a stage further. It wishes to study the fashion in which these
religions actually function in the different cultures in the world
where they are now practised. It is in this sense that 'the new
comparative religion' finds its practitioners from 'the social
sciences' more often than it does in 'the humanities'.

There is a further distinguishing feature in this newer approach.
It sees what is happening today, not only in Africa and in Asia but
in Europe, both East and West, as in the Americas and Australasia,
as legitimate parts of the field which the discipline of the
comparative study of religion seeks to study. In modern Western
society various religious patterns from the religions in the ancient
Near East, from Africa and from Asia, repeatedly recur. The
passionate devotion of the West to the nation is much nearer to
Shintoism than it is to Christianity, whilst Communism in many of
its forms is a return to a deification of the political community
which appeared again and again in the early empires of the ancient
Near East. Similarly, the cult of adjustment of some schools of
psychology sounds like Taoism, whilst the modern funeral parlour
of contemporary America caters for something in modern man
which the ancient Egyptian religions understood well; the cult of
lucky charms and astrology in British newspapers is illustrative of
animism; the modern worship of sex as the road to salvation is a
reflection of what many religions of the world have tried to deal
with in more conscious terms in (miscalled) temple prostitution;
and the peace of mind cults are much nearer to Buddhism and
Hinduism than they are to Judaism or Christianity.

Thus to the contemporary sociologist of religion the political
clash between Communism and the democratic way of life or the
struggle on the campus of an American university or what goes on
in the mind of a lady in a beauty parlour reading an astrological
column is just as relevant for him as a practitioner of the new
comparative religion as what is happening in the bazaars of
Baghdad, the plains of India or the jungles of Burma. He finds, too,
that theological categories of thought such as idolatry, syncretism
and polytheism provide him with the most illuminating mode of
interpreting religion as he finds it in the Western world.

But the Christian apologist cannot stop there, for what are these reversions to earlier and more distant religions but the results of genuine attempts to deal constructively with the ultimate problems of human existence in the light of an affirmation – however halting – of the final positive meaning of such existence?

It is at this point that the apologist will vigorously part company from 'comparative religion' as it initially emerged on the scene a century or so ago, in its claim that by following the natural sciences it could be 'impartial', 'neutral', 'objective' and the like. And this will be true even when he has taken into account the fashion in which the *study of religion* as distinct from *theology* appeared in Western thought.

For many centuries – as is still the case in very wide circles – prior to the emergence of modern modes of scientific thinking, Western thought had dealt with 'religion' primarily in terms of the acceptance or rejection of certain 'doctrines'. These were to be understood as beliefs which could be put in the form of propositions, for example, 'Jesus Christ is the Son of God'. In the light of such a view of the matter, Christianity was regarded as the true religion and the other religions of the world were viewed, at worst as devices of the devil, or at best as examples of human error. The shattering effects of the breakdown of Christendom in the sixteenth century precipitated a radically different temper of mind when a new set of questions about God, man and his place in the universe was being asked. Religion and its place in human life began to be investigated.

It was in England that the most revolutionary step at this point was taken by Lord Herbert of Cherbury. His *De religione gentilium* was not published until twenty-five years after his death in 1638, but he has the best claim to be regarded as the first thinker who sought to undertake the study of religion itself as a 'natural' phenomenon. But it was natural in the older sense of the term, not in the sense in which today we talk about the 'natural' sciences but in the sense that 'dogs delight to bark and bite, for 'tis their nature to'. For Lord Herbert, religion, however finally to be understood, is a distinguishing feature of man wherever he is to be found as a human being.

During the following century or so, progress along this line of thought, even though the Renaissance had revived interest in classical thought and in pre-Christian mythologies, was slow. The Reformation tradition did not help, for it was primarily a movement *within* Christendom. Renaissance and Reformation alike quickened up biblical study enormously by stressing the need for expert knowledge in the languages used by the original authors of the Old and New Testaments. Thereby the discipline of theology was transformed; but it did little for the study of religion in general or of the non-Christian religions of the world in particular. Europe knew less in the sixteenth century about its religious rivals than it did in the thirteenth century. It is illuminating to remember at this point that as late as two hundred years after the death of Martin Luther there were fewer than two hundred Protestant missionaries operating in the whole of the world. The real push came from the growth of trade and commerce which was accelerated by – as it had, in turn, inspired – the exploration of the world by Portuguese, Spanish and then by British, French and Dutch sailors.

The most influential development of Herbert's line of thought subsequently came with the Deists, the school of thought which furnished the basic intellectual patterns for the American founding fathers; in particular I have in mind Thomas Jefferson. His essential purpose at the point of our concern here was to discover, under the name of 'natural religion', the common residuum in *all* religions, Christian or non-Christian. But these approaches to the matter were soon left behind in the nineteenth century as new disciplines, inspired by Darwin's revolution in thought and knowledge, emerged. Anthropology and sociology, soon to be followed by ethnology, came prominently on the academic scene as attempts to study 'scientifically' the religions of the world. It was in this context that 'comparative religion' appeared. The name is, grammatically speaking, inept. It should be 'the comparative study of religions'. But there were more serious shortcomings than grammatical ones. Almost from its origins the approach was shot through and through with two deficiences.

The first of these we have already seen. What I have called 'the old comparative religion' neglected the earlier insight of Lord Herbert and the Deists who at this point had followed him. They had rightly taken for granted that the range of study involved men and religious experience wherever man was to be found, East or West. However, during the last century, as we have seen, there came to be rivetted in the minds of those academically responsible for this field of study the notion that the significant data in this realm are to be obtained from the exotic East, from the monasteries of Tibet, or the jungles of Africa, or the river basins of China. Hence they did not perceive that 'religion' *anywhere* is equally relevant. Hence, as we have seen, the idea of the 'new comparative religion' as an attempt to correct this deficiency about the geographical range of fact to be studied. Let me expand on this point by noticing the revealing use of this fresh approach as it is furnished by those who have applied it to the university scene itself. I think, for example, of Robert Hamill of Boston University, a theologian, in his *Gods of the Campus*, or of Chad Walsh of Beloit College, a literary critic, in his *Campus Gods on Trial*, or of Andrew M. Greeley of the University of Chicago, a sociologist, in 'There's a New-Time Religion on the Campus'.[6] Of course many significant differences have emerged among these writers and others as, starting with the new premise indicated, they go their different ways. Yet, whether they are with Trueblood, a philosopher, or with Hamill, a theologian, or with Walsh, a literary critic, or with Greeley, a sociologist, each of them is concerned – at least to begin with – with the function of religion in human life rather than with the truth of the particular doctrines of a religion.

From Britain I will seek an illustration a long way from university life. One significant social movement which seemed to demand 'religious' language for its description and interpretation is that of the Beatles and their successors. A cautious-minded sometime professor of the philosophy of religion at Oxford, the late Bishop Ian Ramsey (whose reputation significantly enough is based upon the application of linguistic analysis to religious phenomena), in a speech to the Modern Churchmen's Conference a few years ago analysed the 'unexpected significance in the girl who screamed at the Beatles because (she said) they seemed so much bigger than herself'. Here, he concluded, was a 'cosmic disclosure . . . !'[7]

A similar personal testimony about the Beatles appeared in the correspondence columns of the *New York Times*[8] from a teenager, Lynn Pollack, who vigorously replied to an article, 'Why the Girls Scream, Weep, Flip', which had criticized the behaviour of Beatles fans. She wrote, in her letter of protest to the editor about Mr Dempsey's article,

I'm not suggesting that the Beatles have outstanding talent, and they certainly aren't sexy by any stretch of the imagination. I don't know why girls scream and go into mass hysteria, although Mr Dempsey seems to have it all figured out. All I know is, when I see the Beatles on television, they make me feel happy, enthused, just plain good.

Miss Pollack here is surely echoing William James's well-known words:

To be converted, to be regenerated, to receive grace, to experience religion, to gain assurance, are so many phrases which denote the process, gradual or sudden, by which a self hitherto divided, and consciously wrong, inferior, and unhappy, becomes unified and consciously right, superior, and happy, in consequence of its firmer hold upon religious realities.[9]

But the most weighty contribution to this new turn in thought has come from those who seek to understand the emergence of modern 'political' movements like Communism or nationalism. R.H.S. Crossman and Arthur Koestler significantly used the phrase, *The God That Failed*, twenty or more years ago as the title for their widely-read symposium[10] of such authors as the American novelist Richard Wright or the French literary critic, André Gide, or the English poet, Stephen Spender. Each of these writers, whether he had been a party member or simply a sympathetic 'fellow-traveller', came to the conclusion that the most adequate categories in which he could interpret his experience – conversion, loss of faith, and the like – were drawn from theology and religion.

And this is happening, too, in the Soviet Union. Thus, the brilliant young Communist novelist, Yevgeny Yevtushenko, in his *A Precocious Autobiography*,[11] seeking to defend his 'ideals' against those who argue that the Soviet régime is corrupt, does so in the following terms:

You may say: 'But doesn't it occur to you that Communism itself may be a false ideal?'

If the reader believes in God I will ask him: 'Can you equate the substance of the Christian religion with the swindlers who used to make a handsome profit by selling indulgences, with the Inquisitors, the priests who got rich at their parishioners' expense, or parishioners who pray piously in church and lie and cheat outside its walls?'

Neither can I, a believing Communist, equate the essence of my religion with the crooks who climb on its bandwagon, with its inquisitors, its crafty, avaricious priests, or its double-dealing, two-faced parishioners.

And even in America where the word *religion* is a 'good' word and *Communism* is a 'bad' word, the members of the younger generation of political scientists are finding themselves obliged to interpret Marxism and Communism in 'theological' terms. Thus Robert V. Daniels, a historian of the University of Vermont, after a careful study of Communism as a political creed, as a philosophical system and as an economic order, finally concludes by devoting the closing chapter of his *The Nature of Communism*[12] to 'Communism as a Faith'. Similarly, Robert C. Tucker, a political scientist of Princeton University, in his *Philosophy and Myth in Karl Marx*,[13] points out that contemporary literature on Marxism in the West is full of statements that would have bewildered the earlier generation of Marxist scholars. We now frequently read, says Tucker, that

Marxism is a religion of the age of industrialism, and he concludes
that the search for an understanding of the deeper springs of this
world-view increasingly becomes a search for its moral or religious
meaning.

The second deficiency in the traditional comparative religion
approach which the sociologist of religion must record in working
out the significance of this line of analysis for the apologist is of a
different kind. The first shortcoming was a shortcoming about what
would be studied. The second shortcoming was about how it
should be studied. The name 'comparative religion', so easily used,
implies that the scholar is primarily concerned with *comparing* one
religion with another. What was not seen was that the scholar is
arranging the religions in a hierarchical scale from 'lower' to
'higher' religions according to their ethical content and truth-value.
But to do this is to imply that one has a criterion, a standard of
reference by which one is able to evaluate and compare. Where
does this come from? On what grounds is it held to be the true
criterion? This kind of crucial question was ignored by these
thinkers on the ground that since they were being 'scientific' and
not 'theological' thinkers, they were neutral and objective
observers. Thus they left out of account the fact that their
approach, their emphasis, their criteria and their selection of facts
were determined by their ultimate attitude towards the world and
life, their *Weltanschauung*. They did not realize with the Oxford
anthropologist, Godfrey Lienhardt, that 'each general theory of
religion is thus, in a way, a substitute for any particular religion, an
alternative way of giving an account of those situations which
different tribal religions give accounts of'.[14] To put the same point
in another way, they were too much the children of the nineteenth-
century view of the distinction between science and philosophy. At
this point A.N. Whitehead's vivid language of nearly fifty years ago
is still apposite:

> The old foundations of scientific thought are becoming unintelligible. Time,
> space, matter, material, ether, electricity, mechanism, organism, configuration,
> structure, pattern, function, all require reinterpretation. What is the sense of
> talking about a mechanical explanation when you do not know what you mean by
> mechanics?[15]

Indeed the situation in science is more serious than when
Whitehead wrote. It is the whole scientific venture whose future is
at stake. Students with the intellectual calibre to become Fellows of
the Royal Society are not as prone today to take their 'A' levels in
physics, chemistry and mathematics, for like their fellows on the

other side of the Atlantic they question the worthwhileness of a scientific career. This is a problem which already has come to perplex in America the leaders of the National Science Foundation. Similarly in England it is reflected in the issues raised by an eminent chemist, Sir Frederick Dainton (just to mention one example), in his Fawley Foundation lecture three years ago at the University of Southampton, *Science: Salvation or Damnation*. His use of theological language to describe the situation in science is significant. The old issue of science versus religion is about as relevant on the contemporary intellectual scene as is the phlogiston theory in a chemistry laboratory today. Here again the task of the Christian apologist is one needing complete re-orientation.

The 'God is dead' movement may have lost its public acclaim, but the issues it raised, like the attraction of Eastern mysticism for the Liverpool Beatles or Hollywood movie stars, force us to ask for theology in crisis questions similar to those which Whitehead had in mind. We can paraphrase his sentences and say that God, man, salvation, the church, peace, democracy 'all require interpretation'.

The reason why both the scientific establishment and the Christian establishment in the West are in the same plight is a question to which the Christian apologist must give attention in the light of the consideration that there are three major religious traditions which have appeared in the world since man became 'civilized' and these three traditions radically differ in their interpretations of man's attitude towards the natural order. There is first the monotheistic tradition of which Judaism, Christianity, and Islam are illustrations. There is next Hinduism· and its offshoot, Buddhism, as instances of the second major religious tradition, for which, as distinct from the monotheistic tradition where man's highest good in a real world of space and time is to echo in his life the goodness of a Creator God, the world is to be transcended by man in mystic union with that which is beyond all else. The third tradition in classical religion is the one which differs as much from either the tradition of Hindu immanentism or the threefold monotheistic tradition, as each of these in their turn differs from the other. I refer to the Chinese religious tradition, where the keynote thought is that of the golden mean, as it manifested itself in its own form on the mainland of China and as it subsequently spread to Japan and Korea.

Irrespective of how in Old Testament thought or New Testament thought or Koranic thought these scriptures present the matter, the theistic tradition in actual fact has taught that nature is to be conquered and utilized for man's purposes; whereas the Hindu tradition has taught that nature should be negated and transcended; while in Chinese tradition man should neither masterfully seek to conquer nature for his own purposes as in the West nor seek, as in India, to transcend it in a mystical vision of that which lies beyond nature; instead man should seek to live in harmony with nature, neither conquering it nor ignoring it but contemplating it in self-confident awe and joy. Well may contemporary Chinese Communism attack Confucianism as Mao Tse-tung and his followers seek to subject nature to technological ends and exploitation.

NOTES

1. W.R. Inge, *The Idea of Progress*, Clarendon Press 1920; Reinhold Niebuhr, *Reflections on the End of an Era*, Scribner 1934; Paul Tillich, *The Religious Situation*, Eng. trs., 1932 (reissued Meridian Books 1956); Nicolas Berdyaev, *The End of Our Time*, Eng. trs., Sheed and Ward 1933.

2. It is conventional among Protestants, especially in the USA, to make Constantine the chief scapegoat for all the subsequent failures of the Christian church, but in point of fact he and his bishops simply acted on a theory that even today we still unconsciously believe when we try, for example, to influence the social and economic order.

3. *New York Times*, 9 December 1974.

4. M.V.C. Jeffreys, *Education – Christian or Pagan*, University of London Press 1946.

5. Russell R. Dynes, 'Sociology as a Religious Movement', *The American Sociologist* 9, 1974, pp. 169ff.

6. Robert Hamill, *Gods of the Campus*, Abingdon Press 1949; Chad Walsh, *Campus Gods on Trial*, rev. ed., Macmillan, New York, 1962; Andrew M. Greeley, 'There's a New-Time Religion on the Campus', *New York Times Magazine*, 1 June 1969.

7. I.T. Ramsey, 'Towards the Relevant in Theological Language', *Modern Churchman*, New Series VIII, 1964, p. 55.

8. *New York Times*, 15 March 1964.

9. William James, *The Varieties of Religious Experience*, Longmans, Green and Co. 1902, p. 189.

10. *The God that Failed*, ed. R.H.S. Crossman, Hamish Hamilton 1950.

11. Yevgeny Yevtushenko, *A Precocious Autobiography*, Eng. trs., Harvill Press, 1963, pp. 41-3.

12. R.V. Daniels, *The Nature of Communism*, Random House, New York, 1962.

13. R.C. Tucker, *Philosophy and Myth in Karl Marx*, Cambridge University Press 1961, pp. 13f., 25f.

14. Godfrey Lienhardt, 'Religion', in *Man, Culture and Society*, ed. Harry L. Shapiro, Oxford University Press, New York, 1956, p. 320.

15. A.N. Whitehead, *Science and the Modern World*, Cambridge University Press 1927, p. 21.

~ 11 ~

Higher Education in the Post-Robbins Era

ROY NIBLETT

The Robbins Report on Higher Education[1] was presented to Parliament in October 1963, publication of the twelve additional volumes of evidence and statistical data being completed within a further year. The whole represents – it still does – the most massive attempt by a single nation, through an officially appointed committee, to consider how its higher education system should be planned and should develop. The report, with its supporting background of material, was quickly recognized as a document of weight and authority, its recommendations as enlightened and far-sighted.

Yet now the Robbins Report seems to speak to us, however lucidly, from a different world. Some of its most imaginative proposals are, if remembered at all, regarded as biased and elitist, 'university minded' in a narrow sense. Indeed it is now rather carefully neglected. Such treatment has nothing to do with merit. Nor can it be said in excuse that the way forward which it advocated broke with the main lines of our development of higher education up to 1963. Both in its spirit and its practical recommendations the report pointed vigorously in a direction which then seemed progressive and logical. After all, it was the thinking of the University Grants Committee itself which had led to the planning and foundation of a group of eager new universities in the early 1960s, doing many of the things Robbins wanted. It was the McNair Committee's Report of 1944 which had urged the need for universities to take more responsibility for the education of teachers – a responsibility extended in the Robbins recommendations. Within the National Council for Technological Awards itself there was opinion which supported the Robbins view that the way ahead for the colleges of advanced technology was for most of them soon to become technological universities.

Why then the break with the Robbins idea and the manifestly different pattern to which our higher education system is developing – on a binary principle not envisaged by Lord Robbins and his committee and with no minister of education separately responsible for the universities and other autonomous institutions of higher education and research? Why the loss of faith in the power of higher education to do what they hoped? What factors have proved influential which they did not take sufficiently into account?

Admittedly, there are some who would maintain that we are going in just the direction the Robbins Committee really intended. It is true that student numbers increased even more rapidly during the 1962-72 decade than their conservative forecasting allowed. Though perhaps they did not fully see the consequences of encouraging the birth of a Council for National Academic Awards, though they did not envisage and could not have envisaged the creation and rapid development of an Open University – by no means all of whose consequences for other universities are even yet manifest – and though no doubt they did not reckon enough with the burgeoning demands of the later sixties for student participation in university government, some maintain that we *are*, by and large, following the Robbins line. I do not think so, and neither does Lord Robbins himself, as his hard-hitting speech in the House of Lords in 1965 makes clear. After speaking of the rejection by the Government of the recommendation in his Committee's Report that the colleges of education should come within the university ambit, and be supported by grants from the University Grants Committee, he went on:

> But to no avail. The proposal did not commend itself to ministers and . . . the proposal for transfer of administrative responsibility was rejected . . . It is now clear that it is all part and parcel of a much wider policy which is deliberately intended to take us in a direction completely different from, and indeed completely opposed to, the conceptions underlying the Report of the Committee on Higher Education. In his now famous exposition of what he called the Binary system, the Secretary of State proclaimed an eternal separation between the autonomous universities and the rest of the system, that is to say the Colleges of Education and the institutions of Further Education – the Regional, Area and Local Technical Colleges. The universities under the UGC are to go their own ways. The rest are to be built up into a self-sufficient, complementary, if not rival, system; and administratively there is to be nothing in common between them . . . There is to be a gulf between the two systems, a gulf which, for the Secretary of State at least, is not to be at all deplored but positively to be welcomed as the sign and symbol of superior organization; and any hopes of greater intimacy fostered by an academic and frivolous Report are to be stilled for ever. I am tempted to quote from Matthew Arnold's famous lyric:

Who ordered that their longing's fire
Should be, as soon as kindled, cool'd?
Who renders vain their deep desire?
A God, a God their severance ruled
And bade between their shores to be
The unplumb'd, salt, estranging sea.

My Lords, as I have said, all this is diametrically opposed to the conceptions which inspired our recommendations.[2]

The different direction we have taken in developing our higher education system and the different 'look' of the higher education landscape now is by no means all due to a rejection by the government of some of the key Robbins recommendations, very deliberate though that rejection was. It is not a consequence of a political decision only. A bleaker economic wind has started to blow and there has been a change too in the ideological climate. I shall consider five factors which have had their part to play in producing the present state of things, and shall give a little more space to the fifth, which I regard as the most influential. But I would emphasize that each of them has its importance; different diagnosticians might well give them different relative weightings.

The Extent of the Provision of Higher Education

One of the causes of the criticism directed against the Robbins Report in the middle sixties was, ironically, its very success in encouraging an expanded rate of recruitment to both under-graduate and graduate numbers. As compared with the tentatively made Robbins forecast of 390,000 full-time students by 1972/3, there were already 463,000 by 1971/2 – as compared with only 193,000 ten years earlier. The proportion of the eighteen to twenty-two age-group entering higher education increased faster between 1962 and 1972 than Robbins forecast – from some 8% to some 16%. But while there is no reason to think that the average intellectual capacity of entrants declined – if at all, certainly not appreciably – there may be doubts if the motivation of students for being at places of higher education may not have altered somewhat. In the early seventies it had become much more 'normal' than it was in the early sixties for an intelligent young person to find himself reading for a degree; most of his closest school friends were probably doing so, and his chances of 'getting ahead' without higher education were fewer. Not merely did professions like medicine, the administrative civil service, law, engineering, analytical chemistry, geological surveying, demand degree or degree equivalent entry status, but many others had raised their sights: teaching, social work, transport planning, computer science, the defence services – with nursing and institutional management eager to recruit what they now thought of as their fair share of graduates. There were many more students, but of these a larger proportion were consciously choosing courses because they would be useful and because they would be useful soon after graduation.

It was, significantly, in terms of a job rather than more pretentiously in terms of a profession that the large majority thought of, and described, their intended career – whether they were at a polytechnic, a college of education or a university. The idea of a liberal higher education was not much in people's minds. The proportion of students even at universities taking qualifications in applied subjects – both applied sciences and applied arts – rose greatly in the twenty years 1952-1972, in spite of the vastly increased total student numbers. This indeed may be very much to the good if the usefulness is seen in large enough terms. But a technological outlook and ideals limited to material and technological advance are apt to breed an exclusively technological frame of reference which can be dehumanizing. If boys or girls have been for two or more years in a large sixth form studying competitively for GCE 'A' levels of the maximum grade within their capabilities; or have left school, as many now do, to take their 'A' levels from a technical college, they may, long before entering a place of higher education, have gained as immature rats considerable experience of the rat race. The penalty for failure becomes higher and higher in our type of society.

But today the attraction of full-time higher education to school leavers seems itself to have begun to decline. In 1968 87% of boys and girls in Britain with 'A' level grades good enough to secure entry went into some form of full-time higher education. In 1973 the corresponding figure was 80% in spite of there being many empty places in universities and polytechnics – 2,000 of them in engineering and technology courses, 3,000 in science, and 1,500 in arts.[3] No one knows with certainty the relative strengths of the factors accounting for this drop, which, since it is paralleled in a number of other industrialized countries, may be significant of a powerful social trend. Some causes can be advanced which will partially explain it – the identification of 'students' in the minds of some parents with undesirables, the preference for a safer job now (e.g. in banking) rather than the possibility of a better job after graduation ('a bird in the hand is worth two in the bush'); the inadequacy of the level of student grants; the opportunity newly opened up of working for a degree later in life, perhaps at the Open University, if one finds that a degree is necessary and desirable after all. And so on. But it is doubtful if all these causes fully explain the present loss in the power of institutions of higher education to attract the numbers of students which a few years ago everyone, like Robbins, still so confidently foresaw.

Financial Limitations

There is no doubt that to implement *in toto* the original Robbins proposals would have been expensive. The creation of five SISTERS (Special Institutions for Scientific and Technological Education) is a case in point. Even more costly in the long run would it have been to provide colleges or halls for the numbers of students for whom the report, with justice, thought it desirable if not indispensable to provide them. By the middle sixties it was already apparent that the nation was unlikely to be able to stand such costs. Many more students, therefore, if they were to take courses of higher education at all, would have to take them in places cheaper to run than universities. By the middle seventies it has become clear that cutting of costs must be far more drastic than would have been found tolerable even three years earlier. More students will in future have to live at home for the whole of their courses (with all the subtle curtailments of freedom and independence that this involves); more must study for their degrees part-time; there must be a lower proportion of post-graduate students doing research; and the ratio of students to members of staff must increase. Little new building at all can be done and there must be much more 'crowding up' of accommodation.

Unwillingness on the part of places of higher education to accept such tightening of the belt does not appeal to public opinion or the taxpayer. The consequences to their capacity to give easily a general education of high quality should not, however, be underestimated. Part of the Oxford and Cambridge secret has been the leisure and the space they provided for mind as well as body, the escapes from the everyday which they made possible. Contacts between teachers and taught may be closer if some of those contacts are casual. The opportunities offered people to become educated are greater in libraries that are spacious, well stocked, and have browsing rooms. It is difficult to believe that a congested Students'

Union building is a cultural asset of high potency.

With the further economies which are inevitable in the period ahead, there is a greater danger than before that the environment in which higher education takes place will become more Spartan. It is not physical luxury that is needed, rather a productive climate of ideas. But the contribution (whether it be large or small) made by space and grace to the education of the unconscious mind is going to be reduced.

Influence of the Central Government

The creation of a binary system of higher education, whatever the motives, was certainly not, as we have seen, envisaged by Lord Robbins himself.

> The Secretary of State may . . . paint the most splendid picture about the future of the so-called 'public' sector of his Binary system. But he will not convince either the teachers or the students that the picture is a true one. He will not prevent most students, with the necessary qualifications, from first seeking entrance to the universities, traditional or technological. If he wishes to force then into his sector, he will have to raise the requirements of the university sector and thus intensify the disparity of esteem which he professes – I don't doubt sincerely although confusedly – to wish to avoid ...
>
> My Lords, I do not believe that the Binary system will be a success. I do not think that the 'public sector', as the Secretary of State conceives it, can be built up to match the status or the efficiency of the autonomous sector. I do not believe that this will be so, either as regards research or as regards training. Nor do I believe that the prospective higher education population, especially the prospective students, can be brought to regard them in this light. I am confident that the system, as at present conceived, is not ultimately viable.[4]

But a number of reasons can be put forward for the introduction, revolutionary in its short-term consequences, of a binary system of higher education with the universities no longer the sole providers. The first of these reasons springs from remediable deficiencies in the universities themselves.

To many people, universities seem stand-offish institutions, proud of their separateness, loving to draw their skirts about them. The Robbins Committee was overwhelmingly made up of university dons or ex-dons – there was only one person on it well able to speak with intimacy from an LEA viewpoint – and may have found it difficult fully to allow for the wish of industry, students, or the LEAs to have a greater say in controlling the direction in which higher education as a whole should develop.

But the more important reasons for the introduction of the binary system are not so negative. They have prevailed in other countries too: in a number of industrialized nations – the USA, Canada, France, Australia, increasingly Japan – there has been a movement during the last decade in much the same direction. If universities no longer represent a coherent ideology that is respected within the nation as a whole; if they and we inhabit a plural society with rival philosophies; if many more technically trained experts are needed than universities are supplying, the provision of such trained and educated people must be under planned and flexible control for the requirements to be met. Must not in these circumstances the state have greater power within the total higher education system than in the past? But the more the universities are put into a position of final responsibility for meeting the demands of the state for educated manpower of this, that or the other sort, the less freedom universities will have to educate their students in ways they really believe right, to conduct the research their departments think most needed, or to criticize the doings of the state with the detachment that is most likely to be of benefit in the long run to the state itself.

In the past Britain may have unloaded more or less successfully upon the universities the responsibility for ensuring that a sufficiency of educators, scholars, nuclear scientists, economists and other fit persons was available, especially when there was no likelihood of a glut. The UGC has been an admirable go-between and buffer. But it is difficult to credit that either the UGC or places of higher education themselves would be capable of determining the levels of supply needed of, say, teachers for the nation's children, or of trained electrical, mechanical and civil engineers of every grade. Nor would they wish to take on such duties. The task is manifestly harder still when cuts become necessary in what for years may have been an expanding field. The greater the proportion of the young having a period of vocational tertiary education and the greater the tax burden involved, the stronger the argument for allowing the state more power to exercise control over numbers of entrants and standards of qualification.

Through the binary system and its relation to the CNAA a way has been opened for more control to be exercised by the central authority over the provision of courses. In fact, no major course is put on by a polytechnic or technical college without approval from the appropriate regional inspector. Regional inspectors today are very much the eyes and ears of the Department of Education and Science in this matter. They derive their power from the central authority and can exercise it to veto courses that they know the

DES may regard as unnecessary or inexpedient. Of course the UGC has a certain amount of power to influence universities in the provision of degree courses. But it can do this, and wishes to do it, only very indirectly – by giving advice or by slow-acting financial sanctions. Because of the respect in which it is held, its advice will usually be taken, but it is unlikely except in rare cases actually to prohibit the putting on of any course which a university wishes to offer.

Even the UGC, however, is in these days more immediately in touch with DES opinion than in the past, and there is not the separate Minister for Higher Education that Robbins wanted. For many years, of course, the Permanent Secretary of the Ministry of Education or his representative has attended meetings of the UGC and has indeed been frequently appealed to for facts known to his ministry and needing to be taken into account. Though he has never had a vote, he could and did from time to time take a valued part in the discussions which went on. But until December 1963 the UGC functioned under Treasury auspices. Only from that year did it come directly under the Department of Education and Science, with the Permanent Secretary of that Department henceforward the Accounting Officer for the Universities Vote; he is 'the opposite number' of the Chairman of the UGC (and incidentally paid at a higher rate of salary).

The polytechnics have developed rapidly since the first was designated in 1969. There are now thirty of them, and five Central Institutions in Scotland. Most of these cater increasingly for people studying a wide range of science and arts subjects. In the polytechnics – itself a misleading word to describe what they are fast becoming – the over-all ratio of students taking courses in the arts and social sciences as compared with courses in the pure sciences and technology is already about the same as in the universities and it is tending to go further in an arts direction. Both student and public opinion are favourable to sandwich courses, in which students work for a quarter or more of their time as undergraduates in an industrial or other job related to their theoretical studies. The sandwich principle is common to many courses in both technological universities and polytechnics, but it is more publicized by the polytechnics. Difficulties of placement are, however, reducing the proportion of sandwich course students.

There has been a good deal of pressure from central government quarters to persuade colleges of education to join polytechnics in future. Such a transfer is in keeping with the provisions of the

White Paper *A Framework for Expansion*,[5] which is the official statement by the central government of future policy for the development of higher education along a different line from that which Robbins (or McNair) proposed. In this it is clearly said (para. 120) that the government are planning that the fastest expansion should be in the polytechnics and other non-university colleges with the intention that by 1981 there might be an approximate balance of about 375,000 places in each of the university and non-university sections in Great Britain. With the financial difficulties which threaten, it seems certain that this is an overestimate; but even so a more or less equal balance of student numbers between the sections is likely to remain.

Student Attitudes

The predominating modes of perception of any generation are products of a number of circumstances. But if a man is to be of his age with power to affect others because they understand him, he has to come to belong to it, to accept many of its presuppositions, to look for the most part in the direction in which it is looking. Transplants of outlook are not easily acceptable by a society, hardly more easily than transplants of organs to one human body from another which is foreign to it. Personal autonomy, fairness, equality of rights, these are ideas of paramount importance to the young today, both in universities and outside them. The degree of insulation between universities and society outside is less than it used to be; and as Gusfield points out,[6] there is less and less chance of a decompression occurring between home and the establishment of a new self in a place of higher education. Many students wish to give priority to a common endeavour which unites rather than to a competition between themselves which individualizes and at worst can alienate them from their fellows. They accept the need for an analytic approach to the world and to knowledge while believing, to use the Keatsian phrase, in the sacredness of the heart's affections.

The widening social range from which students come and from which it is right they should come; their aims and purposes in studying; their lessened withdrawal from the world during their undergraduate years: these are among the factors making for a different experience of higher education from that obtained by their less numerous predecessors, even though entry standards have not declined. The growth of the habit of going away from their university or polytechnic each weekend during term; the far greater numbers of students living in lodgings; cafeteria type feeding: these are all elements which make higher education a less segregated process than it used to be. As we have seen, students do not feel themselves to be as different from their non-student contemporaries as they used to do. Nor do they *want* to feel separate or privileged: that would be to pretend to deserve a special status in a society in which, on the whole, one wishes to accept one's contemporaries as equal human beings.

Since the early nineteen-sixties many students have wanted more control over the content of the higher education provided. A higher proportion, both men and women, have confidence in themselves but less confidence in institutions than their predecessors had. They are little impressed by dignity. They feel less dependent on employers for a job than previous generations (though with the threat of graduate unemployment this, of course, may change again). They like – as do their contemporaries in industry – to be recognized personally and treated as individuals. They wish quite often to choose for themselves what they shall study, though with the aid of advice, if they think the counsellors concerned can be trusted to give advice that is not self-interested. But by and large students do not wish to be dependent on others to tell them what to do or to be compelled by others to do what they find distasteful. They seek subjects for study which are 'relevant', that is, useful for furthering social and practical ends; for one purpose of all study, they argue, is to lead them to know, and be in control of, the modern world. Who, they ask, is deciding what should be taught? The traditional curriculum in higher education has consisted of a body of knowledge to be passed on and disciplines to be mediated on the decision of scholars, experts and members of an academic hierarchy who were masters of the mysteries. Some of the student protest of the later sixties was directed against the whole assumption, stemming from mediaeval times, that the elders represent all that is fit in our civilization to be passed on. It was not right, they held, that higher education should be so identified with the industrial-capitalist ethos; that it should neglect the contemporary situation; that it should be so exclusively conceptual in its intellectuality; and that it should be so merely impersonal in its apprehension of significances.

Be this a biased analysis or not, it remains true that as the university works today the content of what shall be taught still rests almost entirely with the teachers, influenced no doubt by social demand but only influenced by that in so far as the teachers are themselves sensitive to it – and they may well not be sensitive enough. It is not trustees or councils, presidents or vice-chancellors, certainly not students, but faculties and departments which have power over the curriculum.

In the USA a percipient observer remarked in 1972 that we were seeing in the curriculum of many institutions a shift of emphasis (i) away from books and towards action; (ii) away from analysis and criticism towards affirmation and commitment; (iii) away from solitary work toward collective enterprises and the pleasures of co-operative sociability; (iv) away from the competitive pursuit of grades toward informal non-graded 'evaluations'; (v) away from what is defined as an arid and spurious objectivity, marked by the search for negative evidence, towards the rewards of engagement and membership, and the definition and confirmation of appropriate moral positions.[7] We have not gone as far as this in Britain but we are certainly going some distance down the same road. Maybe the next few years with their reduced employment prospects for graduates, their increasing economic constraints, will prevent much further travel, but this is the direction which attracts very many.

The plea of the Robbins Committee was that universities should give more attention to general education, less to specialist. One reason for the failure to give more weighting to general degrees, as Robbins wanted, is the manifest prestige which specialist and academic attainments bring, not least in fitting the ablest specialists for research studies, for adding to knowledge through publication and for becoming qualified as academics themselves. Had universities moved more quickly to raise the standing of their general degrees there would possibly have been less need for introducing curricula based on a modular principle, popular with students though that has become and is likely to remain. Among the encouragements to places of higher education to offer degrees made up of units – an educational currency which the student theoretically can take with him at the end of a year if he moves elsewhere – are the increased mobility of society; student pressures against authoritarianism and predetermined programmes; and the power of international example. Part of the attraction of courses which are a collection of units lies in the increased freedom given the student himself to decide what he shall study. But the unit principle can also enable the chooser, almost without noticing, to postpone decisions about his career, about hard work and about a deep centre to his intellectual life. Both a preoccupation with what

students want and their own anxiety to have their wants fulfilled
tend to voice a naturalistic philosophy. Levels or depths of wanting
are not involved.

A course made up of modules, even with inbuilt prohibitions to
this combination or that, can still allow bolt-holes into
miscellaneity for those tempted to escape. The chances are no
doubt that older students – such as those enrolled for degree
courses in the Open University or the University without Walls[8] –
will take fewer risks and will be less liable to fall for such
temptations. But even they are only likely to cater for the needs
they recognize themselves as having.

It is significant that students, by and large, approve of colloquia,
discussion groups and working parties. Even with lecturing styles
much more informal than they used to be, many students are
suspicious of lectures, however unjustifiably, as being artificial and
authoritarian. Seminars (even dialogues or confrontations as on
TV) seem more democratic. The danger is that while lessening the
generation gap they too often leave a number of the participants
feeling that no one view has more authority than another.

In their attitudes to examinations, students are pretty strongly in
favour of continuous assessment rather than three-hour papers[9]
and of plain Pass/Fail divisions rather than finer gradings. They
prefer, that is, a reduction in the *distance* between themselves and
their fellows (whether their seniors or their contemporaries) to
being forced into a competitive stance. The distance imposed by
office, or by a frigid tone of voice, or by an Oxford accent, is
suspect. The vice-chancellors and principals most successful with
students are those who depend little for their authority upon their
official position but who win respect as persons. The same tends to
be true in contemporary life for bishops, prime ministers and
presidents of the USA. A modern play written in prose is,
significantly, 'distanced' much nearer to its audience than one
written in verse as in Shakespeare's or Racine's time.

In spite of some ambivalence, student attitudes do adumbrate a
tentative philosophy, vague thought it be. Their intent is to help to
overcome the threats of fragmentation and disillusionment which
menace us all by creating a society with a widespread belief in the
dignity and worth of men and women irrespective of their
particular achievements, talents, status, sex or race. Though the
'openness' they advocate today is often a plea for secularity, there
seems to me no reason why this should be so permanently. Their
demands for their rights and for independence (for example, the

right to choose their own place of residence, to have counsellors, a family planning service, no imposition from outside of a creed) ought to be seen in company with their wish to be real and contributory members of a humane community once a basis of free acceptance has been granted.

Ideology and Higher Education

It is a central focus which universities today, like our civilization, find it so difficult to give. A number of foci can be pointed to as desirable, but it is even more difficult now than it was in the fifties to transmit what the Robbins Report called 'a common culture', even 'common standards of citizenship', for we lack a unifying principle. It may well be that many people in places of higher education, members of staff and students too, exemplify standards of honesty, good taste and breadth of mind which will have their effect upon others. Democratic practices, including genuine consultation with those likely to be affected by new rules or arrangements, are still at least as common in British universities and colleges as in any other institutions in our society. But is this enough to produce people with a faith in democracy or – what is more fundamental – who believe in democracy because they believe in the spirit of man?

Alan Richardson wrote some years ago of an honours degree course in Humane Studies which might band together in a unified purpose many departments within a faculty of arts, and defended it against the charge that it would be too ideological. It was alleged, he said, that such a course would imply taking a particular standpoint to the exclusion of others.

This is true in the sense that there can be no such thing as an absolutely presuppositionless historical study and also in the sense that anyone who wishes to undertake serious study must start with a belief in the value of what he is studying. One presupposition ... is essential to any such study as this, namely, the conviction that truth and value cannot be indoctrinated but must be freely apprehended and freely cherished. If this is an 'ideology', then our study is ideologically oriented. If it rules out alternative ideologies, such as that there is a scientific philosophy which the State has the right to indoctrinate, then we must accept the consequences. But this *is* the humane tradition. It is in conflict with various nationalistic and positivistic philosophies of education which would stifle it. If to study the history of ideas in such a way that the sources of the ideological conflicts of our times may be clearly seen commits us to an ideology, then we are committed. But there are within this commitment the widest possible opportunities for teachers and taught to understand one another's point of view and so to enlarge their conceptions of what is valuable and true in our inheritance.[10]

This is lucidly and eloquently said. But hopes for the success of such a course are based on the presupposition that students will be willing to enter pretty deeply into a humane tradition. The course would be a very different thing in a place of learning where nobody cared passionately about the values encapsulated in what was being studied. Many no doubt still do, but many others will be as likely to pursue their studies with the externality and critical detachment that life in a machine age makes second nature. Simply to study what others have held to be true about the importance of justice, or courage, or music, or religion, without seeing and feeling the actuality for oneself is not enough. What is needed is the realization that these are not only to be approved or disapproved, chosen or not chosen, liked or not liked, but to be loved or believed in profoundly.

To which it can be retorted that the proper sphere for universities is the cognitive, that if they try to enter the non-cognitive they will possibly (at any rate in these days) prove incompetent and that their unique task of teaching the art of rational analysis will be interfered with. I would argue rather that to face all the kinds of fact which need to be faced calls for a greater capacity to enter deeply within human experience than universities and polytechnics often exemplify. To be 'emancipated from' the sorts of reflection which foster self-recognition is a false emancipation, leading in the long run to an emigration from humanity. Detachment is indispensable; but without moments of understanding to precede and follow it its value is utilitarian, not educational. 'We live, after all, in an age of "behavioral science", not of "the science of mind",' remarks Chomsky penetratingly. 'There is some significance in the ease and willingness with which modern thinking about man and society accepts the designation "behavioral science".'[11] An adequate higher education for our time must mean one that really involves its students both intellectually and imaginatively. Where but to universities and polytechnics can we look as vehicles for it?

Among the reasons why the Robbins Report has lost some of its potential influence is the vast decline in confidence regarding what education, including higher education, can achieve. Some of this loss of confidence comes from evidence that earning power for many will not be much enhanced by it. But some is due to creeping disappointment with the results at a different level. There is widespread suspicion that the meaningfulness and therefore the personal relevance of the studies and researches pursued by many students is very limited. The higher education which universities and polytechnics offer needs to be socially relevant and socially useful, but ought to lead to greater self-realization for more people ·than it does. Relevance must often be long-term, not short-term only, if it is to matter or be more than evanescently satisfying.

The social consensus upon which we depend in the education we give at both the secondary and the higher stage is wearing thin. At bottom a curriculum is only likely to be educative if those taking it feel it in their bones to be worthwhile. It is obviously not possible to maintain by law a climate of confidence in the endless benefits to be conferred by progress. Nor can one compel by edict a general acceptance of a moral code which most people have ceased to practise or believe in. To be trained to play a *role* in a society whether as a professional or a worker is an important part of the higher education process, but it is not by itself enough. Yet that is what many now assume the whole intention to be. The only recipe for social recovery is a credible new vision, widely shared.

Clearly places of higher education must be concerned with adding to knowledge and to techniques for applying that knowledge in the service of our own and succeeding generations. No doubt what control over the future is possible is largely in the hands of man. There is no conceivable solution to problems regarding population, migration, food supply, health, climatic conditions, peaceful co-existence, without planning, and that means intense thought brought to bear on them largely by highly trained minds. Herein lies the justification of research as one of the primary tasks.

One argument for the development of a binary system was that in this new public sector it would not be necessary to give much attention to research and that money could be saved by curtailing it. But even if this were viable as a long-term policy, it would only have the effect of making the institutions in the public sector intellectually second-rate. Polytechnics which are themselves second-rate will be in no position to give a soundly-based lead or one that really has authority.

Yet to confine research to what is useful is not enough, nor is it enough to concentrate too exclusively upon single disciplines. Places of higher education which are largely collections of departments held together for self-protection or by self-interest are too fragmented. Multiversities may have been legitimized in a plural society, but they may add to its plurality at a cost to its unity which it cannot afford.

The complexity of a large university or polytechnic makes it imperative in our time for its principal to be an able administrator, skilled in the arts of management. It is asking a great deal to demand of him that he shall also powerfully present university opinion to the outside world, especially if the opinions within his own university on many important issues differ widely or are fragmentary. The seventy-four vice-chancellors and directors of polytechnics in office today may admirably represent our culture at the beginning of the last quarter of the twentieth century. But this implies among other things that they will not wish to pretend that higher education will have a charismatic quality for more than a few of its students.

Can places of higher education in this cultural climate, while remaining in close touch with the real world and supplying it with the technological experts it must have, do much to meet men's need for some more comprehensive overview of things informed by thought? Universities and polytechnics cannot do so, I suggest, if their examination of the world is as confined to the external as it so often tends to be and if the only authorities they recognize are those of fact and logic – authoritative indeed as those are.[12] The modern mind has high standards of truth in observation and of recording with accuracy what has been observed. But it is less sensitive to the place of values and of purpose in a world heavy with facts that have been ascertained; nor is it happy in dealing with phenomena that can neither be explained nor described, that is, essentially, with wholes instead of with the parts of things. Yet people, individuals, experiences, defy complete analysis, however systematic. And this, it may be, is what contemporary students are trying to draw our attention to, though they may not be entirely conscious of the fact. Obviously the university must join and join massively in the intellectual endeavour which the sciences, including the social sciences, represent. Unless it did, it would cease to practise the form of thought most distinctive of the modern world and cease thereby to be part of that world or able to contribute to it. This, however, is not its whole duty. Not all knowledge is to be obtained by ratiocination. Universities need to use the word 'discover' in its older sense of uncover and understand as well as its modern, more confined, sense of find by search.

Departments of theology have rightly emphasized the importance of ascertainable and objective evidence. They have done this as robustly as any other university departments and so have abundantly justified their right to a place, comparatively minor though it may be, in the university of the seventies. Can they now show a wider potentiality?

Theology is an intellectual and imaginative subject, inescapably involved with great questions of human destiny, the 'intention' of the universe, the nature of God. But it has to cope with mysteries as well as problems, and the mysteries may not be greatly diminished by a solution to any of the problems. In the history of university education theology, philosophy, the study of classical literature and mathematics have been traditionally the key subjects, all in their various ways having size and intellectuality, giving exercise to a roaming imagination but disciplining by their own content and shape any desire of that imagination to escape into a void. The usefulness of these subjects has never been their main point, though inducements to their study have included the standing and even the jobs in society which students successful in mastering them could expect to obtain.

Today our open and plural society, using a hundred technological means for the solution of its problems, tends to define all the problems it can in forms that are amenable to such a solution. It requires large numbers of graduates equipped to cope, and pays them for coping in status and salary. But the higher education they receive may not have involved 'the great questions' at all. That makes it the more important that in whatever place of higher education they are members there should be subjects which conspicuously face such questions. Theology is one of these. It must be a respected, modern, tough, academic study, but it also needs to stretch the boundaries of what is in 1976 accepted as respectable.

Among the precursors of any perception of what religion is really about is a sense of awe and of the unknown. We have more evidence of the unimaginable scale of creation today than any of our predecessors had: of the vast extent of space, the incredible size and complexity of the universe, of the almost infinitely little – smallnesses within smallnesses – as well as the enormously large. Some of the books of the Bible, some parts of the great classics of advanced religions other than Christianity, draw upon the sense of the numinous: one of the fundamentals in need of nourishment if theology is to be both properly an academic study and (like literature and music too) more than an academic study. What constantly needs to be borne in mind is that what is said about God (or the gods) cannot all be understood by a purely external approach. Michael Polanyi has given the name 'reductionism' to the tendency by which 'all things whatever are held to be intelligible ultimately in terms of the laws of inanimate nature. . . In the light of such a reductionist programme man's moral and aesthetic ideals, the fact of human greatness, seem anomalies that

will be removed eventually by further progress.'[13] Yet some of the
most fashionable departments of theology are among those
concentrating exclusively on phenomena that can be examined
historically and sociologically for their truth, as if *every* kind of truth
were detachable from imagination, and as though truth could be
important if importance itself were not. They are so uptight about
sheer knowledge! There is something to be said for including in
theological syllabuses books by men of religious insight who have
new understandings of some Christian doctrine to offer: Dante and
Pascal, for instance, T.S. Eliot and W.H. Auden. It is the nature of
goodness and of evil, the relation between love and meaning with
which, among many other matters, the philosophy of religion is
concerned. One will not get far in treating such things unless one
can draw upon a fund of introspected experience, in oneself and
those taking part in the discussion. The study of religion should at
least give students a chance to raise basic questions about life and
human identity, questions which, as Harvey Cox once remarked,
'some other departments have discarded as being too imprecise for
scholarly scrutiny'.

Departments of theology in universities could do much to ensure
that they work within the kind of philosophy of higher education
needed in coming years. What is required is a wider, more inclusive
and more liberal education for many students, which should be in
touch with the country's needs at the level both of the indispensably
useful and of the moral and imaginative. The danger is that places
of higher education may have to give in to catering for shorter-term
needs only. With a binary system under a control which could in
conditions of increasing economic stress be even closer than it yet
is, with student attitudes ambivalent and disparate modular
courses chosen because the easiest seem most attractive, we may be
in danger of giving many young people a higher education which is
magnificently irrelevant to anything but superficial and temporary
human need.

The Robbins Report rightly emphasized the necessity for the
expansion of our system of higher education, but paid too little
heed to the consequences of educating two and a half times as many
students in a society more and more pluralist, less and less sure
what 'the transmission of a common culture' could mean and what
'the general powers of the mind' include.[14] The division of higher
education into two sectors is, as Robbins saw, a nonsense if it is
more than a passing phenomenon. But if the division is to be healed
the universities will have to show a good deal more willingness to be

concerned about questions of value, to give a coherent lead, than they have yet done. The Robbins recipes might have been acceptable, and have worked, in a more stable society, even our own society as it was in 1960. It is more difficult in the mid-seventies to know precisely what direction to take if we are to go 'ahead'. We are not likely to find it without a more disciplined self-recollection and a humble willingness to change.

NOTES

1. *Higher Education*: Report of the Committee appointed by the Prime Minister under the Chairmanship of Lord Robbins, 1961-1963, HMSO 1963.
2. Lord Robbins, *The University in the Modern World*, Macmillan 1966, pp. 145f.
3. Cf. Gareth Williams, *Higher Education Bulletin* (University of Lancaster), 4.1, 1974, pp. 17-26.
4. Lord Robbins, op. cit., pp. 150f., 156.
5. *A Framework for Expansion*, Cmnd 5174, HMSO Dec. 1972.
6. Cf. Joseph Gusfield in *Journal of Higher Education*, 41.1, Ohio State University Press, 1969.
7. Martin Trow, 'The Expansion and Transformation of Higher Education', *International Review of Education* 18, Nijhoff, Den Haag, p. 71.
8. The University without Walls was started in the USA in September 1971. It is conducted by twenty co-operating colleges and universities with grants from the Ford Foundation and the US Office of Information. Each student may tailor his course to suit his needs, using the facilities of more than one college or university; and, if he prefers, may carry on much of his undergraduate work away from any campus.
9. Cf. for example the Report *Student Questionnaire on Assessment*, University of Edinburgh, April 1974, p. 32.
10. Alan Richardson, *University and Humanity*, SCM Press 1964, p. 37.
11. Noam Chomsky, *Language and Mind*, Harcourt, Brace and World, Inc., New York 1968, p. 58.
12. Cf. Liam Hudson, *The Cult of the Fact*, Jonathan Cape 1972.
13. At a meeting of a Joint Study Commission of the World Council of Churches and the World Council of Christian Education; see the summary of their findings in *Study Encounter* II.4, 1966, especially pp. 189f., 196.
14. See the Robbins Report, ch. II, p. 7.

CURRICULUM VITAE

Born 17 October 1905 in the parish of Highfield within the County Borough of Wigan, Lancashire.

University of Liverpool, 1923-27: BA with First Class Honours in Philosophy; Edward Rathbone Prize in Philosophy, 1927; MA, 1929.

Ridley Hall, Cambridge, 1927-28. Ordained deacon in Liverpool Cathedral, 1928; priest, 1929. Curate of St Saviour, Liverpool, 1928-30; Intercollegiate Secretary of the Student Christian Movement in Liverpool University, 1928-31; Assistant Chaplain of Liverpool Cathedral, 1930-31.

Exeter College, Oxford, 1931: BA with First Class Honours in Theology, 1933; MA, 1937; BD, 1941; DD, 1947. Chaplain of Ripon Hall, Oxford, 1931-33; Tutor of Jesus College, Oxford, 1934.

Vicar of Cambo, Northumberland, 1934-38.

Study Secretary of the Student Christian Movement of Great Britain and Ireland, 1938-43.

Sixth Canon of Durham Cathedral, 1943-53.

Visiting English Lecturer, Berkeley Divinity School, New Haven, Conn., USA, 1949.

Hon. D.D., University of Glasgow, 1952.

Professor of Christian Theology, University of Nottingham, 1953-64.

Honorary Canon of Derby, 1954-64.

Dean of York, 1964-75.

Knight Commander of the Order of the British Empire (KBE), 1973.

Hon. D. Univ., University of York, 1973.

Died 23 February 1975 at York.

BIBLIOGRAPHY OF THE WRITINGS
OF ALAN RICHARDSON

BOOKS

Creeds in the Making, SCM Press 1935; 2nd edition 1941; 8th impression 1968

The Redemption of Modernism, Skeffington 1935

Gospels in the Making: An Introduction to the Recent Criticism of the Synoptic Gospels, SCM Press 1938

History and the Kingdom of God: Bible Studies with questions for discussion, SCM Press 1939

The Miracle Stories of the Gospels, SCM Press 1941; 10th impression 1972

The Message of the Bible in Wartime, SCM Press 1940

Preface to Bible Study, SCM Press 1943; 8th impression 1972

Christian Apologetics, SCM Press 1947; 8th impression 1970

Science, History and Faith, Oxford University Press 1950 (published in USA under the title, *The Gospel and the Modern Mind*)

The Biblical Doctrine of Work, SCM Press 1952; 3rd impression 1963

Genesis I-XI (Torch Bible Commentaries), SCM Press 1953; 9th impression 1974

Science and Existence: Two Ways of Knowing (Technics and Purpose Series), SCM Press 1957

An Introduction to the Theology of the New Testament, SCM Press 1958; 6th impression 1974

The Gospel according to St John (Torch Bible Commentaries), SCM Press 1959; 6th impression 1974

The Bible in the Age of Science (Cadbury Lectures in the University of Birmingham and Burns Lectures in Knox College, Dunedin), SCM Press 1961; 3rd impression 1968

History Sacred and Profane (Bampton Lectures, Oxford 1962), SCM Press 1964

University and Humanity, SCM Press Broadsheets, 1964

Religion in Contemporary Debate (Lectures in Queen's College, Dundee), SCM Press 1966; 2nd impression 1968

The Political Christ, SCM Press 1973

BOOKS EDITED BY ALAN RICHARDSON

A Theological Word Book of the Bible, SCM Press 1950; 11th impression 1972

With Wolfgang Schweitzer, *Biblical Authority for Today: A World Council of Churches Symposium on the Biblical Authority for the Churches' Social and Political Message Today*, SCM Press 1951

Four Anchors from the Stern: Nottingham Reactions to Recent Cambridge Essays, SCM Press 1963

A Dictionary of Christian Theology, SCM Press 1969

`        ` CONTRIBUTIONS TO OTHER BOOKS

'Marriage and the Family in the New Testament' in collaboration with Professor C.H. Dodd (Norris-Hulse Professor of Divinity in the University of Cambridge) in *Education for Christian Marriage: Its Theory and Practice*, ed. A.S. Nash, SCM Press 1939, pp. 57-81

'Une interprétation anglicane de l'Eglise' in *La Sainte Eglise Universelle: Confrontation oecuménique*, ed. J.-J. von Allmen, Delachaux et Niestlé, Neuchâtel, 1948, pp. 133-74

'Naturlig Lov og aabenbaret Lov' in *Saertryk af Dansk Teologisk Tidsskrift*, Gads Forlag, København, 1948

'Die Authorität und Bedeutung des alttestamentlichen Ethos heute' in *Der Weg von der Bibel zur Welt* (Study Department of the World Council of Churches: report of conferences), Gotthelf-Verlag, Zürich, 1948, pp. 42-4

Contributions to *Chambers's Encyclopaedia*, 1950 edition

'The Gospel in the New Testament' in *The Enduring Gospel*, ed. R. Gregor Smith (essays in honour of Hugh Martin), SCM Press 1950, pp. 36-51

'An Anglican Contribution' in *Biblical Authority for Today*, 1951 (listed above), pp. 112-26

'Reinhold Niebuhr as Apologist' in *Reinhold Niebuhr: His Religious, Social and Political Thought*, eds. Charles W. Kegley and Robert W. Bretall, Macmillan, New York, 1956, pp. 215-28

'The Rise of Modern Biblical Scholarship and Recent Discussion of the Authority of the Bible', ch. VIII in *The Cambridge History of the Bible: the West from the Reformation to the Present Day*, ed. S.L. Greenslade, Cambridge University Press, 1963, pp. 294-338

'God: Our Search or His?' in *Four Anchors from the Stern* (listed above), pp. 5-14

'Is the Old Testament the Propaedeutic to Christian Faith?' in *The Old Testament and Christian Faith*, ed. Bernhard W. Anderson (Preacher's Library), SCM Press, 1963, pp. 36-48

'The Place of a Department of Theology in a Modern University' in *Theology and the University*, ed. John Coulson, Darton, Longman and Todd, London, and Helicon Press, Baltimore, 1964, pp. 162-73

'Die ökumenische Bewegung im Licht des historischen anglikanischen Kirchenbegriffs' in *Konfession und Okumene: Aspekte – Probleme – Aufgaben*, ed. H. Ristow and H. Burgert, Evangelische Verlagsanstalt, Berlin, 1965

'A Third View' and 'Suggestions for a Lay Ministry' in *Women and Holy Orders: Report of the Archbishops' Commission*, Church Information Office 1966

'York against its Background' in *The Noble City of York*, ed. Alberic Stacpoole, OSB, Cerialis Press, York, 1972, pp. 1-22

'History, Humanity and University' in *Our Secular Cathedrals: Change and Continuity in the University* (Franklin Lectures in the Sciences and Humanities), University of Alabama Press 1973, pp. 1-21

'What is New Testament Theology?' in *Studia Evangelica VI*, ed. E.A. Livingstone (Texte und Untersuchungen zur Geschichte der altchristlichen Literatur, Band 112), Akademie-Verlag, Berlin, 1973, p. 455

'Religious Thought and the Idea of Evolution' in *The Crisis of Evolution*, The Open University Course in the History of Science and Belief from Copernicus to Darwin. AMST 283, 12-14, 1974

ARTICLES

The Liverpool Review

'1932: Good Friday Falls on Lady Day: a Meditation', Vol. VII, No. 3, March 1932, p. 91

Radical Religion (later *Christianity and Society*), New York

'Was Jesus a Social Reformer?', Vol. 2, No. 1, Winter 1936

'A Survey of Britain', Vol. 7, No. 4, Fall 1941

'The British Political and Religious Situation', Vol. 8, No. 1, Winter 1942

Theology

'An American Prophet of Social Righteousness' (Reinhold Niebuhr), Vol. XXXI, No. 182, August 1935, p. 180

'The Kingdom of God and the World', Vol. XXXV, No. 208, October 1937, p. 226

'Surveys (A): Some Recent Books on Doctrine', Vol. XXXVIII, No. 224, February 1939, p. 136

'The Nature of the Biblical Theology', Vol. XXXIX, No. 231, September 1939, p. 166

'Biblical Theology and the Modern Mood', Vol. XL, No. 238, April 1940, p. 244

'Theology in Modern Universities', Vol. LXI, No. 453, March 1958, p. 95

'The Death-of-God Theology', Vol. LXXI, No. 571, January 1968, p. 2

'The Resurrection of Jesus Christ', Vol. LXXIV, No. 610, April 1971, p. 146

Religion in Education

'Our Theology in Wartime' (with questions for discussion and suggested books), Vol. 7, No. 1, January 1940, p. 9

'The IVF *New Bible Handbook*', Vol. 16, No. 1, Autumn 1948, p. 11

Theology Today (Princeton, N.J.)

'British Theology in the War Years', Vol. II, No. 3, 1945, p. 367

'Whose Architect and Maker is God', Vol. VIII, No. 8, 1951, p. 155

Internationale kirchliche Zeitschrift

'Britische Theologie 1939-1945', Jahrgang 36, Heft 4, November-December 1946, p. 214

Interpretation (Richmond, Va.)

'Instrument of God: The Unity of the Biblical Doctrine of Salvation', Vol. III, No. 3, July 1949

'The Feeding of the Five Thousand: Mk 6, 34-44', Vol. IX, No. 2, 1955, p. 144

Duke Divinity School Bulletin (Durham, N.C.)

'The Conception of Revelation', Vol. XV, No. 3, 1950, p. 55

The Churchman

'The Fullness of Christ', Vol. LXV, No. 2, 1951, p. 87

Frontier

'The Biblical Doctrine of Work', Vol. II, No. 3, 1951, p. 109

The Cambridge Review

University Sermon, 15 November 1952, Vol. LXXIV, No. 1798, p. 150

University of Nottingham publication

'Religious Truth in an Age of Science', Inaugural Lecture in the University of Nottingham, 1954 (15 pp.)

Canadian Journal of Theology

'Historical Theology and Biblical Theology', Vol. I, No. 3, 1955, p. 157

Scottish Journal of Theology

'Gnosis and Revelation in the Bible', Vol. 9, No. 1, 1956, p. 44

The Expository Times

'Present Issues in New Testament Theology', Vol. LXXV, January 1964, p. 109

The Listener

'When is a Word an Event?' Vol. LXXIII, No. 1888, 3 June 1965, p. 819

Religion in Life

'The Death-of-God Theology', Spring 1967, p. 70

Ampleforth Journal

'Man, The Universe and the Second Coming'; paper delivered at the Maynooth Union Summer School, August 1967, Vol. LXXII, Part IIIB, Autumn 1967, p. 300

'To Save What Was Lost: the Structural Crisis of York Minster', Vol. LXXIII, Part I, Spring 1968, p. 25

'The Earliest Hymn of Christ'. A review article of *Carmen Christi: Phil. II. 5-11 in Recent Interpretation*, by R.P. Martin; ibid., p. 67

'Ian Ramsey of Durham: An appreciation and review', Vol. LXXIX, Part II, Summer 1974, p. 65

Scripture Bulletin

'The *Bauer Encyclopedia*' [*of Biblical Theology*], ed. Johannes B. Bauer; Vol. II, No. 4, October 1970, p. 108

The Southern Humanities Review (Auburn University, Alabama)

'The Humanities in the Enlightenment' in a series 'The Humanities: Yesterday, Today and Tomorrow' (to be published in 1976)

REVIEWS

Theology

The Priest as Student by various writers, ed. H.S. Box; Vol. XL, No. 236, February 1940, p. 150

Christ and 'The Spirit': An Essay in New Testament Christology by William Samuel Bishop; Vol. XLIV, No. 260, February 1942, p. 113

The Virgin Birth in History and Faith by Douglas Edwards, CR; Vol. XLVII, No. 277, July 1943, p. 160

The Intention of Jesus by John W. Bowman; Vol. XLIX, No. 311, May 1946, p. 154

The Coming Great Church: Essays on Church Unity by Theodore O. Wedel; Vol. XLIX, No. 313, July 1946, p. 216.

The New Modernism: An Appraisal of the Theology of Barth and Brunner by Cornelius van Til; Vol. LI, No. 331, January 1948, p. 30

The Triumph of God: a series of essays, ed. Max Warren; Vol. LI, No. 339, September 1948, p. 344

Equilibrium by Richard Webster; *Butler and Hume on Religion: a Comparative Analysis* by Anders Jeffner; Vol. LXX, No. 566, August 1967, p. 368

New Directions in Theology Today: Vol. I, Introduction, by William Hordern; Vol. II, History and Hermeneutics, by Carl E. Braaten; *God-Talk: An Examination of the Language and Logic of Theology*, by John Macquarrie; Vol. LXXI, No. 581, November 1968, p. 512

True Resurrection by H.A. Williams; Vol. LXXV, No. 625, July 1972, p. 376

Journal of Theological Studies

The Challenge of New Testament Ethics by L.H. Marshall, *The Way of Life: a Study of Christian Ethics* by C.J. Barker; Vol. XLIX, Nos. 193-4, January-April 1948, p. 87

The Christian Way: A Study of New Testament Ethics in Relation to Present Problems by S. Cave; New Series, Vol. I. Part 2, October 1950, p. 226

The Doctrine of Atonement by L. Hodgson; *Some Tendencies in British Theology*, by J.K. Mozley. Vol. III, Part 1, April 1952, p. 138

The Nature of the Church, ed. R.N. Flew; *Intercommunion*, ed. D. Baillie and J. Marsh; Vol. IV, Part I, April 1954, p. 136

The Image of God in Man by D. Cairns; Vol. V, Part 1, April 1954, p. 142

Corpus Christi by E.L. Mascall; Vol. VI, Part 2, October 1955, p. 326

The Doctrine of the Trinity by C.C. Richardson; Vol. X, Part 1, April 1959, p. 199

Visible and Invisible by G. Miegge; *Kierkegaard's Dialect of Existence* by H. Diem; Vol. XI, Part 1, April 1960, p. 226

The So-called Kerygma and the Historical Jesus by P. Althaus; *The New Testament and Mythology* by B.H. Throckmorton; Vol. XII, Part 1, April 1961, p. 81

The Interpretation of the New Testament 1861-1961 by S. Neill; Vol. XVII, Part 1, April 1966, p. 131

The Theology of Rudolf Bultmann ed. C.W. Kegley; *The Church in the Thought of Bishop John Robinson* by R.P. McBrien; *Theology of Hope* by J. Moltmann; *A Handbook of Theological Terms* by V.A. Harvey; Vol. XIX, Part 2, October 1968, p. 693

An Outline of the Theology of the New Testament by H. Conzelmann; *Systematic Theology* by G.D. Kaufman; Vol. XXI, Part 1, April 1970, pp. 169, 261

Christian Theology since 1600 by H. Cunliffe-Jones; Vol. XXII, Part 2, October 1971, p. 655

New Testament Theology I by J. Jeremias; Vol. XXIII, Part 1, April 1972, p. 214

The Philosophical Quarterly

An Existentialist Theology: A Comparison of Heidegger and Bultmann by John Macquarrie, Vol. 7, No. 27, April 1957, p. 189

The Expository Times

Christian Doctrine of History by John McIntyre; Vol. LXX, October 1958, p. 7

St Thomas Aquinas' Commentary on the Nicomachean Ethics, trans C.I. Litzinger,Vol. LXXVII, October 1965, p. 24

The Theology of the Resurrection by W. Künneth; Vol. LXXVII, June 1966, p. 269

Theology in Reconstruction by T.F. Torrance; Vol. LXXVII, July 1966, p. 302

Signs and Wonders by L. Monden; Vol. LXXVIII, June 1967, p. 280

The Word of Reconciliation by H.H. Farmer; *Prospect for Theology*, ed. F.G. Healey; Vol. LXXIX, January 1968, p. 111

The Historian and the Believer by V.A. Harvey; Vol. LXXIX, March 1968, p. 172

Introduction to the Theology of Rudolf Bultmann by W. Schmithals, Vol. LXXX, February 1969, p. 142

The Question of God by H. Zahrnt; Vol. LXXX September 1969, p. 366

Catholic Theories of Biblical Inspiration since 1810 by J.T. Burtchaell; Vol. LXXXI, March 1970, p. 171

Sacra Doctrina: Reason and Revelation in Aquinas, by P.E. Persson; Vol. LXXXII, November 1970, p. 56

Rethinking the Church and *Rethinking the Priesthood* ed. F.V. Johannes, Vol. LXXXII, February 1971, p. 154

Basic Questions in Theology I by W. Pannenberg; Vol. LXXXIII, October 1971, p. 25

The Path of Biblical Theology by W.J. Harrington; Vol. LXXXIII, August 1972, p. 345

The Theology of Wolfhart Pannenberg by E.F. Tupper; Vol. LXXXV, September 1973, p. 381

New Testament Studies

The Person of Christ in New Testament Teaching by Vincent Taylor: Vol. 8, No. 1, October 1961, p. 99

The Ampleforth Journal

A New Catholic Commentary on Holy Scripture: Old Testament ed. Leonard Johnston, New Testament ed. Conleth Kearns; Vol. LXXV Part I, Spring 1970, p. 41

Revelation as History, ed. Wolfhart Pannenberg; Vol. LXXV Part III, Autumn 1970, p. 424

Hort and the Cambridge Tradition by E.G. Rupp; Vol. LXXVI Part II, Summer 1971, p. 105

Hope and History by Josef Pieper; Vol. LXXVI Part III, Autumn 1971, p. 96

The New Testament Christological Hymns: their Historical Religious Background by Jack T. Sanders; Vol. LXXVII Part I, Spring 1972, p. 87

Christ and Spirit in the New Testament: Studies in Honour of C.F.D. Moule, ed. Barnabas Lindars, SSF, and Stephen S. Smalley; Vol. LXXIX Part. III, Autumn 1974, p. 56

Biblica (Pontifical Biblical Institute, Rome)

The Mystery by William A. Van Roo; Vol. 55, Fasc. 1, 1974, p. 134

Journal of Ecclesiastical History

Biblical Inspiration by Bruce Vawter; Vol. XXIV.3, 1973, p. 322